Writing your MA literature review

Richard Malthouse

First published in 2014 by Thalassa Publishing

All rights reserved. No part of this publication may be reproduced, stored in a retrieval system or transmitted in any form by any means, electronic, mechanical, photocopying, recording, or otherwise, without prior permission in writing from Thalassa Publishing, London.

Cover design by Richard Malthouse

© 2014 Copyright Richard Malthouse

ISBN-13: 978-1495995590

ISBN-10: 1495995593

The rights of Richard Malthouse to be identified as the authors of this work have been asserted by them in accordance to the copyright, Design and Patents Act 1988

CONTENTS

	Acknowledgments	i
1	Writing your literature review	3
2	Sarah Quinn - *Has inclusive educational policy led to the inadvertent exclusion of some SEN children in schools?*	17
3	Bhavisha Soma - *A critical review of the literature surrounding the Excellence in Cities policy, 1999 and the education of gifted and talented children.*	43
4	Shika Joshi - *All for one and one for all: exploring New Labour's educational policies; inclusion, exclusion and the standards agenda*	63
5	Paula Quigley - *The Impact of Ofsted on Schools*	89
6	Richard Lester - *A critical review of Ofsted's impact since its commencement in 1992.*	110
7	Suh-lyn Park - *Evaluating the implementation of Section 176 of the 2002 Education Act*	132
8	Usman Ahmed Choudhury - *Are we educating for the knowledge-driven economy?*	152
9	Mariam Khoker - *The changing role and effectiveness of partnerships following the 1988 Education Reform Act.*	172
10	Danica Hines - *An Investigation into the Impact of the Local Management of Schools Policy Established in the 1988 Education Reform Act and The Critical Comparison to the 2010 Academy Act.*	198
11	Alexander Petrovic – *Education Attainment and the Education Reform Act 1988*	219
12	Mohd Syafiq Aiman Mat Noor – *Scientific Enquiry and its Place in the National Curriculum*	241
13	Anna Wright – *Chief Teacher or CEO? Seat of Learning or Business? A Critical Evaluation of the Impact of the 1988 Education Reform Act on Leadership in Education.*	263

ACKNOWLEDGMENTS

Thank you to all my students who have contributed to this publication

1 WRITING YOUR MA LITERATURE REVIEW

Don't look behind you when you are sweeping leaves in the wind.

Chapter contents:

Introduction...	4
What is a literature review?...	4
Preflection and Planning..	5
This first steps...	8
Collaborative and individual learning..	9
Searching..	9
Mind maps..	10
Filing system..	10
Early stages of writing..	11
Writing the introduction...	12
Writing the main body..	12
Levels within the cognitive domain..................................	12
Analysis..	13
Synthesis..	13
Argument...	14
Writing the conclusion..	14
Style...	14
English as a second language...	16
Exemplars..	16

Introduction

Students frequently face two problems when embarking on a literature review, where to start and when to finish. As you search through the countless books, papers and articles it may feel that you are literally surrounded by so much material that you can't find a way to begin. Remember though the advice above, 'Don't look behind you when you are sweeping leaves in the wind.' The allusion to leaves on a windy day is that you cannot hope to read each and every paper available to you on electronic media and at some stage you are going to have to start writing; although frequently the two run concurrently.

Typically you will be concerned by the potential size of the project. As a result, adopting a systematic approach to your research will reap rewards. This chapter has been written to guide you through that process. Writing the MA literature review can be a daunting task, you will be aware that the writing must be at a higher level than the BA or BSc, but how high exactly and what does the finished assignment actually look like? This chapter explains what a literature review is, it offers practical advice in relation to what to include, how to get started, the various things to consider and how to write at an appropriate level. Further, it offers guidance in relation to the format of your writing and provides advice on how to perform a literature search. To enable you to recognize the shape and form of the literature review, 12 MA students' works are offered. They employ various styles and consider a broad spectrum of subjects. It is hoped that by observing how others have approached the literature reviews you can perhaps emulate these.

What is a literature review?

As the name suggests a literature review consists of an evaluation of the academic material available on a given subject following a comprehensive search. The literature review consists of three characteristics:

1. Identification of relevant literature
2. Analyses of the circumstances
3. Synthesis of the analysis

You will notice that the literature review is not simply a list or an account of what has been written. Instead it seeks to identify the chosen subject in a critical way, employing the use of analysis and synthesis. It indicates to the reader that you have thoroughly reviewed the topic and that you understand how the literature relates to you own study.

The literature review is employed to:

- Compare and contrast various authors' opinions
- Assemble authors who share opinions
- Comment upon disagreements
- State how your study relates to previous studies
- Identify gaps or inadequacies in the research

The literature review defines the limits of the study and builds on the existing body of knowledge.

Preflection and Planning

It is imperative to give some thought about what you intend to do; getting this right will reap rewards later. To assist you with this process a model is offered relating to preflection. Preflection, (Malthouse and Watts in conversation, 2014) occurs prior to the planning stage of a project; in this case your literature review. It differs from simple, everyday thinking as it considers a topic, issue, course of action or project from multiple perspectives. For example, it asks a circle of questions in a structured form:

Preflection model

Normally the first question that would be asked is '**What**?' In this case, relating this model to your literature review, it would be the subject to be studied. This is your most significant question and all other questions follow from this.

'**When**?' considers temporal issues. It quantifies your time frame identifying the available time you can offer your project. It contemplates the start and completion dates and the availability of the time in between.

'**How**?' ponders the practicality of your study; is it doable? It asks what strategies you have in place to ensure success.

'**Why**?' reflects upon your motivation towards the task and identifies the underlying preferences you have towards the subject; it is your motivator.

'**Where**'?' can refer to you and to your study. For example, where will you study? Where will you collect your data? This asks about the nature of your available environments.

'**Which**?' raises the question in relation to the selection from the various possibilities available to you. Normally there is more than one possibility from which to choose.

'**Who**?' recounts to the main players within the project. This can include the gate keeper, those from whom you will need to gain permission, or those who you will rely on to assist you look after the children when you need space; this is the selection question.

'**Would**?' is a preflection which considers the appropriateness of an idea. You can ask, would it be appropriate at this time, for these people, at this place? Would it be OK? Would I be able to? Would I want to?

'**Could**?' concerns the possibilities of your idea. It asks whether what you are thinking about can actually occur. It is the realist type of question.

'**Should**?' asks if what you are considering is ethically sound. Should you be doing it? What would be the consequences of your actions? This is a form of critical question.

'**What**?' You start again. Here you ask what have I forgotten? What should I be thinking about? What else should I consider. The process begins again.

Akin to reflecting, preflection is a deep deliberation of a phenomena prior to an event. It is similar to Situated Reflective Practice (Malthouse and Roffey-Barentsen 2013) in as much as it is anticipatory in nature. Preflection is what you do as you muse over the possibilities in advance of starting a project, getting this right enables you to plan effectively in the knowledge that you have considered all eventualities.

It is an old cliché but it is applicable to your writing:

Fail to Plan – Plan to Fail.

There will be a number of considerations that you can reliably predict. For example, the hand in date. This is fixed and so you can count the days available to you and identify when certain tasks must be completed. Some activities are dependable upon others being completed, these can also be taken into consideration. A Gantt chart is a useful tool used for many forms of project management. Gantt charts can be easily down loaded from the internet to assist you with planning. They are named after the person who designed them Henry Gantt in the 1910s to identify start and completion dates within a project, activities which are dependent upon other actions are also included. A very simple version is offered below:

Time in weeks

	1	2	3	4	5	6	7	8
Literature search	■	■	■					
Attend library		■		■				■
Design mind map		■	■	■	■			
Outline policy/topic etc.			■					
Review of the Literature				■				
Organise themes						■		
Conclusions etc.							■	
References and hand in								■

Simple Gantt chart

The first steps

The very first step in writing a literature review is to identify the assessment criteria. This will be identified within the module guide. Some universities include a module specifically aimed at writing a literature review, in which case the criteria will be specific to that module. The criteria indicate the indicative content of your written work against which you will be assessed. They will inform your writing and guide your approach to your study. For example, typical criteria may include the following:

You will be expected to:

- Demonstrate a clear understanding of the topic
- Contextualise that topic
- Identify the relevant themes within the literature
- Group the relevant literature appropriately
- Analyse and synthesise your argument
- Communicate your ideas effectively

If your university does not offer a module for a literature review, then you will be expected to complete this as a part of your dissertation. In this case the criteria will be more general and relate to the dissertation as a whole. In respect of the literature review, typically you will be required to:

- State the previous research relating to the chosen topic
- Identify the relevant theory, practice and context
- Identify a critical and sophisticated understanding of the chosen subject
- Develop a highly systematic and logical and/or insightful argument

If you do not understand an element of the criteria then ask your tutor for an explanation. Having read and understood what is being asked of you, the next step is to discover what has been written on the subject. It is likely that you will not be aware of the full content of the subject you are researching. As a result, you will be looking for something without knowing what it is you are searching for. This is referred as the Meno Paradox or the Paradox of Inquiry. During a conversation with Socrates in about 340 BC, Meno asked how he could find something if he did not know what he was looking for and further he enquired, how would he recognize it as the thing he was looking for once he had found it. Your search for the information you require will lead you to the answer to this paradox. The best place to start your literature search will be via a search engine supplied by the university library, for example, Encore, Summons or Octopus etc. Only suitably academic sources should be employed, in other words academic books, academic e-books, archives and manuscripts, articles, journals and e-journals etc. The majority of the resources from the library will be available to you online.

Collaborative and individual learning

Remember the method of assessment when marking your work in university is criterion referenced and not norm referenced. The implication of this is that you can work collaboratively with your peers by sharing resources, ideas and best practice. This means that, in theory, if everybody meets the criteria and produces excellent assignments, then all could achieve an A+. That is provided the assignments were not subject to plagiarism, so although you have worked together, ensure that the assignments are individual.

Another form of assessment is referred to as ipsative and identifies how an individual performed in relation to their previous efforts. This is useful to you as you reflect on your performance and identifying what needs to be achieved in future.

Searching

At the start of your search you will be conducting a form of environmental scanning. In other words, you will be sweeping the terrain to see what exists, what is important and what is less so. When embarking on your search be as specific as you can as a search engine is capable of providing literally millions of results which is not helpful. For example, typing the words 'Literature Review' into a library search engine provided 5,350, 823 results. A search using the words 'Neo liberalism' provided 35,394 results and 'Neo liberalism Thatcher 1979' reduced the results to 3,968 which is beginning to become a little more manageable; but only just. If your module relates specifically to conducting a literature review then your module guide will offer direction in relation to the indicative reading and it is sensible to identify and include the key sources. However, elements of your specific subject will obviously not be defined within the module guide (as with a dissertation), in which case you can employ a different strategy. Where you chose a subject of study yourself it is useful to begin from the known and then continue to the unknown. It is highly unlikely that you will choose a subject about which you know nothing, however, if this were the case you would search on the various terms relating to your chosen topic until you found a suitable book or journal; the known. From that point you would identify the sources used within that material from the reference section contained within the document you have discovered; the unknown. Try to find up-to-date material as ideas and practices can change quickly in some cases. For more information on searching see the publication Academic Skills: Contemporary Education Series by Malthouse and Roffey-Barentsen (2013).

Mind maps

It is recommended that a mind map be considered for the task of recording the available information. At MA level, your chosen subject will take the form of a series of sub-sections and it is useful to record these. Further, it is likely that areas you had not at first considered will emerge as being suitable for inclusion. Placing the topics and issues in graphic form will assist you further to identify the associations, relationships and connections that exist. The mind map will grow exponentially as you research the topic. Colour coding is another useful tool, enabling differentiation at a glance within your mind map. At this stage it would be unwise to begin the writing process until you have formed a comprehensive view of the subject. Again the Meno Paradox is pertinent, as you don't know what you are looking for, anything can become a significant feature of your subject.

Filing system

If you are saving documents to your home computer then a suitable filing system will need to be developed. It makes sense to mirror the mind map in terms of topics and subtopics. In your saved files a file can be easily placed within the layer of word documents to ensure that the sub-topics are kept in the correct place. It is recommended that frequent use is made of sub-folders as a list of files reached from top to bottom of the screen is unhelpful.

Early Stages of writing

The introduction and conclusion are written last. This is because your research and writing often occur concurrently and you will not know where you are going until you reach the end of your research journey. Initially consider writing about the subject under related topics. These can be cut and pasted easily if necessary. It is useful to think about the structure of your writing as you begin because you will be restricted to the amount of words available to you. Going over the word count will mean that your final mark will be reduced.

The format below is designed to be used with a 5,000 word literature review as a single module:

1. Front Section

    a. Title Page

    b. Abstract (100-word summary of your topic)

2. Introduction (2 pages)

3. Outline of the policy/topic and relevant contexts (5pages)

4. Critical Review of the Literature, organised in themes (10 pages)

5. Conclusions with suggestions of future research directions (2 pages)

6. References, presented alphabetically

Although this plan refers to the completed literature review, when you begin the writing process, you will start at number 3 or 4. It is acknowledged that if your literature review is used as a part of your dissertation then the above model is adapted:

1. Introduction

2. Outline of the policy/topic and relevant contexts

3. Critical Review of the Literature, organised in themes

4. Conclusions with suggestions of future research directions

The number of pages credited to each section will be dependent upon the word count of the finished dissertation. Typically an MA dissertation will be 15,000 words in length. According to Professor Mike Watts from Brunel University, typically chapter 2 (literature review) and chapter 4 (data analysis)outweigh the others. The chapter lengths for a 15k dissertation may be:

1. 2,000
2. 4,000
3. 3,000
4. 4,000
5. 2,000

Writing the Introduction

The introduction is your opportunity to state your chosen theme and to justify your choice. What is your perspective, viewpoint or standpoint in relation to the literature? Explain the structure of the review, guide the reader through the sequence of your review. Justify the limitations and scope of the review. For example what you have omitted and why. Do not write this until you have finished writing the main body of your literature review. (Section 1 above)

Writing the main body

The structure of your writing should support your argument, consider the order of the themes introducing them as required (Sections 2 and 3 above). Sign post your writing with mini conclusions and detail what will be considered next. Your writing should move from the general to the specific. In other words, the general trends should be stated and then broken down to their specific characteristics. Identify the relationships between topics, but be careful with causal relationships as frequently, on closer examination, there is no actual causation. Just because things happen one after another does not mean that one is a consequence of the other. Remember, what is required is not an example of what you know about the subject, that is not academic writing. What is required is what you know about what others have said about the subject studied. Use the words of the authors within the literature to make your point. This can be done by citing directly or paraphrasing what has been said. Where more than one author makes the same point, be sure to include all who support an idea.

Levels within the cognitive domain

As you are aware, there are three domains in relation to education, namely Cognitive (thinking), Affective (Attitude), Psycho-Motor (Skill/doing). When writing your review, you are tested upon your cognitive ability. It was Bloom (1956) who subdivided the cognitive domain into the following hierarchy with evaluation ranking highest:

6 Evaluation	Judging and evaluating concepts and ideas, ranking, appraising
5 Synthesis	Creating new concepts from old ideas, modifying, combining
4 Analysis	Identifying patterns, recognising trends, organizing ideas
3 Application	Using and applying knowledge, problem solving
2 Comprehension	Understanding, demonstrating, discussing
1 Knowledge	Simple recall of information, listing, naming

Analysis

You assignment should be sufficiently analytical. This is achieved by showing relationships between pieces of information, by comparing and contrasting. Comparing is the process of identifying similarities and contrasting is the process of identifying differences. An analogy can be drawn to a car. First you take it apart to see how it works, then you describe the various functions. The functions are then contrasted and compared. You then take another car and do the same, next you compare and contrast the various features of the cars you have studied. These factors then support your argument. However, at MA level you are expected to function in terms of synthesising.

Synthesis

Synthesising is to combine the ideas of more than one source with your own. To return to the car analogy, having analysed a selection of cars you have an informed view because you recognise the advantages and disadvantages of each. However your argument may entail a comparison of certain cars to support your own argument. For example, you compare and contrast a sports car with a four by four and a Multi-purpose vehicle. Your argument may be that family cars can and should be made to be safer for both occupants and pedestrians. You would then select the attributes of the vehicles in support of your argument. Finally, you would take the component parts of each vehicle that supports safety issues and use them in one new car, you introduce the concept of a new car; that is synthesis.

Argument

Argument is the formal presentation of the evidence. In your literature review, it is important that you have an argument, a point of view. However, to complicate things, some authors may agree partly, or disagree partly on something. Other have opposing views and others agree with each other; mostly. You will align yourself to an argument using the literature as your source of evidence.

Writing the conclusion

The conclusion summarises the main argument within the literature and reminds the reader of the main points made within the body of the text (Section 4 above). Here you can evaluate the available literature. For example, you may have identified gaps in the literature, inconsistencies or weaknesses in others' arguments. Some authors may be found to be incorrect in the light of other evidence. Make links between your own and existing research. Lastly give consideration to future study.

Style

When writing academically it is often useful to write in the third person. E.g., 'This assignment will consider...' Rather than, 'In this assignment I will ...' Writing in the third person offers a distance between the writer and the subject. Consideration of the actual words used is an important issue as the day to day style of talking or even texting would be inappropriate within this arena. As you read the associated literature you may notice your style of writing changing as you are influenced by what you are reading. If you have written a passage that you would like to improve, consider the use of the synonyms in a Word Document. To do this highlight the word you wish to change and press the right mouse button. You will see the option 'Synonym' with a small arrow indicated. Click on the arrow and an alternative selection of words will be offered. To include that word click on it:

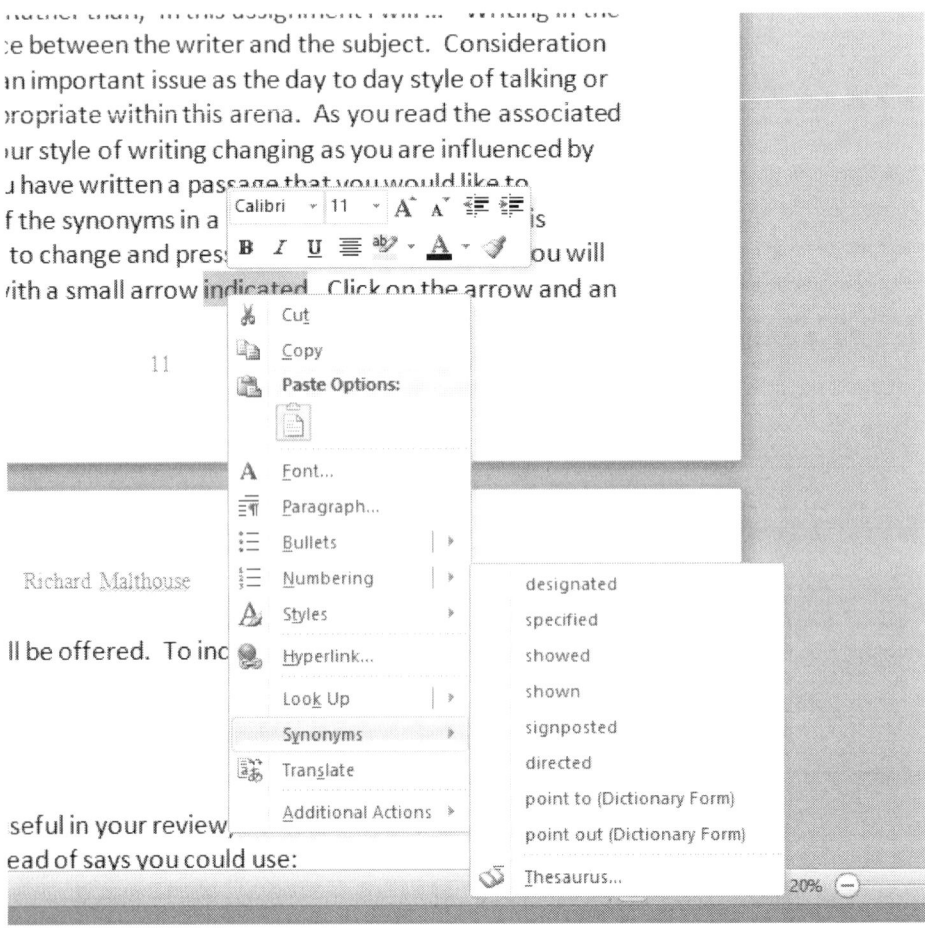

Alternative words for 'says' are useful in your review, due to the fact that so many authors are saying so much. Instead of says you could use:

- Observes
- Considers
- Suggests
- Notes
- Reflects
- Deliberates
- Echoes
- Mirrors
- Emulates
- Disagrees

Your academic style can be improved only if you take an active part in that change. This can be achieved by engaging with what you read and identifying how you can emulate the language used.

You will notice within this book's exemplars that some phrases are quite similar:

- This essay will attempt to examine
- This assignment will consider the
- This assignment will begin by giving an outline of
- This literature review focuses upon
- This essay will analyse the effect and impact that

Above, all five examples employ the third person as a starting point. Consider the 12 exemplars below, what makes the writing academic in style?

English as a second language

The problems of writing academically can be made more difficult if your first language is not English. This is because you may not recognise when and where your written work can be improved. If you are studying in a university, then assistance will be offered to you to improve your written and spoken English from the relevant international department. What is important though is to immerse yourself in the culture and select your influences carefully. BBC Radio 4 offers English spoken in a way suitable for imitation, similarly reading newspapers such as the Times, Guardian or Telegraph will offer an appropriate style of writing.

Exemplars

This book offers exemplars in the following chapters designed to assist you with your writing. As you read through these you may find that certain sentences or phrases have been chosen carefully and that you can use then in your own writing. There is nothing wrong with this as you are improving your written work. The caveat here is to recognise when you are emulating an assignment and when you are plagiarizing it. There exist websites such as Turnitin who are able to not only identify when an assignment has been copied, but where it has been taken from exactly.

The exemplars used within this book consist of only literature reviews. If you would like to see a collection of completed dissertations then the publication Research projects and Dissertations: A collection: Contemporary Education Studies by Malthouse and Roffey-Barentsen (2013) is highly recommended.

References

Bloom, B, S., and Krathwohl, D, R. (1956) Taxonomy of Educational Objectives. The Classification of Educational Goals Handbook.

Malthouse, R. and Roffey-Barentsen, J. (2013) Academic Skills: Contemporary Education Studies. London Thallasa

Malthouse, R. and Roffey-Barentsen, J. (2013) Research projects and Dissertations: A collection: Contemporary Education Studies. London Thallasa

Malthouse, R and Watts, M. (2014) A conversation at Costa Coffee, Brunel University. Latte and an American consumed, 5th March at 10.30 am

2 SARAH QUINN

My name is Sarah Quinn and I am currently a MA student in Brunel University. I am a qualified primary school teacher with a job in a disadvantaged school in Dublin, Ireland. After three years studying English and Spanish in my undergraduate degree, I decided to embark on a post-graduate primary teaching degree. After an intense one and a half years higher diploma I qualified. This time spent in teacher training college in Coláiste Mhuire Marino in Dublin was inspirational both from a lecturing and friendship standpoint. I have cemented lifelong friendships and boulders of support from this short time.

After qualifying in November 2010 I got my permanent job in a DEIS (Disadvantaged) school in Corduff, Blanchardstown in Dublin. I am extremely passionate about this school and its amazing children. I have taught here for three years and hope to continue teaching here for many years to come. After teaching fourth class for two years I was asked to take the special class. In Ireland children with special educational needs are often educated within a mainstream school but given additional support in a special class. It was in this role that I decided to continue my own education and looked towards a Masters. I became interested in the inclusion debate as it directly related to my position as special class teacher in St. Patrick's Corduff. Although the children in my class had SEN, I ensured they were fully immersed in their mainstream class for the majority of the day and merely scaffolded by me to increase their social and academic skills in a smaller group setting. I felt, and still feel, extremely strongly about this. These children need additional help, support and care within school but this is not always possible in the mainstream classroom. I believe that the provision of a special class ensures the best of both worlds for children with SEN. In Ireland there are constant government cuts to the provisions and resources for these classes and children. I felt I needed to gain more universal information regarding the inclusion debate.

I felt under-qualified to teach the children in my special class but also felt Ireland may possibly be somewhat the same in our understanding of inclusion. This is why I decided to study in the UK.

I took a career-break from my cherished Dublin school and moved to London. I began the Masters in Education in Brunel University with an aspiration to specialize in Special Educational Needs. In the short time I have spent in this university I have acquired a wealth of knowledge and hope this will continue to be the case for the remainder of the course. My hope is to bring new research regarding the inclusion debate that will relate particularly to the Irish education system in an effort to enact change in how we work with inclusion.

Title:

Has inclusive educational policy led to the inadvertent exclusion of some SEN children in schools?

Contents:

- Abstract
- Introduction
1. The introduction of SEN legislation into policy
2. Issues with terminology and language in policy leading to possible exclusion
3.1 The effect inclusive policy can have on children with SEN
3.2 The effect inclusive policy can have on children without SEN
3.3 The effect of inclusive policy on parents and teachers.
4. Statementing: A cause of exclusion?
5. The Future of inclusive education policies.
    - Conclusion
    - References

Abstract:

This essay will attempt to look critically at inclusive educational policies and literature. It will focus on how certain Special Educational Needs legislation has led to the inadvertent exclusion of children in UK schools. It will firstly look at the introduction of specific inclusion of all pupils with SEN following the Warnock Report of 1978 right through to the Special Educational Needs code of practice that is in place today. It will focus on the literature surrounding inclusive educational policy and how the language and details of governmental legislation has possibly led to the exclusion of some children with Special Educational Needs. It will examine the current procedure of issuing children with statements of SEN, the inclusion of pupils with SEN into the mainstream classroom and the effect this legislation has on children with and without SEN in special and mainstream classrooms.

Introduction:

This essay will attempt to examine how inclusive educational policy has led to the inadvertent exclusion of some SEN children. It will explore the introduction of SEN policy through the work of Baroness Mary Warnock and her committee in the Warnock Report (1978). It will assess how important this report was and the introduction of new inclusive language and terminology. This essay will then examine the importance of the UNESCO Salamanca agreement and how this influenced pedagogy and practice of special educational needs in the United Kingdom.

Throughout the history of inclusive education the language and terminology used has been problematic (Runswick-Cole & Hodge 2009). Before Warnock the term 'handicapped' was common and arguably denoted very negative images of the educational ability of the child. According to archaic educational policy these 'un-educable' children (Education Act 1944) were completely excluded from the education system until after the Education Act 1981.

This essay will examine the differing definitions of 'inclusion' and how this is reflected in policy. From writers who define inclusion as taking a full and active part in school life (Farrell 2000), to those who argue that inclusion in the mainstream setting is potentially damaging to a child and does not reflect inclusion (Michailakis & Reich 2009, Warnock 2005, Dyson, Farrell, Polat & Hutchenson 2004). Difficulties in the definition and interpretation of the term 'special educational needs' has also led to debate and possible exclusion of children (Runswick-Cole & Hodge 2009).

To examine the possible exclusion of children from the education system this essay will focus on the effects that inclusive policy has on children with SEN, children without SEN, parents and teachers. All of these stakeholders contribute to the inclusion and possible exclusion of children in mainstream schools.

The process of statementing, campaigned for by Warnock (Warnock 1978), has arguably led to the exclusion of some pupils in schools. This element of educational policy is often associated with the labelling children leading to possible stigmatisation (Thomson 2012, Keslair, Maurin & McNally 2012). While some find labelling useful in providing for children's needs, it is often perceived as destructive to a child's 'educational career' (Runswick-Cole & Hodge 2009). Labelling can stigmatise children and influence teacher's teaching methods and attitudes towards them (Keslair, Maurin & McNally 2012).

Finally this essay will examine the future of inclusive education policy. With reference to the issues it will outline, this essay will suggest possible amendments in language and terminology as well as a new 'rights-based' approach to including all children (Runswick-Cole & Hodge 2009). In an attempt to show alternative methodologies with relation to inclusive education this essay will analyse the Reggio Emilia Italian School system and draw on positive directions that may lead to future changes in the way we implement and make education policy inclusive.

1. The introduction of SEN legislation into UK Policy

This essay would argue that within the realm of education the introduction of formal SEN legislation was a vital amendment to dated education policy. After the Education Act of 1970 children became the responsibilities of LEAs and not the health service (Runswick-Cole & Hodge 2009). Following this Baroness Mary Warnock was commissioned to set up the Warnock Committee and subsequently produced The Warnock Report (1978). This committee was set up amid concerns that 'the segregated system of special education was not providing disabled children with positive social and educational opportunities' (Shah, 2007 p.428). The committee made recommendations for the government in relation to the 'education of handicapped children and young people' (Warnock Report 1978). A litany of proposals were suggested by the panel including amending certain dated language and terminology, creating a new system of recording, inservice training for teachers and increased provisions (Warnock Report 1978). Instead of the term 'handicapped' this report adopted the term 'Special Educational Needs' to all children with individual learning needs (Runswick-Cole & Hodge 2009). The Warnock Report was concerned with the approach that wherever possible children should be educated in the mainstream class, achieving inclusion (Roulstone & Prideaux 2008). The committee decided that one fifth of children would, at some point in their educational lives, experience some form of special educational need (Tomlinson 2012). Tomlinson argues that to this day the variation and discrepancy in local authorities and schools deciding on figures and percentages of children requiring SEN provision is a constant difficulty for policy makers (ibid).

The Warnock Report also introduced a form of identification of SEN in children. According to Shah (2007) this form of recording could assure parents that their child was receiving the SEN provisions they required in mainstream schools.

The production of the Warnock Report and the subsequent Education Act 1981 had a prominent effect on inclusive education debates in the United Kingdom. Many argue that the move towards full inclusion in mainstream schools and the elimination of special schools can be detrimental to all children (Farrell 2000 and Dyson et al 2004). Warnock herself in a later publication questioned the notion of full inclusive education. She stated that "Government must come to recognise that, even if inclusion is an ideal for society in general, it may not always be an ideal for school" (Warnock 2005 p.2). It has been argued that the reality is many schools cannot afford adequate provisions for children with SEN, coupled with the fact that the social constructs and beliefs about social justice of segregation are changing constantly (Roulstone & Prideaux 2008). Despite the Government's determination towards inclusive education for all, mainstream schools are not always accessible, as those who are responsible for the expansion of inclusion still think in terms of ramps and rails (Burgess 2003). For example many organisations representing the deaf community argue that they only way full inclusion is possible is through separate, specialist provision in sign language (Freire & César 2003).

A number of stakeholders in inclusive education have argued for the advantages of segregated special schools as opposed to inclusivity in mainstream (Shah 2007). This essay will further examine the inclusion/segregation debate in later chapters.

The next influential landmark in inclusion policy was the Salamanca Statement and Framework for Action (Gibb et al 2007). Regarded by many as imperative to the global re-thinking of inclusion it has been described as 'the most significant international document that has ever appeared in the field of Special Education'

(Ainscow & Miles 2008 p.16). This was the first policy to regard children with SEN with utmost importance and it offered a clear, concise framework of inclusive education focusing on children's strengths and abilities (Hunt, 2011). The policy was a key international educational policy (Gibb, Turnbridge, Chua & Fredrickson 2007) that called on Governments worldwide to recognise and 'adopt as a matter of law or policy the principal of inclusion education' (UNESCO, 1994, p.ix).
The policy has shaped current philosophy of inclusive education placing the onus on the individuals that constitute society:

> 'While inclusive schools provide a favourable setting for achieving equal opportunity and full participation, their success requires a concerted effort, not only by teachers and school staff, but also by peers, parents, families and volunteers. The reform of social institutions is not only a technical task; it depends, above all, upon the conviction, commitment and good will of the individuals who constitute society'
>
> UNESCO 1994, p.11

The Salamanca Statement proposes that schools must actively adapt to the individual requirements for the learning of children with SEN in order for every child to be included and reach their personal potentials (Michailakis & Reich 2009). This international policy was accepted and was a turning point in the inclusive education debate (ibid).

Following the Salamanca Statement under the Labour government subsequent policies emerged such as Excellence in Schools (DfEE 1997) and Meeting Special Educational Needs: A Programme of Action (DfEE 1998) promoting inclusive education for all within the mainstream setting. These policies arguably underpin inclusive education and special educational needs policy that exists today. They enforce the concept that inclusive education is ensuring every child can be educated in the mainstream classroom where it is feasible. The responsibility lies with the school to re-structure itself to ensure inclusion for all children regardless of disability or background (Frederickson & Cline 2002). There are debates that argue that these inclusion policies of past and present and their ideologies of full inclusion in the mainstream classroom have possibly led to the inadvertent exclusion of some children. There are some going so far as to say that pursuing full inclusion can be damaging to the entire special education community (Hornby, 2011).

2. **Issues with language and terminology in policy leading to possible exclusion.**

The language and terminology surrounding inclusive education and special education needs is often contentious and confusing (Florian 2008). Notably the two concepts have been confused and considered the same in many policies and literature and according to Slee (2011 p.155) 'inclusive education needs to be decoupled from special education'. According to Booth et al (2000) inclusion should not be considered just another name for special educational needs. This perplexity in separating the two definitions can arguably create difficulties for policy makers and those who attempt to interpret them. This chapter will critically analyse the issues with language and terminology of Special education needs and Inclusion. It will firstly focus on the issues surrounding the definition and interpretation of inclusive education.

Inclusion has been described as 'an international buzzword' (Benjamin, 2002, p. viii). The difficulty in defining it lies in its ever-evolving state. Inclusion is not a fixed term but is a changing, developing, evolving and even "becoming" as it is lived (Sikes et al. 2007 p.367). Sikes et al (2007) elaborates on this stating that inclusion is an internationally used term yet its interpretations differ not only from country to country but also from city to city and school to school. The interpretations are not mutually agreed upon. Conferences held on Inclusive Education become fixated on definitions so that all theories and conjectures are included and permitted under the umbrella term of inclusion (Slee, 2009). Even throughout the history of educational policy in the United Kingdom the term inclusion is vague and loosely used and explained. Sikes et al explores these differences:

- Inclusion is about equal opportunities for all pupils, whatever their age, gender, ethnicity, attainment and background (OFSTED, 2001, p.4).
- Inclusion is much more than the type of school that children attend: it is about the quality of their experience; how they are helped to learn, achieve and participate fully in the life of the school (DfES, 2004, p.28).
- 'Touchstones for effective inclusion' include key ideas about 'the presence, participation and achievement of children with diverse needs, within mainstream schools and settings' (DfES, 2005, p.9).

(as cited in Sikes et al. 2007, p.358)

These slight differences are reflected in the literature and arguments around defining inclusive education (Farrell 2000, Michailkis & Reich 2009 and Bines & Lei 2011). Farrell (2000) describes it as students taking a full and active part in mainstream schools and to become an integral member of the school community. Others have defined inclusion as the attempt to educate people with learning difficulties by involving them as much as possible into the normal education system (Michailkis & Reich 2009). Bines and Lei (2011, p.421) have identified Inclusion as 'a response to the segregation of pupils as well as their teachers in both special and mainstream settings'.

This essay argues that this ambiguity has led to much dispute regarding what is best for children with Special Educational Needs. Those that believe that inclusion should mean all children being educated in a mainstream school (Fredrickson &

Cline 2002, Farrell 2000, Manset & Semmel 1997 and Avramidis 2010) verses those who argue inclusion in mainstream is potentially detrimental to children where the school is unavailable to provide to the child's particular special education need (Michailakis & Reich 2009, Warnock 2005, Dyson, Farrell, Polat & Hutchenson 2004). Fewer arguments have been discussed regarding the definition of Special Educational Needs. The term Special Education Needs is rarely defined as a concept and is usually determined by people's conceptions of 'special needs' and their understanding of that phrase (Wilson 2002). It is generally recognised that a child with special educational needs is any child that requires additional help as a result of physical, sensory, or cognitive difficulties as well as emotional or behavioural issues (DfES 2005). However there have been some disputes that suggest that the language and terminology of 'Special Educational Needs' is in fact dated and in need of reform (Runswick-Cole & Hodge 2009). The language of special and regular schooling originates in an oppressive view of 'normality and abnormality' (Slee 2009). As in 1978 when Warnock argued that terminology such as 'handicapped' was archaic (Warnock 2005), Runswick-Cole & Hodge (2009) argue that language of special educational needs lend themselves to locate the problem with the child. The power of language is such that it assigns an identity to children, creating positive and negative images which in turn can impact on the policy and practice of education (Corbett 1996). Various policies regarding special educational needs defined areas of need, in The Code of Practice 1994, eight areas were identified:

- Learning difficulties
- Specific learning difficulties
- Speech and language difficulties
- Emotional and behavioural difficulties
- Physical disabilities
- Sensory impairments (hearing)

- Sensory impairments (visual)
- Medical conditions

(DfEE, 1994)

These needs were further classified in the Code of Practice 2001 into just four categories:

- Cognitive and learning
- Communication and interaction
- Behavioural, emotional and social development
- Sensor and/or physical.

(DfEE, 2001)

Runwick-Cole & Hodge argue that these categories still place the onus of educational issues on the child rather than on the barriers that may exist to children's learning. The difficulty in the language in current policy is that it is focused on deficits and difficulties in children's learning and therefore is linked to building and maintaining exclusion within schools (Runswick-Cole & Hodge 2009).

3.1 The effect inclusive educational policy can have on SEN pupils in Mainstream classes.

As previously stated inclusive education entails that students with disabilities have the right to an education with their peers in regular classrooms (Erten & Savage 2012). It insists that mainstream classrooms adapt to provide provisions for all children so that children with SEN can then adapt to the regular classroom (Lindsay 2007). It is argued that the school environment is to meet the needs of each individual child rather than attempting to make the child fit the school system (Erten & Savage 2012).

However there are disputing opinions with regard to the effect this interpretation of inclusive policy has on children with special educational needs. It is important to note that the interpretation of inclusive education should not only be considered the physical placement of a child in a mainstream school but also the curricular and teaching methodology adaptations to facilitate children with special educational needs allowing them to develop socially and academically (Gibb et al. 2007). It is argued that if provisions such as resources, differentiation and alternative teaching strategies are employed it is likely child with SEN will make appropriate progress (Manset & Semmel 1997). Dyson et al (2004) disputes that although children can progress academically, often placement in a mainstream classroom can be socially damaging leading to bullying and social rejection. This suggests a high level of social exclusion for children with special educational needs in mainstream classes (Nabuoka 2003 as cited in Dyson et al. 2004). This argument is valid in that the education of children is not only based on academia. On the other hand others contest that children with SEN actually benefit socially from inclusion in the mainstream class (Farrell 2000). Farrell discusses evidence that shows, in general, children in mainstream schools are quite accepting of children with SEN and incidents of persecution or discrimination are rare (Farrell, 2000). Rujis and Peetsma (2009) found corresponding evidence that studies investigating the effect of inclusion have resulted in mostly positive or neutral effects and very few studies report negative effects.

3.2 The effect inclusion policy can have on children without SEN

This essay will outline how less research has been conducted on the effect inclusive education can have on children without special educational needs. If, as Warnock (1978) suggests, up to 20 per cent of children will have a special educational need of some description in their school careers, it implies that the other 80 per cent of children in classrooms will not. Therefore it is imperative to look at the effect inclusion will have on the mainstream pupils. The overriding right is not that all children should be educated in mainstream schools; the right is for every child to have their individual educational needs met (Farrell 2000).

Avramidis questions the sociometric literature that portrays children with SEN 'predominantly as less accepted and marginalised' (Avramidis 2012 p.427). This study on the social relationships of pupils with Special educational needs in mainstream schools reports optimistic findings (ibid). It suggests that a key motive for inclusive educational policy is to reduce prejudice and increase social interaction of all pupils of varying backgrounds and abilities (Avramidis 2012). The results alluded to the positive effects inclusion has on both the children with SEN and those without (ibid). The friendship clusters within classes were of mixed ability and this fosters an inclusive society within the school (Avramidis 2012). It is advocated that this inclusion in schools lends itself to a more inclusive and accepting society; a society government is keen to establish (Avaramidis 2010, Farrell 2000).

3.3 Effects of inclusive education policy on teachers and parents.

According to Every Child Matters (2003) the SEN code of practice recommends a graduated approach to help enable children and provide provisions for those with special educational needs (Keslair, Maurin & McNally 2012). This Code of practice provides educators with some concrete teaching methodologies and strategies such as one to one tuition, special equipment, staff development and training and the creation of individual education plans (Keslair, Maurin & McNally 2012). While these guidelines are practical and useful they are not always feasible. In the 2010 Education for all Global Monitoring Report, *Reaching the marginalised*, teachers were described as 'a reflection of their education systems' (UNESCO 2011, p.462). It could be argued that if the Education system, through its policies, can promote education for all and best practice then it is imperative that teachers implement these ideals in everyday teaching in the classroom. However this requires a reconceptualisation of teachers' attitudes, roles and competencies (UNESCO 2011). The 2010 OECD survey suggested that teachers do not always feel fully qualified to teach those with every special educational need. Although teachers are generally positive about the idea of inclusive education, many feel unable to fully commit to it or insufficiently prepared for it (Farrell 2000, Opertti & Brady 2011).

Many factors affect teachers' attitudes towards inclusion (UNESCO 2011). The diverse nature of special educational needs and their ever-changing nature (ibid) make it extremely difficult to maintain professional development in inclusive education. Professional training and in-service is imperative to strengthening teachers' confidence to implement the inclusive policies in an effort to cater for the needs of all students (Opertti & Brady 2011). Florian and Rouse (2009) argue that specialised teacher training should not be exclusive to certain teachers but should be a basic fundamental aspect of teacher training. It should be an additional resource for all mainstream teachers if we are to achieve inclusion in mainstream classes (Florian & Rouse 2009).

Inclusion policies require that all children be given the opportunity to be educated in mainstream classes (Farrell 2000). Parents have played a major role in the inclusion debate (Scheepstra, Nakeen & Pijl 1999 and Erten & Savage 2012). One of the biggest motivators for parents was the social contact and relations for children with SEN and their placement in mainstream classes (Scheepstra, Nakeen & Pijl 1999). The advocacy of parents can be the most influencing factor in providing legislative policy for children with disabilities (Erten & Savage 2012). Parents wish for their children to have every opportunity available for academic and social growth in school (Scheepstra, Nakeen & Pijl 1999). However having a large proportion of children with special educational needs in a mainstream class can put strain on the class' resources which can lead to parents being deterred from sending their child to that particular school (Crawford & Vignoles 2010).

Similarly some parents are of the view that if all special schools were terminated in favour of full inclusion in mainstream they would not have the opportunity to choose a path of education for their child (Farrell 2000).

Inclusive educational policy has effects on all stakeholders in education. According to Michailakis & Reich (2009) the importance is finding the appropriate balance between the happiness of the individual child with special educational needs and the overall success of the inclusive education system.

4. Statementing. A cause of exclusion?

Looking back to the first introduction of Special Educational needs legislation; the Warnock report (1978) recommended identifying and recording the special educational needs of children who required additional provisions. In 2001 the Special Educational Needs Code of Practice outlined a strategy that the majority of children with SEN would be provided for in mainstream schools. It also stated that a small number of children with special educational needs would require additional support that is identified in a "statement". The resources for which are provided by their local authority. When a child is identified as having SEN a varied approach of teaching methodologies ensues bringing planning and extra resources for the child (DfEE 2001). The Lamb report (2010) identified a number of issues with the classification of SEN and in particular the varying nature of identification across different Local authorities (Lamb, 2010). The local authorities have the responsibility to identify children who require statements and then provide the funding needed (ibid). This, according to Lamb (2010) is a huge incentive for LEAs to under-identify children with SEN, as it can be a potentially substantial sum in their budgets. This is arguably a barrier to inclusion as children who desperately require additional resources and provisions in schools are not obtaining them, due to financial stubbornness of the Local Authority. On the other hand Crawford & Vignoles (2010) express the argument that schools also have an incentive to over-identify children with statemented needs in order to receive additional funding for their school.

One of the biggest issues regarding statements is labelling. It is theorised that labelling contributes to a stigma that may in turn produce low self-esteem and exacerbate outcomes for children with SEN (Keslair et al 2012). This essay will argue that a stigma such as a SEN label can be problematic for children in numerous ways. Children with a Statement of special educational needs are automatically categorised and assigned an identity that may determine the rest of their educational careers (Runswick-Cole & Hodge 2009). Teachers can inadvertently have pre-conceptions of children with statements often believing they are incapable or under qualified to teach these children (Slee 2009). Children with a statement are therefore treated differently and are segregated rather than assisted in adjusting to the regular class (Ho, 2004). Regularly it is the low expectations of schools and teachers when a child is labelled with a specific need that may cause the pupil to attribute their lack of achieving to ability rather than effort (Keslair, Maurin & McNally 2012). There are issues with teachers lowering their accepted level of achievement for a child with a statement and even cases where some school officials still consider these children as 'less competent or inherently inferior' (Ho 2004 p.87). This problem leads to the constructing and sustaining of exclusionary practices within our education systems today (Runswick-Cole & Hodge 2009).

It has been argued that labelling children can lead to the loss of their personal identity or individuality behind the cloak of a syndrome or learning difficulty (Runswick-Cole & Hodge 2009, Van Swet et al 2011). Pre-conceived notions of what children with certain syndromes will behave like induces a practice of 'othering' the child to a fixed classification of syndrome in order to maintain school order (Hehir 2002). The labels can begin to have lives of their own (Dehue 2008 as cited in Van Swet et al 2011). On the other hand Slee (2009) articulates the importance of statementing to offer individual and unique support to children with specific requirements.

5. The Future of Inclusive Education Policy

As it stands inclusive education policy requires schools to ensure that all students have equal access to educational opportunities regardless of special educational needs, disability or backgrounds (Ainscow, Booth and Dyson 2006, UNESCO 2000). The debate of why we should implement inclusive pedagogies has evolved into the more important question of how we can develop inclusive schools (Savage 2006, Erten & Savage 2012).

To examine the future possibilities of inclusive educational policy this essay will examine the literature surrounding the Italian Emilia Reggio schools and their interpretation of inclusive education. Runswick-Cole & Hodge (2009) have advocated for the influence of the Italian schools to permeate the barriers to inclusion in national policy. The Emilia Reggio schools were set up by parents and draw on the work of early childhood psychologists such as Vygotsky, Piaget and Dewey (Runswick-Cole & Hodge 2009). The primary aims of Reggio schools are to ensure every child has a sincere sense of belonging within the class and school community and to reinforce children's sense of identity (Edmiaston & Fitzgerald 2000). Most importantly, for policy debate, it is the rights-based approach of Reggio schools that differs from inclusive educational policy in the United Kingdom(Runswick-Cole & Hodge 2009). In these schools children have special 'rights' not special 'needs'. Runswick-Cole & Hodge (2009) cite this alteration of language and terminology as vital. The exclusion caused by terminology discussed earlier in this essay is almost entirely eradicated with this simple change. Unlike the Individual Education Plan that is used in the UK for children with special educational needs, the Reggio schools have a 'Declaration of Intent' that all pupils attain (Runswick-Cole & Hodge 2009). This focuses attention on every child's strength, eliminating the singling out of children with 'special needs'. This will inevitably lead to less children being excluded in the classroom (Runswick-Cole & Hodge 2009).

This rights based approach has already been endorsed by UNESCO (2007) in a human rights action plan. The progressive plan advocates that educational policies should promote a rights-based approach and that the learning environment should enable the practice of human rights in the whole school community, among other things (UNESCO 2007).

The term special educational needs has led to some children facing exclusion both socially and academically from schools (Runswick-Cole & Hodge 2009). This essay would contest that although a change in language and terminology cannot alone change exclusionary practice within schools, it may lead the way in policy-making for the future.

Conclusion

This essay has attempted to examine how inclusive educational policy may have led to the inadvertent exclusion of some children in mainstream schools. It explored the introduction of SEN policy through the Warnock Report (1978). This paper measured how important this report was and how influential the introduction of new inclusive language and terminology was on policy. It then examined the importance of the UNESCO Salamanca agreement and how this influenced pedagogy and practice of special educational needs in the United Kingdom and internationally.

Before Warnock the term 'handicapped' was common and denoted very negative images of the educational ability of the child. These 'un-educable' children were completely excluded from the education system until after the Education Act 1981.

As shown in this essay language continuously changes and is in constant need of updating.

This essay examined various definitions of 'inclusion' and how they are reflected in policy. From writers who defined inclusion as taking a full and active part in school life (Farrell 2000), to those who argued that inclusion in the mainstream setting can be disadvantageous to children and does not reflect inclusion (Michailakis & Reich 2009, Warnock 2005, Dyson, Farrell, Polat & Hutchenson 2004). Difficulties in the definition and interpretation of the term 'special educational needs' and it's contribution to the possible exclusion of children (Runswick-Cole & Hodge 2009) was also highlighted in this essay.

To examine the possible exclusion of children from the education system this essay focused on the effects that inclusive policy has on children with SEN, children without SEN, parents and teachers. The importance of all of these stakeholders in the quest for inclusion was emphasised.

A major factor in the exclusion of children with SEN is the process of statementing. This element of educational policy has led to labelling children. While some find labelling useful in providing for children's needs, it is often perceived as destructive to a child's 'educational career' (Runswick-Cole & Hodge 2009). Labelling can stigmatise children and influence teachers' teaching methods and attitudes towards them (Keslair, Maurin & McNally 2012). Finally this essay analysed the future of inclusive education policy. While drawing on the issues that were presented in the essay it has suggested possible amendments in language and terminology as well as a new 'rights-based' approach to including all children in inclusive policy (Runswick-Cole & Hodge 2009). It has investigated the Reggio Emilia Italian School system and has drawn on positive directions that could possibly lead to future changes in the way we implement and make education policy inclusive.

References

Ainscow, M., Booth, T., and Dyson, A., (2006). Inclusion and the standards agenda: Negotiating policy pressures in England. *International Journal of Inclusive Education* 10, nos. 4-5: 295-308.

Ainscow, M., & Miles, S. (2008). Making Education for All inclusive: where next? *Prospects*, 38: 15-34.

Avramidis, E. (2010) Social relationships of pupils with special educational needs in the mainstream primary class: peer group membership and peer-assessed social behaviour, *European Journal of Speical Needs Education,* 25:4, 413-429

Benjamin, S. (2002) *The Micropolitics of Inclusive Education.* Buckingham: Open University Press.

Bines, H. & Lei, P. (2011) Disability and education: The longest road to inclusion. *International Journal of Educational Development* 31, 419-424.

Booth, T., Ainscow, M., Black-Hawkins, K., Vaughan, M. & Shaw, L. (2000) *Index for Inclusion.* Bristol: Centre for Studies on Inclusive Education.

Burgess, E. (2003) *Are we nearly there yet? Do teenage wheelchair users think integration has been achieved in secondary schools in the UK?* (Whizz-Kidz No Limits Millennium Award).

Corbett, J. (1996) *Bad-Mouthing: The language of special needs.* London: Falmer Press.

Crawford, C., & Vignoles, A., (2010) An analysis of the educational progress of children with special educational needs. *Department of Quantitative Social Science Working paper* no. 10-19.

DES (1978) *Special Educational Needs: Report of the Committee of Enquiry into the Education of Handicapped Children and Young People (The Warnock Report).* London: HMSO.

DfEE (1994) *The Code of Practice on the Identification and Assessment of Special Educational Needs.* London: HMSO.

Dfee (1997) *White Paper Excellence in Schools.* Cmnd 3681. London. HMSO

DfEE (2001) *The Code of Practice on the Identification and Assessment of Special Educational Needs.* London: HMSO.

DfEE (2003) Every Child Matters. Norwich: The Stationary Office.

DfES. (2005). *Admissions and Exclusions of pupils with Special Educational Needs.* National Foundation for Educational Research, Research Report no. 608, London, DfES.

Dyson, A., Farrell, P., Polat, F., & Hutchenson, G. (2004). *Inclusion and pupil achievement.* Research Report RR578. London: DfES Publications.

Edmiaston, R.K. & Fitzgerald, L.M. (2000) How Reggio Emilia Encourages Inclusion. *Educational Leadership.* Volume 58, Issue 1, pp. 66-69.

Erten, O., & Savage, R.S. (2012). Moving forward in inclusive education research, *International Journal of Inclusive Education*, 16:2, 221-233.

Farrell, P. (2000). The impact of research on developments in inclusive education. *International Journal of Inclusive Education* 4, no. 2: 153-62.

Florian, L., (2008). Inclusion: Special or inclusive education: future trends. *British Journal of Special Education,* Volume 35, Issue 4, 202-208.

Florian, L., & Rouse, M. (2009). The inclusive practice in Scotland: Teacher education for inclusive education. *Teacher and Teacher Education,* 25(4) 594-601.

Frederickson, N. and T. Cline. (2002). *Special educational needs inclusion and diversity: A text-book.* Buckingham: Open University Press.

Freire, S., & César, M. (2003). Inclusive ideals/inclusive practices: How far is dream from reality? Five comparative case studies. *European Journal of Special Needs Education,* 18 (3), 341-345.

Gibb, K., Tunbridge, D., Chua, A., Frederickson, N. (2007). Pathways to Inclusion: Moving from special school to mainstream, *Educational Psychology in Practice: theory, research and practice in educational psychology,* 23:2, 109-127.

Hehir, T., (2002). Eliminating ableism in education. *Harvard Educational Review* 72: 1-32.

Ho, A., (2004). To be labelled, or not to be labelled: that is the question. *British Journal of Learning Disabilities*, 32, 86-92.

Hornby, G., (2011). Inclusive Education for Children with Special Educational Needs: A Critique, *International Journal of Disability, Development and Education*, 58:3, 321-329.

Hunt, P.L. (2011). Salamanca Statement and IDEA 2004: Possibilities of practice for inclusive education, *International Journal of Inclusive Education,* 15:4, 461-476.

Keslair, F., Maurin, E. and McNally, S. (2012) Every Child Matters? An evaluation of "Special Educational Needs" programmes in England, *Economics of Education Review* 31, 932-948.

Lamb (2010), The *Lamb inquiry: Special Educational Needs and Parental Confidence*, DCFS publications, Nottingham, http:www.dcsf.gov.uk/lambinquiry/downloads/8553-lamb-inquiry.pdf

Lindsay, G. (2007). Annual Review: Educational psychology and the effectiveness of inclusive education/mainstreaming. *British Journal of Educational Psychology* 77: 1-24.

Manset, G., & Semmel, M.I. (1997). Are inclusive programs for students with mild disabilities effective? A comparative review of model programs. *The Journal of Special Educaiton, 31* (4), 155-180.

Michailakis, D. & Reich, W. (2009). Dilemmas of inclusive education, *ALTER, European Journal of Disability Research* 3, 24-44.

Opertti, R. & Brady, J., (2011). Developing inclusive teachers from an inclusive curricular perspective. Prospects, Volume 41, Issue 3, pp.459-472.

Roulstone, A. & Prideaux, S. (2008). More Policies, greater inclusion? Exploring the contradictions of New Labour inclusive education policy, *International Studies in Sociology of Education,* 18:1, 15-29.

Ruijs, N.M. & Peetsma T.T.D. (2009) Effects of inclusion on students with and without special educational needs reviewed. *Educational Research Review* 4, 67-69.

Runswick-Cole, K., & Hodge N. (2009). Needs or Rights? A challenge to the discourse of special education, *British Journal of Special Education,* Volume 36, number 4, 198-203.

Scheepstra, A.J.M., H. Nakken, and S.J. Pijil. (1999) Contacts with classmates: The social position of pupils with Down's syndrome in Dutch mainstream education. *European Journal of Special Needs Education* 14, no.3: 212-20.

Shah, S. (2007). Special or mainstream? The views of disabled students, *Research Papers in Education*, 22:4, 425-442.

Sikes, P., Lawson, H. & Parker, M. (2007) Voices on: teachers and teaching assistants talk about inclusion. *International Journal of Inclusive Education*, 11 (3), pp.335-70.

Slee, R. (2009). Beyond special and regular schooling? An Inclusive education reform agenda, *International Studies in Sociology of Education*, 18:2, 99-116.

Slee, R., (2011). *The irregular school.* London. Routledge.

Thomson, M.M. (2012). Labelling and self-esteem: Does labelling exceptional students impact their self-esteem? *Support for Learning*, Volume 27, Issue 4, 158-165.

Tomlinson, S. (2012). The irresistible rise of the SEN industry, *Oxford Review of Education*, 38:3, 267-286.

UNESCO and Ministry of Education and Science Spain. (1994). *The Salamanca Statement and Framework for Action on special needs education.* Spain: UNESCO.

UNESCO IBE (2011). *Developing inclusive teachers from an inclusive curricular perspective.* Geneva: UNESCO IBE.

UNESCO (2007). *Human Rights Action Plan.* Available at:

(http://unesdoc.unesco.org/images/0015/001548/154861e.pdf)

Van Swet, J., Wichers-Bots, J. & Brown, K. (2011). Solution focused assessment: rethinking labels to support inclusive education, *International Journal of Inclusive Education*, 15:9, 909-923.

Warnock, M., (2005). *Special Educational Needs: A new look.* London. Philosophy of Education Society of Great Britain.

Wilson, J., (2002) Defining 'special needs', *European Journal of Special Needs Education*, 17:1, 61-66.

3 BHAVISHA SOMA

My name is Bhavisha Soma and I am a primary school teacher. Before this I enjoyed working with children on various drama projects and also at a martial arts club. Through these experiences I became interested in how children develop academically and socially to become adult citizens. I was particularly interested in what constitutes a 'gifted' and 'talented' child and how these labels might affect a child's learning and their later opportunities in life. This inspired me to do my Masters in Gifted Education.

The literature surrounding educational policy for the 'gifted' and 'talented' has been fascinating to read and I find myself keen to explore further into the effects of policy on practice and how this ultimately affects the lives of children as they grow up. My ongoing learning is helping me to ensure that I provide an opportunity for all my children to develop their own gifts, whatever they may be, and to reach their full potential.

A critical review of the literature surrounding the Excellence in Cities policy, 1999 and the education of gifted and talented children.

Abstract

This assignment will consider the literature surrounding New Labour's Excellence in Cities policy, launched in 1999. It will specifically review the policy in relation to the education of gifted and talented children. Beginning with an outline of the policy and its relevant context, this assignment will reflect on several aspects of the policy. These aspects are political, social and economic context, area-focused intervention, identification of the gifted and talented, provisions for the gifted and talented at school (school policy, school co-ordinator, school register, teaching and learning strategies and the curriculum and also resources), absence, multi-agency working and effects on pupil attainment. The assignment will then conclude that for the short time EiC was in operation, not enough research was carried out to definitively assess its long-term impact. Finally, this assignment will make some suggestions for further research.

Introduction

The Excellence in Cities (EiC) initiative has been highlighted by many authors, such as Cooper et al. (2003) and Machin et al. as 'one of the U.K government's flagship education policies' (2004: 396). Casey and Koshy describe the initiative as a 'milestone' (2013: 46) in gifted and talented education as it was 'the first time that the topic of improved provision for these pupils had been placed firmly within the national agenda' (ibid.: 44). On the other hand, some authors such as Whitty, highlight the 'limitations of the initiative in terms of raising attainment and improving skills and attitudes across all pupils, especially among the most disadvantaged' (2008: 172). Both these perspectives will be examined further throughout this assignment.

This assignment will begin by giving an outline of EiC and its relevant context. Several thematic strands, as identified in the literature surrounding the policy, will then be explored with analysis and synthesis of various viewpoints in regards to the education of gifted and talented children. In this way, the assignment will illustrate the debate surrounding this policy, before drawing some conclusions on the policy and the education of gifted and talented children. Finally, this assignment will make some suggestions for further areas of research.

Outline of Policy and Relevant Context

According to Lowe, 'the 1990s saw an increasing recognition that the needs of able pupils were not being adequately served' (2002: 88). In contrast, after 2003 a commitment to provision for gifted and talented children was expected from all local authority schools in England (Casey and Koshy, 2013). Furthermore, co-ordinators to implement this area of policy were appointed at both local authorities and school (ibid.). The role of these co-ordinators is discussed later in this assignment.

Bailey et al. state that the EiC policy 'adopted a multi-strand approach' (2004: 134). The different elements of the policy, as identified by many authors including Lowe (2003) and Whitty (2008), are Gifted and Talented, City Learning Centres, Learning Support Units, Education Action Zones, Specialist Schools, Beacon Schools, Learning Mentors and the Excellence Challenge, which provided post-16 provision. Much of the literature available on EiC (Machin et al. (2004) and McNally (2005), for example) focuses not on these individual aspects of EiC, but on the policy as a whole. As a result of this characteristic of the literature, this assignment will also refer to EiC in this overarching and all-encompassing way.

Exploration of the literature surrounding the EiC policy and the education of the gifted and talented reveals seven thematic strands. These strands are political, social and economic context (Lowe, 2002), area-focused intervention (Raffo, 2009 and McNally, 2005), identification of the gifted and talented (Casey and Koshy, 2013 and Bailey et al., 2004), provisions for the gifted and talented at school (Casey and Koshy, 2013 and Lowe, 2002), absence (Cooper et al., 2003), multi-agency working (Ball, 2013) and effects on pupil attainment (Machin et al., 2004 and McNally, 2005). This assignment will now consider each of these areas in turn.

Political, Social and Economic Context

Politics

As indicated by Halpin (1997) and Goodwin (2011) the fact that EiC was implemented at a time when a New Labour government was in power, can be said to be indicative of its design. Casey and Koshy state that EiC was 'at the heart of Prime Minister Tony Blair's vision of a meritocratic society' (2003: 47) and that this drove the EiC principle of children being rewarded based on merit, regardless of social background. In reference to the relationship between politics and policy, Ball goes so far as to say that 'education policies construct the 'problems' they address and thus the solutions they propose' (2013: 103), suggesting that an issue might be problematised simply so that a way out can be put forward. This idea is further supported by Ball's writing on the dissemination of the EiC policy (2013).

> '...the document was widely circulated (and was available at supermarket checkouts)...lively coloured photographs, taken in schools, are interspersed throughout; mini-case studies of good practise are contained in colour-coded bordered boxes.'
>
> (Ball, 2013: 100)

This very public distribution of EiC is also highlighted by Machin et al. (2004), illustrating the political significance of the policy document. Politics and policy are inextricably linked and as stated by Lowe, 'social policy, economic policy and educational policy must be linked if things really are to change for the better.' (Lowe 2002: 93). This assignment will now examine these linked relationships and go on to explore how things might have changed after the introduction of the EiC.

Social Issues

Bailey et al. claim that EiC is 'embedded within a specific social and political context' (2004: 138). Further investigation is needed into what that social context could be and Raffo emphasises the vital link between education and social opportunity claiming that 'education plays a crucial role in social inclusion because it is the principal passport to opportunity.' (2009: 66). Casey and Koshy expand on what that opportunity might be, stating that EiC was launched to 'tackle "disadvantage" through educational social mobility... encouraging more children from poorer backgrounds toward higher education and, potentially a more fulfilling adult life' (2013: 45). Ball explains how EiC aimed to achieve this goal through schemes such as the Education Action Zones (EAZs):

> Specific initiatives like EAZs and Excellence in Cities (EiC) were targeted at areas of social disadvantage. In turn, these initiatives were part of a broader social policy strategy of tackling 'social inclusion'... social and economic goals were interrelated.
>
> (Ball, 2013: 176)

Whitty (2008), however, dismisses EAZs as having little noticeable impact on the education of the gifted and talented. Lowe suggests that the nature of provision for the gifted and talented was 'paradoxical' (2002: 88), stemming from 'the uneasy relationship between questions of class and questions of educational policy and provision' (ibid.). Having explored the political and social context, this assignment will now examine the economic context.

Economic Issues

During the 1980s and 90s, the Conservative Governments that preceded New Labour had implemented a number of public spending cuts (Ball, 2013). Goodwin develops this by stating that, in contrast to the 1980s and 90s, New Labour's 'focus on public service delivery as the as the core business of government was informed by a relatively prosperous and stable economic environment' (2011: 408). The economic strength might even have been the driving force behind the newly elected government's educational policies (Goodwin, 2011). New Labour 'invested significantly in the development of the 'gifted and talented' strand within the education policy' (Koshy et al., 2012). Indeed, Cooper et al. underline the fact that 'as of July 2002, the government had made £511.2 million available for Excellence in Cities, a figure intended to rise to over £300 million a year by 2003-2004.' (2003: 84). Machin et al. project a more long term spending forecast stating that 'in the 2002-2003 financial year the resources devoted to the scheme were about £300 million, and this is set to more than double to £700 million by 2006' (2004: 397). Both sets of statistics demonstrate a strong financial commitment to EiC initiatives (Copper et al., 2003 and Machin et al., 2004). However, Machin and McNally (2012) draw attention to the relationship between the funding available and EiC policy provisions, noting its sometimes restrictive impact on material factors such as resources. The issue of resources and their use for gifted and talented children will be discussed later in this assignment.

It is in this context of political, social and economic affairs that the EiC came into effect. This assignment will now consider the various components of the policy.

Area-focused Intervention

EiC has been labelled by both Raffo (2009) and McNally as an 'area-based education initiative' (2005: 292), drawing attention to the way in which EiC was largely focused on urban areas (Whitty, 2008 and Bailey et al., 2004) and the fact that it took a localised approach. Cooper at al. (2003) cite Hazelbury Infants' School in Edmonton as an illustration of an EiC area specific initiative to help make the most of children's potential. At that school many of the parents speak English as a second language and find it more difficult to help their children with their learning. For this reason, the school runs a scheme whereby numeracy and literacy skills are taught to both the children and their parents so they can help each other learn together (2003). Despite the apparently positive effects of EiC's local interventions, Cooper et al. do stress the 'need for greater fine-tuning of these flagship programmes at the local level' (2003: 87).

Identification of the Gifted and Talented

When reflecting on a policy for gifted and talented children, the importance of a definition and teacher identification of 'gifted and talented' has been highlighted by several authors, such as Koshy and Pinheiro-Torres (2013). One must first have some understanding of what being 'gifted' and 'talented' means before then considering how such children can be identified (Bailey et al., 2004). Bailey et.al note that 'the broad area of 'Giftedness and Talent' is littered with linguistic and conceptual difficulties' (2004: 134) and much research supports this (Dai and Chen, 2013 and Renzulli, and Reis, 1991). Casey and Koshy (2013) explain that at that time the government clarified that 'gifted' referred to those learners who excelled at academic subjects such as English and 'talented' described learners who performed well in applied practical skills, for instance in sports or performing arts. However, in their study into the identification of talented children in physical education, Bailey et al. (2004) discovered that teachers found it hard to convey precisely what talent is and how they recognised it, making it problematic to identify children who might fit into that category. Identification of gifted and talented children is central to a policy that aims to make provisions for their learning and Bailey et al., writing only a few years after the introduction of EiC, make the following claim:

> There is limited guidance available to teachers at the time of writing, regarding best practice in the identification of talent in PE, sport, or any other area of the curriculum...
>
> (2004: 136)

This suggests a significant lack of direction when it comes to identifying gifted and talented children (Bailey et al., 2004). At the same time, in their study they found that there was a 'considerable degree of commonality in teachers' experiences' (ibid.: 133) in relation to when and how they identified talent. In spite of this, the authors felt that the qualitative data they gathered through interviewing teachers revealed that they would benefit from more official guidance to support them (Bailey et al., 2004).

Casey and Koshy emphasise that one study found that the 'predominant method of identification used by the teachers in their national sample was based on national or school test results' (2013: 54). Bailey et al. (2004) also refer to the way in which National Curriculum levels were used as a measure of attainment and giftedness. Koshy et al. question the appropriateness of this and also note that children with creative abilities might not perform well in these tests (2012: 177). In addition to this, a 'study has also documented that tests are not reliable indicators of giftedness in the case of students from socially disadvantaged backgrounds' (ibid.). This is especially problematic when one considers that a major goal of EiC was to minimise the risk of social disadvantage impacting negatively on gifted education (Casey and Koshy, 2013).

EiC sets practitioners the target of identifying 'a gifted and talented population, consisting of 5% to 10% of the top-ability pupils within their school' (Casey and Koshy, 2013: 47). However, as Bailey et al. point out, there is 'no scientific reason for this figure' (2004: 136), it is simply a government target for the purposes of monitoring and evaluation. Arguably, this figure being set in stone can be seen as a 'straitjacket' (Lowe, 2002: 90) that is restrictive towards the identification of gifted and talented children. One example of the constraint described by Lowe (ibid.) is illustrated in the following case, described by Bailey et al. (2004). In one year, the teachers might decide that there are not enough children who fit the criteria to make up the 5 to 10 per cent group of gifted and talented children. However, they would still need to add children (perhaps of lesser ability) to the group to reach the government target set. The following year, there might be more than 5 to 10 per cent of children who teachers feel are gifted and talented. However, some children would not make the group due to there being too many children in the group already. The children who miss out might even be considered by the practitioners to be more able than some of the children who made it into the group last year. In this way, this prescriptive figure of 5 to 10 per cent, brings with it intrinsic difficulties (ibid.). Lowe maintains that the figure 'can be construed as a powerful force for change as a catalyst for challenging underachievement' (2002: 90), a foundation that can be built upon and developed for the education of gifted and talented children. Yet, Casey and Koshy acknowledged that teachers did not like labelling children as gifted and talented and found that 'most had decided to ignore the policy requirement of making a percentage list' of those pupils' (2013: 45), in effect invalidating this particular policy requirement.

Provisions for the Gifted and Talented at School

School Policy

Casey and Koshy state that 'schools were expected to draw up policies outlining how their identification, provision, and monitoring systems would operate and how targets would be set for these pupils' (2013: 47). In a study examined by Casey and Koshy, they found that 90% of the sample had a 'written school policy for gifted and talented education' (ibid.: 50), which was an increase on 32% of schools having a policy in an earlier study. This can be seen as a positive outcome of EiC on the education of gifted and talented children (Casey and Koshy, 2013), yet there is little in the literature to indicate the specifics of each school's individual policy. In addition to this, there is the possibility that the policy will be either ignored or 'interpreted in the light of teachers' particular beliefs about teaching, learning and giftedness' (Koshy et al., 2012: 170). This is perhaps where the role of school co-ordinator could offer some guidance on interpretation and implementation of the policy.

School Co-ordinator

Lowe argues that amongst all the considerations in education for the gifted, there is a 'need for well-trained and informed staff and collaborative cultures in and across schools' (2002: 93). Lowe emphasises the importance of staffing, highlighting the significance of a 'high-status' (2003: 126) school co-ordinator who would be an expert in their field and someone who can easily facilitate changes within the school. On-going professional development plays a considerable part in this and Wilson (2009) claims that as part of EiC, over two thousand primary school teachers participated in specialist training. However, there is little information in the literature as to how these trainees went on to use their new learning to benefit the gifted and talented children. In fact, in their evaluative report into EiC, the Department for Education and Skills (DfES), found that some school co-ordinators believed they did not have enough time to adequately perform their role.

School Register

Teachers were required to choose gifted and talented children and put their names on a register (Casey and Koshy, 2013). Placing a select group of children on this register has been described as posing 'the greatest challenge to the teaching profession and to the schools involved since the introduction of the gifted and talented initiative in the UK (Koshy et al., 2012: 175). Much of the reason for this was based on the confusion surrounding the terminology and identification of gifted and talented (Koshy, et al., 2012). The validity of the register has been questioned by Koshy et al. and they suggest that the emphasis of gifted education should be on 'enriched provision rather than selection' (2012: 178). The nature of the register can also be questioned as Koshy et al. found that many schools did not monitor socio-economic background on their register, suggesting that 'the issue of inclusion which is at the heart of government policy does not seem to be addressed' (ibid.). Thus, EiC's aim of facilitating social inclusion (Ball, 2013) is not being realised.

Strategies and Curriculum

The nature of the curriculum for the gifted and talented is a recurring theme in the literature (Casey and Koshy, 2013). Casey and Koshy note that schools were expected to put together 'a distinct and discernibly different teaching and learning program to address the needs of these pupils' (2013: 47).

In reference to specialist schools for the gifted (one of the strands of the EiC), Kaplan makes the following claim:

> Some of the special schools for the gifted have maintained their reputation on their abilities to define themselves as separate educational settings because their population comprises the gifted and not because they have a differentiated curriculum appropriately aligned to the gifted.
>
> (Kaplan, 2013:204)

Kaplan's assertion (2004) draws attention to the issue of a lack of a separate curriculum for the gifted and talented. Lowe (2002) agrees that some schools and teachers are reluctant to teach to a special curriculum for the gifted. Nonetheless, Lowe acknowledges that the use of ICT is one strategy that has been applied to enhance the education of the gifted and talented. Another strategy consists of teachers using materials and challenges from the next level up in the National Curriculum (Casey and Koshy, 2013). However, Bailey et al. point out that there are 'some tensions, especially with regard to the interplay between professional judgements and National Curriculum guidelines' (2004: 133). Indeed, Dai and Chen warn against the use of a 'one-size-fits-all, age graded curriculum' (2013: 158), meaning that the curriculum might not be the definitive indicator of which level a child is working at, or should be working at. According to Casey and Koshy (2013), an expert panel on a government select committee claimed that implementation of EiC at a classroom level was inconsistent and disjointed. This view is supported by Machin et a. (2004) and Lowe, who states that schools have taken 'different and varied approaches according to their particular context' (2002: 91). According to Lowe, 2002, HMI 'commended the quality of work which is being undertaken in out-of-hours and enrichment activities in Excellence in Cities schools' (2002: 93) but maintained that this level of challenge should be integrated into daily practice within the classroom. As this section of the assignment has illustrated, according to the literature, the implications of EiC on classroom strategies and curriculum has had varied consequences.

Resources

A 'difficult empirical issue in this area is that additional school resources are often disproportionately allocated to disadvantaged students' (Machin and McNally, 2012: R18). Arguably, those gifted children who did not receive additional resources might then be put at a disadvantage compared to those who did receive them and this would create difficulties in comparing the achievements of both groups and linking attainment exclusively to EiC (Machin and McNally, 2012).

Absence

As part of the EiC initiative, the government set local education authorities the challenge of cutting unauthorised absences by a third, with the aim of raising attainment and 'reducing antisocial behaviour also commonly associated with truancy and exclusion' (Cooper et al., 2003: 85). Cash incentives such as the 'truancy buster' awards (ibid..: 86) were given to schools that succeeded in cutting truancy rates. In keeping with the area-focused approach of EiC, a number of schemes were implemented, which were specific to their locality. This is exemplified by an arrangement in the London borough of Tower Hamlets, which 'with its 40 per cent Muslim population, uses the local mosque' (ibid..) to tackle truancy. Imams have stressed the importance of education in their sermons and even made home visits and attended parents' evenings. This has been reinforced by the mosque's radio station, which awarded certificates and pens to children who improved their school attendance (ibid..). Cooper et al. acknowledge that these interventions meant that 'primary school attendance has increased by an estimated 5-10 per cent' (ibid..). McNally (2005) and Machin et al. (2012) also suggest that introduction of the EiC led to improved attendance at school, but this does not necessarily boost the attainment of the group of children labelled as gifted and talented.

Absence was the focus of an article by Cooper et al. (2003), in which they examined the effect of several factors, including absence, on pupil attainment in Greater London. They found that for every one percent increase in 'unauthorised half days missed at secondary school' (ibid.: 83), the percentage of pupils gaining five GCSEs A*-C was reduced by over 9 percentage points, suggesting that absence does indeed have an impact on pupil attainment. However, when considering the findings of a study such as this one, one must contemplate the validity of the data and any potential problems associated with the variables:

> The existence of statistical relationships between a dependent variable (educational attainment) and one or more independent variables (proxies for material/social deprivation) does not, of course, necessarily capture cause and effect. (ibid.)

Consequently, it is important to remember that there might be other factors that also contribute to poor pupil attainment, some which may be linked to absence and some which might not be linked (Copper et al., 2003). Thus, evidence to show the direct impact of reduced absences on the education of the gifted and talented, appears to be lacking.

Multi-Agency Working

Ball claims that 'multi-agency working, business participation, attempts to engage local people in decision making' (2013: 178) were central to New Labour educational policies. Lowe (2002) and Bailey et al. (2004) agree that educational partnerships and sharing good practice are a key principle of EiC. Bailey et al. (2004) found that many teachers felt that they were lacking in this 'collaborative culture' (Lowe, 2002: 93) and would benefit from closer relationship with their primary feeder schools, so that they could offer more continuity to those children identified as gifted and talented at an earlier stage. One could argue that policies are simply suggested ways forward (White, 2012), nevertheless one cannot ignore the fact that there is little literature available that illustrates multi-agency working in practice.

Pupil Attainment

Lowe acknowledges that it is important to 'gain an understanding of the impact of the Excellence in Cities strategies on achievement and attainment of pupils' (2003:128). It has been argued that there are differences in pupil attainment before children begin their schooling and that these gaps, particularly ones associated with social disadvantage, become wider as a child grows up. (Machin and McNally, 2012). EiC aimed to bridge the attainment gap caused by social disadvantage (Ball, 2013) and some authors argue that to a certain extent the policy did do this (Machin et al., 2004). Machin et al. interpreted their findings as 'evidence that policies like EiC can impact positively on pupil attainment and attendance' (2004: 396) and this viewpoint is supported by McNally (2005). Conversely, Whitty argues that due to misconceptions of the education market there has been 'at best only a very modest reduction in the attainment gap between pupils from advantaged and disadvantaged backgrounds under New Labour.' (2008: 166).) Similarly, Lowe (2002) lists a number of findings that suggest pupil attainment was not improved as a result of EiC. These findings include stagnant or worsening progress at Key Stage 3, children at schools in the inner city continuing to achieve less than those that are not, low attainment of some ethnic groups and 'a continuing gap between boys' and girls' achievements' (2002: 91). This gender gap in pupil attainment is supported by the research of Machin et al. who found that 'Maths attainment show larger effects for boys than for girls' (2004: 404). The views of Whitty (2008) and Lowe (2002) would suggest that the attainment of gifted and talented children was not greatly increased by EiC.

Conclusion

This assignment has considered the education of gifted and talented children in relation to the EiC policy. Several thematic strands are present in the literature. Firstly, it has been argued that the political, social and economic context is of great relevance (Lowe, 2002) and it is under this umbrella that the EiC came into effect. Secondly, the concept of EiC as an area focused intervention has been explored and there is some evidence that this helped gifted children make the most of their potential (Raffo, 2009 and McNally, 2005). Thirdly, the definition and identification of the gifted and talented was reviewed this area of the policy appears to be fraught with difficulties (Casey and Koshy, 2013 and Bailey et al., 2004), meaning that the EiC can be seen as no more than a stepping stone to catering more fully for the needs of gifted and talented children (Lowe, 2002) . Fourthly, provisions for the gifted and talented at school were put under scrutiny and it was noted that the interpretation and implementation of EiC was inconsistent (Casey and Koshy, 2013 and Lowe, 2002). Then the issue of absence was addressed and there is some evidence that this was tackled by EiC (Cooper et al., 2003). Next, multi-agency working was investigated (Ball, 2013) and while this key principle of EiC, there were few specific examples of it in the literature. Finally, pupil attainment was inspected (Machin et al., 2004 and McNally, 2005) and the evidence that this was improved, remains as having mixed results in the research available. On the one hand policy can 'help to lay, on philosophically thought-through foundations, pathways towards a better education for all' (White, 2008: 515). On the other hand, in their report evaluating the impact of EiC in primary schools, Ofsted found that some schools 'believed that the gifted and talented strand of the programme was not conducive to promoting equal opportunities' (Ofsted, 2004). Tomlinson states that 'despite a rhetoric of inclusion... education remains divided and divisive' (2003: 195). In summary, the literature surrounding the Excellence in Cities policy paints a blurred picture as to what the conclusive outcomes were for the education of gifted and talented children. As Casey and Koshy point out, there is in fact 'very little published research or evaluative data on how schools interpreted and implemented the policy' (2013: 49). It is only in the consistent, rigorous and on-going application and continual evaluation of all aspects of 'policy formulation, policy interpretation and policy implementation' (Koshy et al., 2012) that it would be possible to more fully assess its long-term impact on the education of the gifted and talented children. However, as governments continually change, so do their policies (Ball, 2013) and this can make it difficult to review what potentially could have been achieved.

Suggestions for Future Research

Lowe asserts that there is still much to be done in regards to research into the education of the gifted and talented (2003: 128). Through conducting this critical review of existing literature on EiC, it is possible for this assignment to make some suggestions for future research. As noted by Koshy et al., 'there is only a very small body or research available to practitioners on different models of provision and their effectiveness' (2012: 182) and so further research is recommended in that area (Koshy et .al, 2012).

> Teachers need to create their own intelligible map of the different conceptions of ability and apply their own understanding in practice. It is only by engaging in debates and discussions about different models and approaches to provisions and how these relate to their own contexts that teachers can make a significant contribution to the new and challenging task of educating our most able pupils.
>
> (Casey and Koshy, 2013: 61)

This quotation highlights the important role relationship between research and practitioner and the intended benefits for gifted and talented children. In their study, Machin et al. (2004) identified differences in attainment between different groups of children. This is significant because understanding differences particularly 'among subpopulations such as girls and disadvantaged and minority populations, is critical in planning appropriate curriculum for them' (VanTassel-Baska, 1991). Thus, perhaps more research could be conducted into why certain groups within the gifted and population achieve better or worse than others and how this can be effectively addressed by policy provisions.

References

Bailey, R., Tan, J. E. C. and Morley, D., 2004, Talented Pupils in Physical Education: Secondary School Teachers' Experiences of Identifying Talent within the 'Excellence in Cities' Scheme, *Physical Education and Sport Pedagogy*, 9 (2), pp.133-148.

Ball, S. J., 2013, *The Education Debate*, 2nd ed., Bristol: The Policy Press.

Casey, R. and Koshy, V., 2013, Gifted and Talented Education: The English Policy Highway at a Crossroads?, *Journal for the Education of the Gifted*, 36 (1), pp.44-65.

Cooper, M., Lloyd-Reason, L. and Wall, S., 2003, Social Deprivation and Educational Underachievement: Lessons from London, *Education and Training*, 45 (2), pp. 79-88.

Dai, D. Y. and Chen, F., 2013, Three Paradigms of Gifted Education: In Search of Conceptual Clarity in Research and Practice, *Gifted Child Quarterly*, 57 (3), pp.151-168.

DfES, 2005, *Excellence in Cities The National Evaluation of a Policy to Raise Standards in Urban Schools 2000-2003 Report Summary*, London: DfES.

Goodwin, M., 2011, English Education Policy after New Labour: Big Society or Back to Basics?, The Political Quarterly, 82 (3), pp.407-424.

Halpin, D., 1997, New Labour: New Hope for Education Policy?, *British Journal of Educational Studies*, 45 (3), pp. 231-234.

Kaplan, S. N., 2013, Special Schools and the Differentiated Curriculum The Issues, *Gifted Child Today*, 36 (3), pp.201-204.

Koshy, V. and Pinheiro-Torres, C., 2013, 'Are we being de-gifted, Miss?' Primary School Gifted and Talented Co-Ordinators' Responses to the Gifted and Talented Education Policy in England, *British Educational Research Journal*, 39 (6), pp.953-978.

Koshy, V., Pinheiro-Torres, C. and Portman-Smith, C., 2012, The Landscape of Gifted and Talented Education in England and Wales: How Are Teachers Implementing Policy?, *Research Papers in Education*, 27 (2), pp.167-186.

Lowe, H. 2002, Excellence for All: Able Pupils in Urban Secondary Schools, Support for Learning, 17 (2), pp.88-94.

Lowe, H., 2003, Excellence in English Cities: Gifted and Talented Education and the National Training Programme for 'Gifted and Talented Co-Ordinators', *Gifted Education International*, 17 (2), pp.120-129.

Machin, S. and McNally, S., 2012, The Evaluation of English Education Policies, *National Institute Economic Review*, 219, pp.R15-R25.

Machin, S., McNally, S. and Meghir, C., 2004, Improving Pupil Performance in English Secondary Schools: Excellence in Cities, *Journal of the European Economic Association*, 2 (2-3), pp.396-405.

McNally, S., 2005, Reforms to Schooling in the UK: A Review of Some Major Reforms and their Evaluation, *German Economic Review*, 6 (3), pp.287-296.

Ofsted, 2004, *Excellence in Cities: the Primary Extension Real Stories*, London: Crown Copyright.

Raffo, C., 2009, Interrogating Poverty, Social Exclusion and New Labour's Programme of Priority Educational Policies in England, *Critical Studies in Education*, 50 (1), pp.65-78.

Renzulli, J. S. and Reis, S. M., 1991, The Reform Movement and the Quiet Crisis in Gifted Education, *Gifted Child Quarterly*, 35 (1), pp.26-35.

Tomlinson, S., 2003, New Labour and Education, *Children and Society*, 17, pp.195-204.

VanTassel-Baska, J., 1991, Gifted Education in the Balance: Building Relationships with General Education, *Gifted Child Quarterly*, 35 (1), pp.20-25.

White, J., 2012, The Role of Policy in Philosophy of Education: An Argument and an Illustration, *Journal of Philosophy of Education*, 46 (4), pp.503-515.

Whitty, G., 2008, Twenty Years of Progress? English Education Policy 1988 to the Present, *Educational Management Administration and Leadership*, 36 (2), pp.165-184.

Wilson, H., 2009, Challenge and Creativity: Making the Links in Balchin, T., Hymer, B. and Matthews, J. (eds), *The Routledge International Companion to Gifted Education*, Oxon: Routledge, pp.235 – 242.

4 SHIKHA JOSHI

I graduated with a Law Degree in 2009, however then changed my field of work to education and I am currently an Infant School teacher, teaching Year 2. I am currently studying for an MA in Education to further enhance my professional practice through greater theoretical understanding of historical and current educational issues alongside developing extensive and through knowledge of teaching and learning pedagogy.

All for one and one for all: exploring New Labour's educational policies; inclusion, exclusion and the standards agenda

Contents

Introduction

From integration to inclusion: inclusion in policy

What is inclusion?

The broadening horizons of inclusion

Inclusion, New Labour and the plethora of policies!

The inclusion agenda versus the standards agenda – can both prosper?

Conclusion

Introduction

This literature review focuses upon New Labour's educational policies concerning inclusion. Specifically, interpretations of inclusion, contradictions in New Labour's educational policies and the relationship between the inclusion agenda and the standards agenda are debated.

The *de rigeur* of inclusion in policy has witnessed unparalleled growth and has been subject to a 'progressively broadening compass' (Thomas and Loxley, 2007:1). Inclusion is now 'embedded in a range of contexts – political, social...and educational' (Thomas and Loxley (2007: vii).

It is against this background that this review is presented. Beginning with a brief historical overview of the origins of inclusion, the following themes are then examined and explored:

1. The contentious issue of the absence of any consistent meaning and definition of inclusion.
2. The evolution of inclusion to a broader subject that encompasses social, emotional, and moral concepts.
3. The inconsistencies and inadequacies of the plethora of policies established by New Labour and their impact on inclusion.
4. The impact of the 'third way' ideology of New Labour's policies on pre-existing conceptions of inclusion.
5. Whether the inclusion agenda and the standards agenda work in opposition, or are complementary as government rhetoric suggests.

Finally, conclusions are drawn from the body of evidence and opinion critiquing 'policy' and 'inclusion' as documented in this review.

From integration to inclusion: inclusion in policy

Inclusion, or integration as it was formerly known, was conceptualised by the *Warnock Report* (DES, 1978) (Hodkinson, 2010; Powell and Tutt, 2002; Lloyd, 2000) which criticised the 'orthodoxy of segregation' (Hodkinson and Vickerman, 2009:67) and recommended that a child's special educational needs (SEN) should be met 'through a continuum of *integrated* provision that should be mainly delivered in ordinary schools' (ibid). The subsequent 1981 Education Act enshrined recommendations of the Warnock Report by legalising the need for children with SEN to be educated in mainstream schools if their needs could be reasonably met without detriment to the learning of others (DES, 1981). Hence, the notion of segregation was replaced by the concept of integration (Powell and Tutt, 2002; Warnock, 2010; Glazzard, 2013). However, educational change and policy reform has now moved away from the 'integration' and firmly toward inclusion (Dunne, 2009; Hodkinson and Vickerman, 2009; Powell and Tutt, 2002; Thomas, 1997).

Powell and Tutt (2002) have commented inclusion that necessitates schools must become supportive communities and successfully cater for a range of diverse needs - implying a proactive approach by schools in meeting the needs of children with SEN (Corbett and Slee, 2000). This 'sharply contrasts with the notion of integration' (Glazzard, 2013:183) which focuses upon individual children assimilating into an 'unchanged system' (ibid).

England's subscription to the Salamanca Statement (United Nations Educational, Scientific and Cultural Organisation [UNESCO], 1994) acted as a catalyst for contemporary inclusive educational policy within the UK (Hodkinson and Vickerman, 2009; Lindsay, 2007; Sikes, Lawson and Parker, 2007). The statement called for 'inclusion to become quite simply the norm' (Clough, 1988: 2) by expressing the rights and entitlements of those with SEN (Dunne, 2009). The *Code of Practice for the Identification and Assessment of SEN* (DfEE, 1994) followed, which ensured those children identified as having SEN would remain in mainstream schooling and 'access the same, albeit modified, curriculum entitlement as their peers' (Lloyd, 2000: 134; Hornby 2011).

New Labour, elected in 1997 is perceived to have expeditiously committed themselves to the inclusion agenda through a plethora of policies and publications (Roulstone and Prideaux, 2008; Thomas and Loxley, 2007). Soon after election, *The Green Paper, Excellence for All Children: Meeting Special Educational Needs* (DfEE, 1997) was published, expressing strong support for inclusion:

> we want to develop an education system in which special provision is seen as an integral part of overall provision aiming wherever possible to return children to mainstream.
>
> (DfEE, 1997: 44)

A revised curriculum (DfEE, 1999) followed focusing upon three core inclusion-oriented principles:

1. setting suitable learning challenges;
2. Responding to pupils' diverse needs and overcoming potential barriers to learning;
3. Assessment for individuals and groups of children

(Dunne, 2000: 43)

New Labour continued with the inclusion agenda through *The Special Educational Needs and Disability Act* (2001); *Every Child Matters* agenda (Department for Education and Skills [DfES] (2003) and the *Strategy for SEN: removing barriers to achievement* (DfES, 2004). Dunne argues that within the remit of ever growing policy 'inclusion is presented as a 'strategy' that is linked to achievement, confidence and intervention' (ibid).

What is inclusion?

The term "inclusion" dominates 'the political landscape' (Glazzard, 2013:182, Sikes, Lawson and Parker, 2007)) and is a 'buzz word' (Evans and Lunt, 2005: 41; Hodkinson and Vickerman, 2009; Benjamin, 2002) which has become normative in government policy and discourse. Dunne (2009:44) however argues that due to the inherent lack of a singular definition in policy, 'inclusion appears to remain a generalised, disputable concept that is wide open to interpretation'. Terzi (2010:3) is supportive of Dunne's view, arguing although 'there is a general consensus on the value of inclusion, there is little agreement on what this actually means'. Furthermore, Avramadis, Bayliss and Burden (2002:158) state 'inclusion is a bewildering concept which can have a variety of interpretations and applications'. This suggests politicians, policy makers, educators and parents may all perceive inclusion to mean something different (Glazzard, 2013; Armstrong, Armstrong and Spandagou, 2011, Slee, 2010). Therefore, the imperative question remains, as articulated by Hodkinson (2012:5) 'what then is…inclusion?'(Hornby, 2011; Terzi, 2010; Armstrong, Armstrong and Spandagou, 2011).

Clough (2000) suggests inclusion cannot be perceived as a fixed state with clear parameters; Sikes et al (2007: 367) taking this further proposes that the concept of inclusion evolves over time and is developed as 'understandings of inclusion…are articulated and lived'.

Dyson (2001a) argues there are a number of common interpretations of the term inclusion. Firstly, that inclusion can be perceived to include a range of identified 'groups' with 'diverse needs' within the UK school population (Dunne, 2009; Hornby, 2011, Dyson, 2001b). Secondly that inclusion is irrevocably entwined with wider issues of race, ethnicity and gender (Black-Hawkins, 2007; Sikes, Lawson and Parker, 2007; Thomas, 2007). Lastly, and contrary to other views, is that inclusion has a strong conflation with SEN (Cole, 2005; Simmons and Bayliss, 2007). This perception, which is perhaps the most contentious (Cole, 2005) can be traced back to the Warnock Report which originally proposed an inclusive ideology; stating those identified with SEN had 'a right to be included in mainstream schools, provided they did not adversely affect the learning of others' (Warnock, 2010).

This ideology continues to develop; the Centre for Study of Inclusive Education (CSIE, 2004) regard inclusion as a fundamental human right and propose any segregation of children should be abolished – thereby evidencing support for the abolishment of any form of "special schooling". However, Powell and Tutt (2002) argue that this view emphasises the location of where children with SEN are educated as being paramount whilst failing to consider issues of social cohesion or where needs can be best met. In opposition to the CSIE (2004) and *The Warnock Report* (1978) which suggest that inclusion plays a crucial role in normalising those with SEN, Low (2007) argues that it is essential to remain aware that inclusion is not absolute.

Therefore it is evident that 'there is a plethora of definitions of inclusion and...this is a concept that may be defined in a variety of ways' (Hodkinson and Vickerman, 2009:76).

The broadening horizons of inclusion

Warnock (2010) who originally advocated the concept of inclusion as the right of every child to be educated in a mainstream class room, now views that as a 'disastrous legacy' (Warnock, 2010:19). She has now concerted her efforts in advocating that inclusion should be viewed beyond the sole aim of a right to be educated alongside peers and rather should focus upon 'children...truly experiencing a sense of belonging' (Terzi, 2010:5). In support, Slee (2011) contends that inclusion should be seen as a means to eliminate injustice and promote social wellbeing. Similarly, Armstrong, Armstrong and Spandagou (2011) propose inclusion encompasses social cohesion and the role of education in promoting this must be explored. This view is supported by Carrington and Elkins (2005) who emphasise that 'inclusion is about a philosophy of acceptance where all pupils are valued and treated with respect' (Carrington and Elkins, 2005:86); highlighting the social aspect of inclusion as opposed to the educational.

Warnock (2010) suggests that 'schools should not be seen as microcosms of society' (Warnock, 2010:32) but that 'inclusion should mean being involved in a common enterprise of learning, rather than being necessarily under the same roof' (ibid). However Norwich (2010:61) argues that Warnock's concept of inclusion does not 'extend to the common social learning' which is an essential derivative of participation 'in common learning'. Norwich (2010) addresses the possible costs of segregation 'in terms of lost opportunities for a sense of social belonging...as well as lost opportunities for other children to socialize and learn together' (Norwich, 2010: 62). Hence it can be observed that the concept of inclusion, within education, appears to have evolved to include social notions of justice, fairness and opportunity (Glazzard, 2013; Dyson, 2001b; Roulstone and Prideaux, 2008).

Conversely some commentators have explored how inclusion can inadvertently lead to exclusion (Evans and Lunt, 2007; Roulstone and Prideaux, 2008; Powell and Tutt, 2002, Warnock, 2010). Powell and Tutt (2002:45) consider inclusion to be a 'social concept' which 'requires that the person feels a sense of social belonging'. They contend that feeling a sense of belonging, respect and value are intrinsic to inclusion and such feelings are most likely to be achieved in special settings where 'differences do not militate against feelings of acceptance and belonging (ibid). Furthermore they comment that full inclusion can lead to a child feeling excluded as they are perceived as different and odd in comparison to others. In support, Warnock (2005) contests that although 'the concept of inclusion springs from hearts in the right place but it's meaning...is far from clear, and in practice it often means that children are physically included but emotionally excluded' (Warnock, 2010:32). Powell and Tutt (2002) advocate Warnock's position, noting that physical inclusion does not necessarily translate to emotional and social inclusion.

On the contrary, Thomas (1997) promotes inclusion as a necessity arguing it is 'at the heart of any society...and must be at the heart of a truly comprehensive education system' (Thomas, 1997:106) therefore advocating full inclusion. In opposition, Hodkinson and Vickerman (2009) argue that Thomas' view purports to remove differences based upon 'predicted equality and not those based on outcomes' (Hodkinson and Vickerman, 2009:127). However Thomas (1997) argues 'there is no doubt that a non-segregated, diverse school population...will produce schools which are more sensitive and more humane...in inclusive schools all will thrive' (ibid). Conversely Oliver (1992) notes inclusion places the impetus for change on the pupil and not the schools thereby promoting intolerance. Furthermore, Evans and Lunt (2002) and Baker, (2007) argue inclusion is 'fundamentally a question of ethos and attitude' as a child can 'be in a mainstream class, yet still be excluded because of the attitude of teachers or other children in the class' (Evans and Lunt, 2002:9) – thereby supporting Oliver's (1992) that observation often inclusion reinforces and perpetuates segregated practices. Warnock (2005) supports this stance by expressing that 'including all children under the same roof' (Warnock, 2005: 13) is a naive ideal of inclusion and that special schools have a crucial role to play in developing inclusive practices, as those children who feel excluded within a mainstream school will be in a position to 'embrace a feeling of belonging' (ibid) in a special school.

Low (2006) developing upon this, argues there is still a very real need for special schools - as mainstream schools cannot meet the needs of every child with a special need. Supporting Low (2006), Baker (2007) takes the view that 'special schools and inclusion should be two sides of the same coin' (ibid) and should work in cohesion to support vulnerable children in their learning. However, Vaughn (2005) maintains that all special schools should be closed, as by segregating children they become the subjects of discrimination. The position of New labour on this issue is contradictory. The Green Paper, *Excellence for All Children* on one hand supports inclusion, whilst on the other advocates the need for special schools:

> There are strong educational, as well as social and moral grounds for educating children with special educational needs with their peers. We aim to increase...inclusion within mainstream schools, while protecting and enhancing specialist provision for those who need it
>
> (DfEE, 1997:43)

Thus it is evident that under New Labour there is still disparity regarding the role and need of special schools (Baker, 2007).

Inclusion, New Labour and the plethora of policies!

Throughout New Labour's power there has been unprecedented growth in education policies regarding inclusion (Hodkinson and Vickerman, 2009; Thomas and Loxley; 2007). However, there is no singular definition of the term (Lloyd, 2008; Terzi, 2010; Hodkinson, 2012, Glazzard, 2013). Shortly after coming into power, New Labour published The Green Paper entitled *Excellence for All Children* (DfEE, 1997) which provided the following definition:

> By inclusion, we mean that pupils with SEN should, wherever possible receive their education in a mainstream school, but also that they should join fully with their peers in the curriculum and life of the school . . . . But separate provision may be necessary on occasions for specific purposes.
>
> (DfEE, 1997: 44)

Lloyd (2000) interprets this to mean that children with SEN should receive 'the same educational diet and experiences as peers with some compensatory support, and/or extra resourcing as a means to accessing their entitlement' (Lloyd, 2000:134; Dunne, 2009). However, Powell and Tutt (2002), supported by Hodkinson and Vickerman (2009), observe this implies the idea of 'locational inclusion' (Hodkinson and Vickerman, 2009:77) – meaning greater weight is given to children being educated together and less to the 'attitudes or environment that each child is subjected to' (ibid). This perception of inclusion conflicts with Warnock's - which emphasises belonging and social acceptance (Powell and Tutt, 2002).

With the election of New Labour, it was hoped that the education agenda would address issues relating to 'social injustice and inequality in education' (Lloyd, 2000:134) and although the Green Paper (DfEE, 1997) clearly adopted 'the language of 'inclusion'...its focus' was 'entirely upon individual pupils' needs and improving the efficiency and cost-effectiveness of systems for managing those needs' (Armstrong, 2005:138). The Green Paper encompassed 6 themes regarding provision for inclusion:

- high expectations for all children, especially in literacy and numeracy;
- inclusion for children with SEN in the mainstream;
- greater involvement of parents;
- ensuring 'good value for money;
- providing opportunities for staff development;
- greater co-operation between local agencies involved in education pupils with SEN.

(DfEE 1997: 5)

Accordingly Armstrong (2005) is of the view that although the rights of children with SEN to an education in mainstream schooling is advocated, New Labour failed to recognise the principles of an inclusive society and specifically how education can be employed as an instrument to conflate social cohesion and inclusion to promote a society where each individual feels a sense of belonging.

Furthermore, Lloyd (2000) suggests the policy failed to address how all children would access equal opportunities and it's meaning in practice. Rather it can be construed that the policy is focused upon 'concepts of efficiency, value for money, effectiveness, competition etc' (Lloyd, 2000: 137). Ball (2008) supports Lloyd's position, discussing how New Labour's "third way" of politics, which encompass neo-liberal values, is geared towards using education as a vehicle in ensuring citizens have the correct skills for a knowledge-based economy, meaning 'knowledge and education can be treated as a business product, and that educational and innovative intellectual products and services, as productive assets, can be exported for a high value return' (Ball, 2008:19). Thus by 'maximising social, educational and economic participation' (Ball, 2008:17) a society will flourish within the global economy. This perception of education conflicts with the views of commentators such as Warnock (2005); Powell and Tutt (2002); Evans and Lunt (2002); Carrington and Elkins (2005) who value the intrinsic need for inclusion to promote a sense of wellbeing, belonging and value.

Dyson (2001b) recognizes this move towards a 'new discourse' (Dyson, 2001b:27) of inclusion. He proposes that previous interpretations of inclusion; such as the right for SEN children to be included in the mainstream (Warnock, 2010) and the need for children to feel valued, accepted and respected (Carrington and Elkins, 2005) have been replaced with a new third way ideology of inclusion – which promotes social inclusion as the means by which 'potentially marginalised groups' are equipped 'with the capacity to become active citizens' (Dyson, 2001b:27). Dyson (2001b) further argues the inclusion agenda is concerned with creating 'a highly skilled workforce capable of maintaining a high tech economy' (ibid).

New Labour's publication entitled *Removing Barriers to Achievement. The government's Strategy for SEN* (DfES, 2004) stated the government's vision for the education of children with SEN:

> [to] personalise learning for all children with SEN, to make education more innovative and responsive to the diverse needs of individual children, so reducing our reliance on separate SEN structures ad raising achievement of the many – nearly one in six – who are considered to have SEN.
>
> (DfES, 2004, Introduction)

However, Lloyd (2008) argues that this publication again failed to provide a strategy which defined and recognised issues relating to the definition of inclusion and the concept of equal education opportunities. Instead, it again, reaffirmed the idea that inclusion is linked with economic contribution; suggesting 'children with SEN will make an economic contribution to society as adults and their education alongside their peers will ensure that this contribution is better valued and *of better value*' (Lloyd, 2008: 226). Therefore, Lloyd's (2008) view is consistent with Dyson's (2001b) that inclusion is no longer about equal educational entitlement and participation but about the end outcome of contribution to society. Dyson (2001b) and (Lloyd 2008) have been critical of this approach, observing that it 'demonstrates an ambiguous commitment to genuine educational inclusion' (Lloyd, 2008: 226). They suggest that inclusion has the capability to address issues of disadvantage created by issues of 'social deprivation thus implicitly inclusion is conceived as social inclusion' (Lloyd, 2008:225).

Armstrong (2005) supported by Lloyd (2008) and Dyson (2001b) proposes that the strategy 'provides a 'complete articulation' (Armstrong, 2005:44) of New Labour's 'wider ideological vision of the inclusive society' (ibid).

Furthermore, the strategy for SEN (DfES, 2004) adopts the language and ideologies of the *Every Child Matters* (DfES, 2003) agenda; which pledged to ensure that those children considered as most vulnerable would not fall 'through the cracks' (DfES, 2003:5). The strategy states:

> *Removing Barriers to Achievement* sets out the Government's vision for giving children with special educational needs and disabilities the opportunity to succeed. Building on the proposals for the reform of children's services in *Every Child Matters*, it sets a new agenda for improvement and action at national and local level.
>
> (DfES, 2004:6)

Therefore, it can be interpreted that the SEN strategy (DfES, 2004) is rooted in a 'child protection model of inclusion (Armstrong, 2005:44) and SEN intervention is broadened to a wider context, to include social disadvantages. In support, Eggleston (2001) comments that New Labour are aware of the need to provide equal opportunities for all children who are considered to be at a disadvantage – implying the definition of inclusion has been further widened to encompass social disadvantage.

Armstrong (2005) argues that New Labour's strategies fail to discuss and rectify the barriers that create educational disadvantage; instead on one hand policies are understood to focus upon including SEN children in the mainstream; however on the other, there is still 'reliance upon special schools for the more disabled and troublesome pupils' (Armstrong, 2005: 139) - suggesting that there has not been a 'radical departure' (ibid) from past policy. Hodkinson and Vickerman (2009) affirm this commenting that New Labour have essentially 'stopped short to a commitment to full inclusion' (Hodkinson and Vickerman, 2009:79) as inclusion in policy is often riddled with caveats; for example the Green Paper (DfEE, 1997:4) which states that 'children should be educated as far as possible with their peers'.

So, although New Labour have been seemingly committed to inclusion, some commentators observe inconsistencies and contradictions (Hodkinson and Vickerman, 2009; Armstrong, 2005; Dyson, 2001b; Lloyd, 2008). Additionally, Armstrong (2005) notes that the abundance of policy and guidance has certainly 'strengthened the rights of children with SEN to a mainstream education' but that it has 'said little about the nature of the education' – therefore suggesting inadequacies in policy. (Armstrong, 2005: 139). Furthermore, Dyson (2001b) argues traditional concepts and interpretations of inclusion can been seen to have been replaced with a focus upon outcome, productivity and the promotion of social inclusion - again suggesting New Labour have done little to transform inclusion. Support can be found in a report by the Office for Standards in Education (OFSTED) which stated that only a small fraction of mainstream schools were found to be meeting the SEN needs of pupils and that:

> taking steps to enable pupils with SEN to participate fully in the life of the school and achieve their potential still remains a significant challenge for many schools.
>
> (OFSTED, 2004:4)

Therefore although awareness of inclusion has been heightened, the impact on the number of SEN children in mainstream schooling and the effectiveness of their individual needs being met has been marginal (Lloyd, 2008).

The inclusion agenda versus the standards agenda – can both prosper?

Simultaneous to the pursuance of the inclusion agenda, the government have been pursuing 'the standards agenda' (Powell and Tutt, 2002; Glazzard, 2013; Lloyd, 2008; Hornby; 2011). This agenda aims to improve attainment and therefore ultimately increase productivity and competitiveness in a globalized economy (Lipman, 2004). However Hornby (2011) argues that the standards agenda has 'deflected attention away from the broader goals of education, such as...the development of social and life skills (Hornby, 2011:326). Conversely Lloyd (2000), Dyson (2001b) and Ball (2008) suggest the inclusion agenda has been broadened to encapsulate the creation of 'a highly skilled workforce capable of maintaining a high tech economy' (Dyson, 2001:27) – thereby entwining the two agendas. However Slee (2011) contends that inclusion should not be entwined with economic productivity; he is supported by Corbett (2001) who emphasises the need for inclusion to focus upon inclusive communities which promote value and belonging.

Dunne (2009) comments on the key aims of policy relating to inclusion as aiming to 'improve outcomes for pupils' and 'to narrow the gaps between the lowest and highest achievers'(Dunne, 2009:43) – making it abundantly clear that 'inclusion is presented as a strategy that is linked to achievement' (ibid). Armstrong (2005), supporting this view observes that the inundation of policy relating to inclusion is consistently riddled with the 'mantras of 'high expectations', 'standards' and 'school improvement' (Armstrong, 2005: 139). The drive for achievement is challenged by Hornby (2011) who states that the 'major goal of education for many children with SEN must be to produce happy, well-adjusted and productive citizens (Hornby, 2011:326).

Benjamin (2002) comments upon the irony of the juxtaposition of the inclusion agenda and standards agenda – on one hand inclusion policy calls for the full participation of children with SEN in all aspects of school life; however, on the other hand schools are subjugated by the need to compete and continually raise levels of performance and attainment. Dunne (2009) suggests that in order for schools to ensure they are perceived to demonstrate success and achievement for all children a 'powerful othering framework' (Dunne, 2009:49) is employed – meaning children with SEN are 'subjected to intervention programmes and segregated' (Glazzard, 2013:183) or grouped in specific ways, with specified targets to guarantee that 'those children can be seen to progress and achieve' (Lloyd, 2008:227). Therefore, Evans and Lunt (2002) argue this infers that in practice it is difficult for the two agendas to work in tandem; instead it would appear that children with SEN are subjected to what may be perceived as exclusion within the mainstream to ensure that targets are met (Evans and Lunt, 2002).

Another issue in dispute is the way in which attainment is measured – as the criteria is 'concentrated on a narrow view of attainment' (Ainscow, Booth and Dyson, 2006:26) and based upon scores in national tests. OFSTED can be seen to support the government's narrow ideals of attainment; stating that an inclusive school is where 'the teaching and learning, achievement, attitudes and well-being of every person matter' (OFSTED, 2000). Thus it would appear that the 'standards agenda operates as if standards are absolute' (Benjamin, 2002:47) and school improvement is measured by the number of children who attain national averages. Hodkinson (2010) questions this definition by asking, 'whether inclusion should ever be determined by academic standards?' (Hodkinson, 2010: 62). Lloyd (2008) argues government policy dictates that it should and this ultimately creates the greatest barrier to attainment for children with SEN. Supported by Glazzard (2013) she argues that the definition of achievement must be 'reconceptualised' (Glazzard: 2013:184) and the way in which attainment is measured must be altered to ensure children with SEN are not excluded in the mainstream.

Norwich (2002) discusses how the standards agenda is detrimental to the aims of inclusion agenda. On one hand schools are encompassed by an accountability culture (O'Neill, 2002) and on the other are 'required to make themselves attractive to families of children' (Ainscow, Booth, Dyson, 2006) with SEN. However, children who require personalised learning and greater resources become unappealing to some schools – explaining why the assimilation of SEN children into mainstream is seen to have made little progress (Norwich, 2002). Contrarily, Hodkinson (2010) perceives the two agendas as having created a problem within the realm of inclusion, commenting that 'inclusion has become defined and operationalised by governmental targets of accountability and standards' (Hodkinson, 2010:62). Ainscow, Booth and Dyson (2006) however suggest that in theory the inclusion agenda and the standards agenda can be perceived as compatible and argue that the relationship between the two agendas is not a case of 'simple opposition' (Ainscow, Booth and Dyson, 2006:305) but that the two can be entwined within school culture and communities and must 'become a part of a dialogue whose outcomes can be more rather than less inclusive' (ibid). Therefore, they propose (through findings from studies undertaken) a way forward in the amalgamation of the two agendas by implementing the following initiatives which were seen to improve the relationship between the two agendas, promote morale and develop a 'can do' culture for practitioners (Ainscow, Booth and Dyson, 2006):

1. Enhancing participation in learning for SEN children – thus proposing a move away from notion of separately educating SEN children in mainstream classrooms
2. Shifting assumptions – of all involved in the wider school community, to accepting and restricting thoughts to promote inclusion
3. Broadening horizons

Ainscow, Booth, and Dyson (2006:304) conclude that 'fundamental rethinking' and understanding is necessary to reconstruct inclusive practices within the framework of the standards agenda. Lloyd (2008) however argues that current policy is engrossed in target setting, measuring achievement and standards and therefore is contributing to achievement barriers and not removing them. Lloyd (2008) is supported by Croll and Moses (2000) who in a study found that 'attitudes and values' (Croll and Moses, 2000:11) within some schools cultivated 'a competitive ethos' (ibid) which prevented them from fully including and embracing SEN children as those children were seen to negatively affect attainment data.

Thus it can be observed that 'inclusion has become defined and controlled by...accountability and standards' (Hodkinson and Vickerman, 2009:82) causing a serious challenge to the implementation of inclusive education (Lloyd, 2008; Croll and Moses, 2000; Hodkinson and Vickerman, 2009, Ainscow, Booth and Dyson, 2006).

Conclusion

This literature review has examined New Labour's educational policies concerning inclusion and explored the dogma surrounding discourse of inclusion.

The absence of a clear definition of inclusion in government policy continues to cause debate (Lloyd, 2008) and has widened the parameters of inclusion, broadening it to embrace a 'variety of interpretations and applications' (Avramadis, Bayliss and Burden (2002; 158) encompassing social, moral, equitable ideologies (Warnock, 2010, Powell and Tutt 2002; Evans and Lunt 2002; Carrington and Elkins 2005). Consequently the disparities between interpretations of inclusion continue to cause contention (Glazzard, 2013).

It has been observed that policies appear to fully commit to inclusion (DfEE, 1997) whilst also advocating the fundamental need for special schools to remain (DfES, 2004). Accordingly, 'such contradiction within policy has resulted in confused messages' (Glazzard, 2013:183).

Additionally, it has been explored how inclusion can inadvertently lead to exclusion as documented by: Evans and Lunt, 2007; Roulstone and Prideaux, 2008; Powell and Tutt, 2002; Warnock, 2010 and Carrington and Elkins, 2002. They suggest inclusion comprises social well-being, value, a sense of belonging and respect which can only be achieved in 'special settings where differences do not militate against feelings of acceptance and belonging (Powell and Tutt, 2002:45).

The impact of the neo-liberal, 'third way' ideology has been discussed; it can be ascertained that inclusion, under New Labour, has moved beyond issues of SEN and evolved to 'social inclusion' (Dyson, 2001b:27) – whereby the ultimate goal of inclusion is linked to marketization and creating a 'highly skilled workforce capable of maintaining a high-tech economy' (ibid).

The standards agenda is perceived to marginalise children with SEN; rather than removing barriers, it purports to construct them (Lloyd, 2008; Glazzard, 2013; Slee, 2001) through singling out children based upon their inability to achieve a narrow 'set of norm related standards' (Glazzard, 2013:186). Some commentators (Hodkinson, 2010; Lloyd, 2008; Glazzard, 2013; Benjamin, 2002) suggest that the definition of attainment needs to be reconstructed for the inclusion and standards agendas to work in conflation.

Hence, it is pertinent that variances between interpretations of inclusion (Thomas and Loxley, 2007; Hodkinson and Vickerman, 2009) coupled with the 'emergence of the social inclusion agenda (Dyson, 2011b:27) and inconsistencies in policy agendas (Lloyd, 2008; Glazzard, 2013; Hodkinson, 2010; Norwich, 2002) continue to cause debate within the field of inclusion.

References

Ainscow, M., Booth, T. and Dyson, A. (2006) 'Inclusion and the standards agenda: negotiating policy pressures in England', *International Journal of Inclusive Education,* 10 (4-5): 295-308

Armstrong, D., Armstrong, A., and Spandagou, I. (2011) 'Inclusion: by choice or by chance?', *International Journal of Inclusive Education,* 15 (1):29-39

Avramadis, E., Bayliss, P. & Burden, R. (2002) 'Inclusion in action: an in-depth case study of an effective inclusive secondary school in the south-west of England', *International Journal of Inclusive Education*, 6 (2): 143–63

Ball, S. (2008) *The Education Debate*. Bristol: The Policy Press.

Benjamin, S. (2002) *The micropolitics of inclusive education..* Buckinghamshire: Open University Press.

Black-Hawkins, K. (2007) *Achievement and Inclusion in Schools*. London :Routledge.

Carrington, S. & Elkins, J. (2005) 'Comparisons of a traditional and an inclusive secondary school culture', in: J. Rix, K. Simmons, M. Nind & K. Sheehy (eds) *Policy and Power in Inclusive Education: Values into Practice*. London: Routledge, pp. 85-95

Centre for Studies on Inclusive Education (2004) *Article 17 and Inclusive Education in the New UN Disability Convention,* Bristol: CISE
Clough P. (2000) 'Routes to inclusion', in P. Clough & J. Corbett (eds), *Theories of Inclusive Education: A Students' Guide*. London: Paul Chapman, pp.1-33

Cole, B. (2005) 'Good faith and effort? Perspectives on educational inclusion', *Disability and Society,* 20 (3): 331-244

Corbett, J. & Slee, R. (2000) 'An international conversation on inclusive education', in F. Armstrong, D. Armstrong & L. Barton (eds) *Inclusive Education: Policy Contexts and Comparative Perspectives*. London: David Fulton, pp.133-146

Croll, P., Moses, D. (2000) 'Ideologies and utopias: education professionals' views of inclusion', *European Journal of Special Needs Education,* 15 (1): 1-2

Department for Education and Science (DES) (1978) *Special Educational Needs: Report of the Committee of Enquiry into the Education of Handicapped Children and Young People (The Warnock Report)*. London: HMSO.

Department for Education and Science (DES) (1981) *The 1981 Education Act*. London: HMSO. Available at: http://www.educationengland.org.uk/documents/pdfs/1981-education-act.pdf [accessed 30th November 2013]

Department for Education (DfE) (1994) *Code of Practice on the Identification and Assessment of Special Educational Needs*. London:HMSO

Department for Education and Employment (DfEE) (1997) *Excellence for All Children: Meeting Special Educational Needs*. London: The stationary Office. Available at: http://www.educationengland.org.uk/documents/pdfs/1997-green-paper.pdf [accessed 30th November 2013]

Department for Education and Schooling (DfES) (2001) *Inclusive schooling: Children with special educational needs.* London: DfES

Department for Education and Schooling (DfES) (2003) *Every Child Matters: Green Paper on Children's* Services. Norwich: The Stationery Office. Available at: http://webarchive.nationalarchives.gov.uk/20130401151715/https://www.education.gov.uk/publications/eOrderingDownload/CM5860.pdf [accessed 28th November 2013]

Department for Education and Schooling (DfES) (2004) *Removing barriers to achievement. The government's strategy for SEN.* London: DfES. Available at: http://webarchive.nationalarchives.gov.uk/20130401151715/https://www.education.gov.uk/publications/eOrderingDownload/DfES%200117%20200MIG1994.pdf [accessed on 30th Novemeber 2013]

Dunne, L. (2009) 'Discourses of Inclusion: a critique', *Power and Education,* 1 (1): 42-56 Available at: http://wwwords.co.uk/pdf/validate.asp?j=power&vol=1&year=2009&article=5_Dunne_POWER_1_1_web [accessed 1st November 2012]

Dyson, A. (2001a) 'Special Needs Education as the Way Forward to Equity: an alternative approach', *Support for Learning*, 16 (3): 99-104

Dyson, A. (2001b) 'Special Needs in the Twenty-First Century: Where We've Been and Where We're going', *British Journal of Special Education*, 28(1): 24-29

Eggleston, J. (2001) 'New Labour, the market and social inclusion', *Improving Schools* 4(59): 59-60

Evans, J. and Lunt. I. (2002)' Inclusive education: are there limits?', *European Journal of Special Needs Education*, 1(1):1-14

Evans, J. and Lunt, I. (2005) ' Inclusive Education: Are there limits?', in K. Topping and S. Maloney (eds.) *The Routledge Falmer Reader in Inclusive Education..* London: Routledge Falmer, pp. 41-54

Glazzard, J. (2013) 'A critical interrogation of the contemporary discourses associated with inclusive education in England', *Journal of Research in Special Educational Needs,* 13(3): 182-188

Hodkinson, A. and Vickerman, P. (2009) *Key Issues in Special Educational Needs and Inclusion.* London: Sage.

Hodkinson, A. (2010) 'Inclusive and special education in the English educational system: historical perspectives, recent developments and future challenges', *British Journal of Special Education,* 37(2): 61 – 67

Hornby, G. (2011) 'Inclusive Education for Children with Special Educational Needs: A critique', *International journal of Disability, Development and Education.* 58(3):321-329

Lindsay, G. (2007) 'Rights, efficacy and inclusive education', in Cigman, R. (2007) (ed.) *Included or excluded? The challenge of the mainstream for some SEN children.* Oxon: Routledge, pp. 15-22

Lipman, P. (2004) *High stakes education,* London: Routledge Falmer

Lloyd, C. (2000) 'Excellence for all children false promises! The failure of current policy for inclusive education and implications for schooling in the 21st century', *International Journal of Inclusive Education,* 4(2): 133-151

Lloyd, C. (2008) 'Removing barriers to achievement: A strategy for inclusion or exclusion?', *International Journal of Inclusive Education,* 12 (2): 221-236

Low, C. TES (2006) 'Why there's still a case for special treatment'. Available at: http://www.tes.co.uk/article.aspx?storycode=2196460 [accessed 14th December 2013)

Low, C. (2007) 'A defence of moderate inclusion', in Cigman, R. (2007) (ed.) *Included or excluded? The challenge of the mainstream for some SEN children.* Oxon: Routledge, pp 1-14

Norwich, B. (2002) *LEA inclusion trends in England 1997–2001, statistics on special school placements and pupils with statements in special schools.* Bristol: CSIE.
Norwich, B. (2010) 'A Response to 'Special Educational Needs: A New Look', in Terzi, L. (ed.) *Special Education Needs: A New Look,* London: Continuum, pp. 47-113

Oliver, M. (1992) 'Intellectual masturbation: a rejoinder to Soder and Booth', *European Journal of Special Needs Education,* 1(1): 20-28

O'Neill, O. BBC (2002) *Called to account. Lecture 3, Reith Lectures*. Available at: http://www.bbc.co.uk/radio4/reith2002/lecture3.shtml [accessed on 15th December 2013]

OFSTED (2004) *Special Educational Needs and Disability: Towards Inclusive Schooling*. London: OFSTED. Available at: http://www.ofsted.gov.uk/resources/special-educational-needs-and-disability-towards-inclusive-schools [accessed 1st November 2013]

Powell, S. and Tutt, R. (2002) 'When inclusion becomes exclusion', *International Journal of Primary, Elementary and Early Years Education*, 30(2): 43-46.

Roulstone, A., and Prideaux, S. (2008) 'More policies, greater inclusion? Exploring the contradictions of New Labour inclusive education policy'. *International Journal in Sociology of Education*, 18(1): 15-29.

Sikes, P., Lawson, H. & Parker, M. (2007) 'Voices on: teachers and teaching assistants talk about inclusion', *International Journal of Inclusive Education*, 11 (3): 355–70.

Simmons, B., Bayliss, P. (2007) 'The role of special schools for children with profound and multiple learning difficulties: is segregation always best?', *British Journal of Special Education,* 34(1): 19 - 24

Slee, R. (2011) *The Irregular School; Exclusion, Schooling and Inclusive Education*. Abingdon: Routledge.

Terzi, L. (ed.) (2010) *Special Educational Needs A New Look*. London: Continuum

Thomas, G. (1997) 'Inclusive Schools for an Inclusive Society' *British Journal of Special Education,* 24(3): 103-107

Thomas, G., Loxley, A. (2007) *Deconstructing Special Education and Constructing Inclusion*. 2nd edn. Berkshire: Open University Press

UNESCO (1994) *The Salamanca Statement and Framework for Action on Special Needs Education*. World Conference on Special Needs Education, Access and Quality. Available at: http://www.unesco.org/education/pdf/SALAMA_E.PDF [accessed 30th November 2013]

Vaughn, M. TES (2005) 'Wary about Warnock'. Available at: http://www.tes.co.uk/article.aspx?storycode=2110076 [accessed 14th December 2013]

Warnock, M. (2005) *Special Education Needs: A New Look.* London: The Philosophy of Education society of Great Britain

Warnock, M (2010) 'Special Education Needs a New look', in Terzi, L. (2010) (ed.) *Special Education Needs: A New Look..* London: Continuum, pp.11-45

5 PAULA QUIGLEY

My name is Paula Quigley and I was born in 1988. I grew up in a small village in the North East of Ireland called Inniskeen. I attended Primary and secondary school in that area. At the age of 18, I moved to Dublin to attend University College Dublin. There I studied an Arts degree specialising in Irish and Mathematics. Three years later in 2009, I received my Honours Degree. Teaching has always been a passion of mine and spaces on teaching courses in Ireland are quite limited. I then decided to apply to universities in England to complete the PGCE. I got accepted to Edge Hill University outside Liverpool and I completed my PGCE Primary in 2010. That year, I decided that I wanted to move to London to experience teaching in schools in the capital city. For the next three years I taught in a Catholic Junior school in East London in upper Key stage 2. During my time at that school, I was fortunate to lead a number of successful projects. In 2013, I moved to a different area of the South East and at got a job at a Catholic Primary school in West London. On starting this new job, I also decided to complete my Masters in Education at Brunel University

The Impact of Ofsted on Schools

Abstract:

The research gathered will look at the impact that Ofsted have on England's education system. Ofsted have undergone many changes since 1992 and gone through different governments in power. Through this research it is evident that there are tensions between schools and Ofsted. Firstly there is a strain on teachers through different phases of the inspection: before, during and post-inspection. Secondly Ofsted feel pressure as well as they have to ensure that they are rising and sustaining standards in school so that England is able compete on a global scale. This impacts how inspections are managed and the changing Framework.

Introduction:

This essay will analyse the effect and impact that Ofsted has on schools. Ofsted are an outside body that was set up to work for the government inspecting schools (Woods and Jeffrey, 1998). They were first brought about in the 1988 Education Reform Act and later established through the 1992 Education Act (Fulton, 1996). Ofsted have undergone a lot of change through the past years and this has impacted our schools and education system.

There are different ways that Ofsted have impacted the schools in England. Ofsted have working relationships with the government, schools and the public. Each one of these partnerships views Ofsted in a different way. Ofsted are a complex establishment as they are a quasi-autonomous non-governmental organisation (quango) but the government relies heavily on them to influence Education policy (Temple, 2000). This essay aims to look at the literature connected to Ofsted and how we can see its relevance in today's society.

One argument in this literature review will look at Ofsted's driving force, the economy, and making sure that our education is able to compete on a global scale. Baxter and Clarke (2013:702) point out that there is a great need for our education system to be able to compete globally, 'Pressure on England to improve its system of Education has not only emerged from the national need for all schools to serve their pupils well, but has also been prompted by an increasing emphasis on international league tables'. Ofsted are a regulating body and one of the components to inform our Government whether the schools are producing good enough standards to compete in markets globally (Ofsted, 2014).

Secondly, we will focus in the tension between Ofsted and schools. Ofsted are seen as a professional development body that is there to enhance the leadership and teaching in our schools of today (Ofsted, 2014). From the literature in this essay, it is evident that there is major tension between teaching staff and Ofsted. This will be discussed in detail.

There is a lot of criticism towards these inspections conducted by Ofsted and people have questioned whether the impact that they pose on schools in sufficient enough (Stewart, 2013). There are different opinions regarding the impact of the inspection process especially post inspection whereby schools are expected to implement any changes that were suggested by Ofsted (Lonsdale & Parsons, 1998; Cuckle & Broadhead 1999).

Ofsted's current vision for its inspectors state that they 'should evaluate objectively, be impartial and inspect without fear or favour, report honesty and clearly, ensuring that all judgements are fair and reliable, and base all evaluations on clear and robust evidence' (Ofsted, 2012a: 19).

From the research conducted in this essay, the impact that Ofsted have on schools has always been up to debate by the media, schools and parliament. They have all questioned the accuracy of their judgements and how much it is measured to contribute to school improvement (Matthews et al. 1998, Parliament 2004, 2011).

Strain (2009) questions the impact of inspections and through his research, he recommends that the inspections were 'removed and higher priority given to acknowledging the impact of social factors on performance and achievement' (ibid. 2009; 154).

Inspection Process

'Inspection has been a feature of the education landscape in England since its inception in 1838 (Maclure, 2000; 83). It is evident from this that inspections are a key element in schools. 'In September 1992 HMI effectively ceased to exist and the process of inspection was vested in a new body: the Office for Standards in Education (Ofsted), under the direction of Her Majesty's chief Inspector (HMCI)' (Lee and Fitz, 1997; 39).

Ofsted, which stands for Office for Standards in Education was primarily created from the 1988 Education Reform Act but later established through the 1992 Education Act. Ofsted's role when they were set up was to inspect schools throughout England (Cullingford, 1999). They are an outside agency that is not run by the government but they do report directly to the government (Ofsted, 2014). Each school is inspected at least once every four years (Abbott, Rathbone and Whitehead, 2013). Ofsted's main role is to inspect all schools in England. Their duty is to ensure that they are lending themselves to the progress of school improvement (Plowright, 2007; Ofsted 2004b).

Chris Woodhead was the first chief inspector of Ofsted (Fitz and Lee, 1997). The Functions of Chief Inspector was to keep the Secretary of State informed about the standards of education throughout all schools (Parliament, 1992). Sir Michael Wilshaw is the current chief inspector and is responsible for the running of Ofsted inspections and reporting directly annually about the quality of teaching in our schools (Ofsted, 2014).

Ofsted- Initial Government

While conducting this literature review it is important to consider the time when Ofsted was established and look at the relevance that they have in the economy at that present time. Ofsted were introduced during a time where the Conservatives were in power and they were pushing for education to be more centralised (Whitty and Power, 1997). This would thereby take power from the LEAs (Local Education Authorities) and give their government more power in how schools are managed (ibid. 1997). Previous to this establishment, LEAs were able to control the inspections of schools through HMI.

Regulatory Body

Before Ofsted came in, the HMI were responsible for inspecting schools. They were portrayed as inspectors that were there to help develop and advise schools (Lee and Fitz, 1997). Baxter (2013) states that Ofsted were seen strictly as a regulatory body, that was inspecting schools in a bid to raise standards. Ofsted wanted to inform parents, with a more clear vision of the performance of certain schools around the country. In turn this would help parents pick a school which was most suitable for their child (ibid. 2013). This was a factor of the Conservatives view of giving the parents more choice and creating a competitive market amongst schools (Whitty and Power, 1997).

Standardisation

In 1988 an important area was marked in Education as the 1988 Education Reform Act was put into place. Through this Act, a new National Curriculum was established, SAT exams were introduced and a new inspection body (Education Reform Act, 1988). One of the main themes from this policy that was embedded across the strands was standardisation. The government were focusing their attention on this area in a bid to raise standards. By raising standards in our education, it would then result in better educated individuals which in turn with help the economy and our compatibility to compete with other countries around the world. Schools would be inspected and results published publically. The government saw this as one way that would help raise standards. (Abbott, Rathbone and Whitehead, 2013).

Chapman (2002) also agrees that the theme of raising standards was embedded in central government at the time the 1988 Education Reform Act was implemented and Ofsted was created. This policy was able to directly affect teachers and the day to day duties within their profession. It helped to raises standards and expectations in schools across the country (ibid. 2002).

Whitty and Power (1997) all highlight an important aspect of the 1988 Education Reform Act: the introduction of the National Curriculum. This was another assessment tool that the government introduced to help raise standards in education. The School Curriculum Assessment Agency (SCAA) had to work alongside Ofsted to ensure that a true picture of how a school was performing was published. This was published through league tables and inspection reports. These two agencies had the power to determine whether a school was performing at their best. This then fed into the competiveness market that schools were undergoing at that time with the Conservatives in power (ibid. 1997). It is evident that Ofsted have a number of partners that they need to work alongside in order to get a clear vision of achieving a high standard of education (Politics, 2014).

Drive in the Economy

'Policy always has to be viewed in terms of both change and continuity- what changes and what stays the same' (Ball, 2008: p55). During the time of the 1988 Education Reform Act, there was a new reform in the way schools were managed and the marketization of the running of the schools. There are questions of how this has impacted the education that children are receiving. Quasi markets were introduced and competiveness between markets (Whitty and Power, 1997).

Additionally, this competitiveness was becoming more apparent. The economy was changing. Schools were becoming increasingly more important in producing a skills force that could complete with the economy at that time. Tomlinson (2005:3) stated that 'teachers were gradually stripped of their professionalism and policed by new inspection regimes'. Tomlinson, (2005) identifies elements of pressure building amongst schools and Ofsted as the importance was laid on whether schools were producing children that were skilled so that England could complete on a global scale, which was one of the main priorities that the government had at that time. Teachers, schools and local authorities were getting the blame for this and therefore the state employed more private bodies to regulate how our education were preparing for the future economy (ibid. 2005).

From 1944 onwards, it was evident that education policies were changing. Usually the schools and local authorities made the decisions but the government were moving away from decentralisation to a more centralisation approach (ibid. 2005).

Managerial state

Standardisation is seen to operate in bureaucracy where by the skills of the professional bodies are controlled. The professional bodies within education need to be trusted. There must be a balance created between personal and impersonal judgement in the form of bureaucracy (Clarke and Newman 1997).

The decentralisation of working autonomy is a relevant process in the effectiveness of management in the education system. One of their main drives is to improve the standards of service and if the management has more freedom, they can ensure that this is met. Although if managers were given more freedom, they are still limited as they need to meet regulations and they may be limited by their budget. (Clarke and Newman, 1997).

Ofsted are vital in the tracking of England's education. They are a regulating body but they also are core elements 'that constitutes new forms of governance' (Newman and Clarke, 2009; 33). Fitz and Lee (1997) argue that the transfer from HMI to Ofsted also transferred the balance between professional development and advisory to a more direct influence of the education system and the direction that the government wanted it to go in.

Inspectors were initially employed with the aim of being a separate regulating body form the government and decrease inspectors ability to directly influence education policy on a day to day basis (Fitz and Lee, 1997).

Burchill (1991) emphasises the importance that inspectors have in their role and the impact that they bestow on schools. He advises that they should be employed in an unregulated market whereby schools have the authority to choose their own inspection teams (ibid. 1991).

Woods and Jeffrey (1998) question what impact the power of the state is having directly on the way that inspections occur and the way that teachers handle them. 'The values behind the new reforms contrast sharply with the prevailing child-centred discourse preferred by primary school teachers' (ibid. 1998; p.547).

Phases of Ofsted

Ofsted have the ability to give an outsiders view on the performance of the school when inspected from within. They can leave a lasting effect especially with the power of publically displaying the results so that they are open to interpretation to a mass of people. Ofsted are one effective ingredient that helps raise standards in schools (Ball, Maguire and Braun, 2012: 74)

There are different ways and phases that Ofsted operate to have an impact on school improvement. Schools react differently to different phases. The main three phases are; the time prior to the inspection, the actual inspection itself and the time frame after the inspection (Chapman, 2010).

Chapman (2010) conducted research on the impact that Ofsted has on different phases on schools and in his findings he drew against a number of issues. Firstly Chapman (2010) spoke about when an inspection was looming and coming closer to a school, there were different styles adapted for managing the school. This in turn has a major impact on the vision for school improvement as a whole as it becomes more focused on short term thus neglecting the long term vision. This brings up concerns for raising and sustaining standards in schools. Chapman (2010) then spoke about the negative effects that these inspections were having on staff within the school as they felt the pressure to perform. This is especially the case in schools where they are aware that they are under achieving or in special measures. The management look for short term solutions to pass the inspection but this then has an impact on the long term improvement of the school (ibid. 2010).

Gray and Gardener (1999) also agree with Chapman with regards to staff pressure. They speak about the staff experiencing a lot of pressure and stress during the different phases of Ofsted. When teachers are being inspected in their classroom, this is when the anxiety is at its highest. During their study, they also concluded that some inspector's mannerism added to the anxiety of teachers (ibid. 1999).

Teachers

The impact of the 1988 Education reform Act had standards at the core of their policy. As a result Strain (2009) highlights the support that teachers, as a profession, were losing at that time. Their profession was losing status compared to teacher professions in other countries. With Ofsted being introduced to head teachers and teachers, their mood was wary and their voice had reduced in the running of the school (ibid. 2009).

Davies (2000) agrees and also points out that some teachers felt that they were being personally attacked by Ofsted and they felt that their ability to teach was being questioned and under close scrutiny. This then adds to the pressure that burdens teachers as Chapmen (2010) previously spoke about.

From this research, it is evident that Ofsted's relationship with the teachers has an impact on school improvement. Promoting positive interactions and encouraging professional development from Ofsted can lead to teachers being more open to change and open-minded towards new and current ways of practice in their school. With Ofsted only visiting the school on average once every four years, it is much harder to generate this positive working relationship. Especially schools that are struggling to perform and get their school to improve (Chapman, 2010).

Furthermore a large amount of teachers feel that a huge amount of excess pressure is put on them from Ofsted. They feel that they only have a short space of time to perform and ensure that all relevant practices are put in place. This adds to the negative factors that Ofsted bring when inspecting schools (Ouston *et al.* 1996; Earley 1998 and Ferguson *et al.* 2002). It is argued that some teachers leave the profession because of this pressure. This has a negative effect especially in the case of struggling and failing schools. These are the schools that are most vulnerable and need the stability and retention of staff and pupils (Chapman, 2010). Jeffrey and Woods (1996) agree and discussed, in their research, the disheartening impact that inspections can have on staff and how this can lead to a negative view of the profession.

Schools want there to be more opportunities to speak to the inspectors to help with their professional development. This in turn may help both, the teachers and inspectors, have a better understanding of the environment they are working in and help with retention of staff (Ball, 1998; Gleeson and Knights, 2006). Baxter (2013) states that the new framework set in 2012 aims to strengthen the relationship between Ofsted and the teachers in regards to the teacher's professional development. The framework aims to this by putting a stronger emphasis on the teaching and learning.

Governments

It is evident that Governments are definitely in favour of Ofsted and they value their contribution in helping to raise the standards of education in Britain. The Conservatives and Labour party both kept Chris Headwood as Chief Inspector. From this, it is evident that both parties agreed that Chris was doing a sufficient job. Chris later resigned in November 2000. During Chris' time as chief inspector, he heavily criticised schools and their staff which aided the Conservatives and Labour party and give them an insight to what was going on in schools (Tomlinson, 2005). Chris was always open and gave a realistic view of what type of practices he was observing in schools. He had a clear and open focus on the quality of teaching in schools and made it clear to the public and government what direction it should be steering in (Fitz and Lee, 1997). In the Times Educational Supplement (2008), one of Chris's former colleagues publicly disagreed with the way that Chris worked in Ofsted. He stated that: 'Mr. Woodhead's politically-inspired negative comment and highly economical use of registered inspectors' judgments is giving the public a misleadingly gloomy picture of primary teaching and is contributing to the sector's deep malaise' (ibid. 2008).

Ofsted is employed as a regulating agency that informs the government of practice they experience through inspections and the quality of schools. Therefore, they have a direct influence on government education policy (Ozga et al. 2013). It is evident that there is a strong need for regulators but Baxter (2013) argues that to be a successful regulating body, then they should not be influenced by any other agencies. To be an independent regulating body, Ofsted inspectors would then have to rely heavily on their professional judgement and discretion and there are issues surrounding this (Bardach and Kagan 2013).

Baxter (2013) researches Ofsted's current framework implemented in 2012 and the impact that it has on government's education policy. She concludes that Ofsted is a 'credible regulatory body and legitimate tool' (Baxter 2013; 14) to aid the government in England's education system. She also praises the fact that Ofsted continuously reinvent themselves to serve their purpose and create a discourse of inspection (ibid. 2013).

Standards in failing schools

Parliament (1992) stated that the inspectors were responsible for schools that were deemed to be at risk. The inspectors needed to state this in their written report if they felt that the standards in an educational setting were failing (ibid. 1992).

Ofsted have the responsibility to make the Secretary of State aware of schools that are deemed to be at risk of failing and they also have the responsibility to use their professional judgement to recognise failing schools (Gray and Gardener, 1999). This proves that Ofsted were vital in recognising and reporting in the schools that were deemed as failing. They had to intervene and raise expectations and standards in those schools in a certain amount of time. Fitz-Gibbon (1998) argues the effectiveness of inspectors judgements when observing teachers teach. She highlights that inspectors using their professional judgement alone when observing classrooms is not substantial enough to be responsible for deeming a school is at risk (ibid. 1998).

It is evident that keeping up standards was big on the agenda in schools and when New Labour took over in the 90's, they continued to keep this theme on their list of high importance. Ball (2008) highlights that failing schools were reported through the media and policy makers held this theme repeatedly through new education policies. Ball (2008) then states that when a school was deemed to be failing, inspectors had permission to intervene more regularly and help with the plan of removing its failing status. Often failing schools would enter the Fresh Starts Scheme whereby the school undertook new management, staff and name. This information became public information and led to a wider distribution of interest from the media. In turn, this gave the government more power to reform the standards in these education establishments and justify why outside agencies could get involved in the help with failing schools (ibid. 2008).

Ofsted are powerful forces in determining a failing school. They have the power to steer the system. Fitz and Lee, (1997)state that Ofsted have the ability to put fear into schools which hopefully in turn would make schools try their best to steer away from being called a failing school. This is a stronger message than what the HMI were giving out (ibid. 1997).

Self-Evaluation

In the more recent frameworks that Ofsted have created they want schools to be the key developer in their own improvement through self-evaluation. They need schools to work on their own initiative so that they are able to pick out the key areas that are needed for development and improvement. (Plowright 2007; Ofsted, 1999: 138) In 2005, the Department for Education published; A New Relationship with Schools: *Improving Performance through Self Evaluation.* Guidance was given in this to schools on how Ofsted would use this form to assess the overall standard of the school. Schools were advised that this form would give Ofsted a judgement before they inspected the schools and throughout the inspection. It would give the inspectors a clear vision of how the school was performing and their ability to raise standards (Department for Education and Skills, 2005b). This links back to the phases that Ofsted perform in.

It was the headmaster's duty to carry out the self-evaluation form prior to inspection. Ferguson et al. (2000) identifies flaws in this SEF (self-evaluation form) as some schools may think that this will have an influence on what is in the end report produced by Ofsted. Schools needed to ensure that this form give a clear honest view of the school's performance (ibid. 2000). Therefore, Ofsted are giving some control to the school to develop themselves but the power and responsibility still remains with Ofsted.

Move over, in 2010, the government declared a new approach on how they see the SEF form and the impact that it has on raising standards in schools. However, Education Minister, Michael Gove, announced that he wanted Ofsted to get rid of the SEF form. He felt that it was wasting too much of valuable time for Head masters and the cost of it was eating into school's budgets (Department for Education, 2010). Gove said that 'The Coalition government trusts teachers to get on with their job. That's why we are taking steps to reduce the bureaucracy they face and giving them the powers they need to do a good job. We believe that teachers - not bureaucrats and politicians - should run schools' (ibid. 2010).

Dispersal of information

Ofsted have a lot of power in the information that has impact on the discourse in education. They have access to a range of data analysis. Unlike the HMI, they use this information in a more positive light. They publicly publish all their inspectors online on their website (www.ofsted.gov.uk) which allows them as a regulating body to interact publically and inform a variety of persons (Fitz and Lee, 1997). Ofsted continue to research and publicise new findings in Education to help benefit the education system (Ofsted, 2013). There are a number of positives coming from the regulatory body Ofsted. 'Ofsted makes use of educational research, particularly international comparisons, to bolster its data and strengthen its arguments' (Fitz and Lee, 1997; 49).

Current Ofsted

Ofsted in recent years have introduced 'one of the most stringent and demanding inspection frameworks since its interception' (Baxter and Clarke, 2013: 702). There are four main areas that Ofsted are now focusing on compared to the previous inspection framework that had 29 judgements (Ofsted, 2012). In the new inspections, the inspectors play a vital role as there is a lot more emphasis on professional judgement. Baxter and Clarke (2013) argue that this is moving away from the 'tick box' judgement and there are some issues with this new approach and the quality of the inspectors. Their research concludes that although the framework has undergone a lot of positive changes, they recommend that Ofsted still need to develop more worthy professional judgements (ibid).

The Audit Commission also agree that 'skilled and credible inspectors are the single most important feature of a successful inspection service' (Audit Commission, 1999; 9). The reiterate the point made by Baxter and Clarke, that inspectors are the key people in school inspections.

Conclusion

Andreas Schleicher, who works with the Organisation for Economic Cooperation recently pointed out that 'Your education today is your economy tomorrow' (BBC News: 2013).

This essay looked through the literature and argued the effect and impact that Ofsted has had on schools. Ofsted are an outside body that was set up to work for the government inspecting schools. Ofsted have undergone a lot of changes through the past 23 years and it is evident that there has been major impact on schools and our education system in England.

Firstly the relationship between Ofsted, the economy and the government was looked at in detail and what impact that their relationship had on school inspections. It is evident from the literature that the economy will always be a factor in the driving force of Ofsted and their changing framework. Ofsted need to the Education in England to have the ability to compete on a global scale with education systems around the world. Baxter and Clarke (2013:702) have highlighted the importance of this area and how we as a country need to be standing out in the competitive market: 'Pressure on England to improve its system of Education has not only emerged from the national need for all schools to serve their pupils well, but has also been prompted by an increasing emphasis on international league tables'.

Secondly, this essay focused on the tension that has arisen over the years between Ofsted inspectors and school staff. Strain (2009), Davies (2000) and Chapman (2010) all agree that negativity that teachers are experiencing through inspections is having a negative impact on schools. But through the research it is evident that Ofsted's new Framework is aiming to amend some of their breakdown in communications between teachers and inspectors (Baxter, 2013).

'The general managerialist trend continues, with inspectors and teachers coping as best they can, making little real contact across the structural divide' (Woods and Jeffrey, 1998; p.568).

Ofsted also publicly inform the public on their website so that they are aware the progress in schools and current issues. Ofsted are seen as a professional development body that is there to enhance the leadership and teaching in our schools of today. It is evident from the literature in this essay that teachers want to be guided more through the inspection process to help develop them in their profession (Chapman, 2010).

It is evident that Ofsted are heavily criticised from different sources which has been pointed out. There are different opinions regarding the impact of the inspection process especially post inspection whereby schools are expected to implement any changes that were suggested by Ofsted (Lonsdale & Parsons, 1998; Cuckle & Broadhead 1999).

Ofsted's framework has changed throughout the years and currently we can see that there is a focus on developing the schools in four key areas (Ofsted, 2012). It is clear that Ofsted inspector have a very important role to play in the inspection process. Ofsted's current vision for its inspectors state that they 'should evaluate objectively, be impartial and inspect without fear or favour, report honesty and clearly, ensuring that all judgements are fair and reliable, and base all evaluations on clear and robust evidence' (Ofsted, 2012a: 19).

Media, parliament and the public have all questioned the accuracy of their judgements and how much it is measured to contribute to school improvement (Matthews et al. 1998, Parliament 2004, 2011).

Strain (2009) questioned the impact of inspections and through his research, he recommended that the inspections were 'removed and higher priority given to acknowledging the impact of social factors on performance and achievement' (ibid, 2009; 154).

'The new schedule began in January 2012, and since then, data suggests that either schools are regressing or the framework is indeed far tougher' (Baxter and Clarke, 2013; 710). This will be one area that will need to be researched further in the future to measure the impact of the new framework implemented in 2012.

It is also evident through this literature review that the research surrounding Ofsted is limited in the positivity that it is contributing to our society. Ofsted publish a number of publications annually to inform and benefit our education system (Ofsted 2014).

References

Abbott, I., Rathbone, M. and Whitehead, P. (2013) *Education Policy*. London: Sage.

Audit Commission (1999) *Developing principles for Public Inspection: A consultant document.* London: Audit Commission.

Ball, S. (1998) Performativity and fragmentation in 'postmodern schooling'. In J. Carter (Ed.), *Postmodernity and the fragmentation of welfare* (pp. 187-203). London: Routledge.

Ball, S. (2008) *The Education Debate*, Bristol: Policy.

Ball, S., Maguire, M. and Braun, A (2012) *How Schools Do Policy: Policy Enactments in Secondary Schools*. Abingdon: Routledge.

Bardach, E. and Kagan, R. (2010) *Going by the Book: The Problem of Regulatory Unreasonableness.* London: Transaction.

Baxter, J. (2013) An independent inspectorate? Addressing the paradoxes of educational inspection in 2013, *School Leadership and Management,* [Online] Available at: http://www.tandfonline.com (Accessed: 5th January, 2014).

Baxter, J. and Clarke, J. (2013) *Farewell to the tick box inspectorate? Ofsted and the changing regime of school inspection in England*, [online] Available at: http://www.tandfonline.com (Accessed: 5th January, 2014).

Burchill, J. (1991) *Inspecting schools: Breaking the Monopoly*. London: Centre for Policy Studies.

Chapman, C. (2010) Ofsted and School Improvement: Teachers' perceptions of the inspection process in schools facing challenging circumstances. *School Leadership & Management: Formerly School Organisation* Volume 22, Issue 3, pp. 257-272, [Online]. Available at: http://www.tandfonline.com. (Accessed: 30th November 2013).

Clarke, J. and Newman, J. (1997) *The Managerial State: Power, Politics and Ideology in the Remaking of Social Welfare*. London: Sage.

Cuckle, P. and Broadhead, P. (1999) Effects of Ofsted on School Development and Staff Morale in Cullingford C (ed.), *An Inspector Calls*, London: Kogan Page.

Cullingford, C. (1999) *An inspector calls: Ofsted and its effect on school standards*. London: Kogan Page.

Davies, N. (2000) *The School Report.* London: Vintage.

DfES/ Ofsted (2005b) *A New Relationship with Schools: Improving Performance through Self Evaluation. Nottingham*: DfES.

Earley, P. (1998) *School Improvement after Inspections: School and LEA responses*. London: Paul Chapman Publishing.

Education Reform Act 1988, (c.40) London: The Stationery Office.

Ferguson, N., Earley, P., Fidler, B. and Ouston, J. (2002) *Improving Schools and Inspection: The Self Inspecting School*. London: Paul Chapman Publishing.

Fitz-Gibbon, C. (1998) Can Ofsted stay afloat? *Managing schools Today*, 7, 6, pp. 22-25.

Glesson, D. and Knights, D. (2006) Challenging dualism: Public professionalism in 'troubled' times. Sociology, 40, 277-295.

Government UK: Department for Education (2010) *News*. Available at: https://www.gov.uk/government/news/education-secretary-michael-gove-sets-out-the-next-stage-in-a-programme-of-reducing-bureaucracy (Accessed: 24th November).

Gray, C. and Gardener, J. (1999) The Impact of School Inspection. *Oxford Review of Education* Vol. 25 No. 4 pp.455-468 [Online]. Available at: http://www.tandfonline.com. (Accessed: 5th January 2014).

Great Britain. Education (Schools) Act 1992. (c.38). United Kingdom: Controller and Chief Executive of Her Majesty's Stationery Office and Queen's Printer of Acts of Parliament.

Jeffrey, B. and Woods, P. (1996) Feeling deprofessionalised: the social construction of emotions during an Ofsted inspection. *Cambridge Journal of Education*. 26, 3 pp. 325-343 [Online]. Available at: http://www.tandfonline.com. (Accessed: 12th January 2014).

Lee, J. and Fitz, J. (1997)HMI and Ofsted: Evolution or Revolution in School Inspection. *British Journal of Educational Studies*, Vol.45, No.1, pp.39-52. [Online]. Available at: http://www.tandfonline.com. (Accessed: 2nd November 2013).

Lonsdale, P. and Parsons, C. (1998) Inspection and the School Improvement Hoax in Earley P. (ed.) *School Improvement After Inspection*, London: Paul Chapman Publishing.

Maclure, S. (2000) *The Inspectors' calling*. Oxford: Hodder and Stoughton.

Matthews, P. Holmes, J., Vickers, P. and Corporaal, B. (1998) Aspects of the Reliability and Validity of School Inspections Judgements of Teaching Quality. *Educational Research and Evaluation 4 (2)* pp. 1676-188 [Online]. Available at: http://www.tandfonline.com. (Accessed: 8th January 2014).

Newman, J. and Clarke, J. (2009) Public, Politics and Power: Remaking the Public in Public Services. London: Sage.

Ofsted (1999) *Handbook for Inspecting Secondary Schools: with Guidance on Self-Evaluation*. London: The Stationery Office.

Ofsted, (2004b) *Standards and Quality 2002/03: The Annual Report of her Majesty's Chief Inspector of Schools.* London, Ofsted.

Ofsted, (2012a) *The evaluation schedule for the inspection of maintained schools and academies*. London: Ofsted.

Ofsted, (2012b) *The Framework for school inspection 2012*. London: Ofsted.

Ofsted, (2013) *Publications*, Available at www.ofsted.gov.uk. (Accessed: 18th January, 2013).

Ofsted, (2014a) *About Us*. Available at www.ofsted.gov.uk. (Accessed: 19.01.14).

Ofsted (2014b) *How we are structured*. Available at www.ofsted.gov.uk. (Accessed: 19.01.14).

Ouston, J., Earley. P and Fidler, B. (1996) *OFSTED Inspections: The Early Experience*, London: David Fulton.

Ozga, J., Baxter, J., Clarke, J., Grek, S., and Lawn, M. (2013) The Politics of Educational Change: Governance and School Inspection in England and Scotland. *Swiss Journal of Sociology* 39 (2) pp.37-55 .

Parliament, (2004) The work of Ofsted, Sixth Report of Session 2003-4, Report, Together with Formal Minutes, Oral and Written Evidence 2003-4, House of Commons Papers 2003, 04,026. London: Her Majesty's Stationary Office.

Parliament (2011) *The Role and Performance of Ofsted*. London: The House of Commons Education Committee.

Plowright, D. (2007) 'Self-Evaluation and Ofsted Inspection: Developing an Integrative Model of School Improvement, *Educational Management Administration & Leadership* 2007 35: 373, [Online] DOI: 10.1177/1741143207078180, (Accessed: 12th November, 2003).

Politics, (2014) *Ofsted*. Available at: http://www.politics.co.uk/reference/ofsted (Accessed: 12th January, 2014).

Schleicher, A. (2013). How Pisa became the world's most important exam. *BBC News* [Online]. 27th November [Accessed 11th January 2014]. Available from: http://www.bbc.co.uk/news/business-24988343.

Stewart, W. (2013) Ofsted's approach 'is not backed by research' *Times Educational Supplement*. 18th September [Online] Available at: www.tes.co.uk [Accessed: 10th January 2014].

Strain, M. (2009) Education Reform Act 1988: A success or failure? A short report of a BELMAS Discussion Forum. *Management in Education* 23:151 [Online] Available from: http://mie.sagepub.com/ [Accessed: 12th December 2013].

Temple, M. (2000) *How Britain works: from ideology to output politics*. Basingstoke:

Macmillan.

Times Educational Supplement (2008) Chief Inspector's 'distorted' Tactics, *Times Educational Supplement.* www.tes.co.uk (Accessed 10th January 2014).

Tomlinson, S. (2005) *Education in a post –welfare society.* Maidenhead: Open University Press.

Whitty, G. and Power, S. (1997) *Quasi-Markets and Curriculum Control: Making Sense of Recent Education Reform in England and Wales.* London: Sage.

Woods, P. and Jeffrey, B. (1998) Choosing Positions: Living the Contradictions of Ofsted. *British Journal of Sociology of Education* Vol.19, No.4, pp.547-570 [Online]. Available from: www.tandfonline.com [Accessed 12th November 2013].

6 RICHARD LESTER

Born and bred in Cork, Ireland. I moved to the UK in 2002 to study Physical Education in UWIC Cardiff. I have now been teaching for the past 8 years and I am currently working in a faith academy in West London. I trained as a PE teacher but have always had a keen interest in the pastoral side of education leading me to undertake an MA at Brunel in Leadership and Management of Education.

Table of contents

Section 1.0

    Abstract

Section 2.0

    Introduction

        2.1 History

        2.2 The purpose of Ofsted

Section 3.0

    The Impact of Ofsted

    3.1 Staff

    3.2 Results

    3.3 Leadership

    3.4 Problems

Section 4.0

    Development in policy

Section 5.0

    Conclusion

References

1.0 Abstract

School inspections have existed in various forms for over 200 years. Since the creation of the Office of Standards in Education (Ofsted) in the 1992 Education Act school inspections have aimed to improve the quality of education through inspection. Ofsted claim to have improved the teaching and management of schools leading to a superior education system and better exam results for students. This assignment looks at the impact Ofsted has had on the stress levels caused to teachers, the scale of improvement in exam results along with the problems and developments associated with Ofsted since its formation.

A critical review of Ofsted's impact since its commencement in 1992.

Section 2.0

Introduction

> *Ofsted's remit centred originally on: the regular inspection of all schools by independent inspectors; public reporting, with summaries of reports for parents as users; an annual report to parliament, and the provision of advice to ministers. The scope of Ofsted's work has been expanded substantially since 1997 as a result of legislation. 'Improvement through inspection' is a self-selected aspiration over which Ofsted has little direct control except in relation to statutory provisions for the identification and monitoring of schools, colleges and sixth forms causing concern, and the regulation of childcare*
>
> *(Matthews, 2004 :13).*

This assignment will critically review the impact that Ofsted has had since its commencement in 1992. This will be achieved by gaining an understanding of the history of school inspections leading to why Ofsted was created and put into place through the 1992 Education Act. Furthermore the purpose and function of Ofsted will be examined resulting in the impact that the new inspection regime has had upon schools, teachers, senior leaders but more importantly on the results of students. Within this assignment both positive and negative perspectives will be compared to get an overall view on the impact and associated problems inspections have made. Lastly there have been numerous changes to Ofsted over the 20 years of its existence and these developments and their impacts will also be explored.

2.1 History

Ofsted inspections were first carried out in schools in Britain in 1993 (Clarke, 2005, Ouston et al 1997, Matthews and Sammons, 2004). Prior to the creation of Ofsted in 1992, inspections were undertaken in schools in England dating back as far as the industrial revolution in 1839 (Smith, 2000, McLaughlin, 2001, Brighouse, 1995). Shaw et al (2003) explains how early inspections were not through educational legislation but were part of Althorpe's Act 1833 which gave inspectors the power to set up and inspect schools for the children of factory workers.

Kerr (1891) reckons there are few respects where a greater contrast exists between past and present in relation to education in Scotland in the 17th century. The clergy were in charge of everything associated with schools, the suitability of teachers, there appointment and dismissal was all in the hands of the church (ibid). Kerr (1891) suggests this was discharged with by no means satisfactory results or any consistency. Scottish school inspection dates back as far as 1696 where each parish had a school and each school was inspected annually by clergy but supported by government grants (ibid). This continued until the passing of the educational act in 1872. England was different according to Kerr (1891) as the church funded schools until the establishment of the Committee of Council on Education in 1839.

Brighouse (1995) suggests similarities between the inspectors of today and Her Majesty's Inspectorate (HMI) of 1840's as the inspectors upset a lot of people, but specifically at that time by commenting on social conditions and criticising authority. The HMI found that about half of the teachers of that era were completely untrained and the other half had spent a mere one or two months training to understand the schooling system and so the Normal Schools for the training of teachers was established (Kerr, 1891, Brighouse, 1995).

Although HMI inspectors upset people with their findings the inspectors of this time were much respected gentlemen and being part of HMI was often used as a way of progressing up into leading positions in the church until a change in Act in 1870 saw a drop in the status of HMI inspectors (Brighouse, 1995). Inspectors were no longer separated by denomination and they were given specific areas to monitor (Shaw et al 2003, Kerr, 1891).

From as early as the start of the 20th century inspectors themselves were being investigated and it was found that the more appropriate inspectors were all university trained men and as a result of this Shaw et al (2003) explains how local inspectors moved to a more curriculum based focus and concentrated their efforts on curriculum developments instead of whole school inspections.

By 1986 Local Education Authority's (LEA) started taking more responsibility due to government abandoning the national inter-authority arrangements for in-service education and training which led to the expansion of inspectors and advisors (Smith, 2000, Brighouse, 1995, McLaughlin, 2001). Advisors were renamed as inspectors and were to look at and collect data based on individual school visits

(Smith, 2000). In 1988 the Education Reform Act set out a major LEA role in the monitoring, informing and inspecting of schools due to the introduction of the National Curriculum (Harris, 2007). Matthews and Sammons (2004) highlights the problem with this act was that the same inspectors were to help develop a particular school yet at various stages they were to inspect and criticise the school wholly for its faults. On the other hand Ouston et al (1997) looked at this act favourably recognising how it moved the focus of schools accountability into the hands of parental choice. As a result of the 1988 Act grant maintained schools only were allowed to be inspected by HMI and parents could then make judgements based on comparative qualitative data (ibid). Towards the end of the 1980's Bolten (1998) and Rosenthal (2004) highlight how the HMI reports were becoming less popular within the government as they were receiving copious amounts of negative publicity. Recognising it needed help, the government turned to the HMI as reports could not be kept from the public and therefore clearly showed the strengths and weaknesses of the current education system (ibid). The government realised perhaps it needed things to change to keep in line with the 1990 Education Reform Act. According to Bolten (1998) this need for regular inspection and for parents to see the information on their child's school created the need and beginning of Ofsted. HMI would no longer have the same role as the previous 150 years but would oversee, organise and ensure quality of inspection (Bolten, 1998). In the 1992 Education Reform Act a systematic regime of inspections was put into place with the formation of Ofsted (Ouston et al, 1997).

2.2 The purpose of Ofsted

The purpose of Ofsted is to improve standards of achievement and quality of education through regular independent inspection, public reporting and informed advice (Ofsted 1999: 16, Perry, 1995:35).

According to Moon (1995) the establishment of Ofsted was a result of John Major's, the Prime Minister at the time, citizen's character policy for improving all public services and more specifically improving educational standards. The question which needed answering by the government was how inspection can be used more efficiently to raise academic standards and achievements (ibid).

Rosenthal (2004) states that the presumption of Ofsted was that the findings and recommendations to schools will cause improvement to the education for students. Yet only after Ofsted was introduced did schools clearly understand the criteria they would be judged on as it was presented in the inspection handbook (Clarke, 2005). The creation of Ofsted was to give advice to the Secretary of State on the standards of student achievement, the quality of education provided, and the efficiency in management of financial resources along with the provisions for students' spiritual, moral, social and cultural development (Clarke, 2005, Kennedy, 1995, Ouston et al, 1997, Wilcox et al, 1996, Pike, 1999).

Both Pike (1996) and Ouston et al (1997) agree that a clear intention of Ofsted was to increase information for parents on schools. Ouston et al (1997) suggests that it gives parents the knowledge prior to selecting the school they wish their children to attend. Whereas Pike (1996) looks at the actual inspection process and how transparent Ofsted aim to be by having a formal meeting with parents and the lead inspector before the inspection and then insisting that the school send letters to each parent with a summary of the final report.

Section 3.0

The impact of Ofsted

Chapman (2002) states that the introduction of the Ofsted policy has had a weighty effect on schools, teachers and the greater educational context of England and Wales. He continues by stating that Ofsted has played a key role in the reform of education this century holding schools and teachers accountable for their actions and in monitoring long term strategic decision making and progress (ibid, Kennedy, 1995).

3.1 Staff

This accountability has however come at a cost to teaching staff in the form of stress (Perryman 2010). According to James et al (2013) a key feature of the policy since the mid 1990's has been the pressure for schools and teachers to improve performance and he feels that this pressure is unavoidable and likely to increase. Dr Mary Bousted the General Secretary for the Association of Teachers and Lectures in 2012 said Ofsted is to blame for adding to teachers stress and said according to the 2010/2011 HSE figures how teaching is the occupation with the third highest amount of work related stress (Anonymous, 2012). In comparison to this Sir Michael Wilshaw, the head of Ofsted suggested at an education conference in East Sussex that teachers use stress as an excuse for poor performance (Anonymous, 2012).

In contrast Winch (2001) says Ofsted hold teachers accountable and punishes them if they fail to meet criteria. Other services do not undergo the same scrutiny or have the same personal consequences as Ofsted (ibid). Fullan (2001) mentions how moral purpose should mould the teaching profession to have clear visions for students however Rosenthal (2004) points out that during times of inspection teachers and administrators concentrate on meeting Ofsted criteria and requirements and not exam performance. Furthermore a consequence of inspections has caused the people Ofsted aim to improve (the teachers), to seem diminished, betrayed and distorted by their influence (Fielding, 2001).

Perryman (2010) suggests teachers stress stems from the fear of inspection and how some teachers have one off perfect lessons prepared along with rehearsed meetings in place just to get through the inspection. This idea of having prepared lessons leads to what Perryman (2010) describes as a 'performance' by schools for Ofsted. Some members of staff according to Chapman (2002) have witnessed this with Ofsted believing this is how the school works day to day leading to a satisfactory grading when the staff thought they should have been placed in special measures. Perryman (2010) raises her concerns over this performance as the schools that are genuinely in special measures will not get the support they really need.

> 'The need to be permanently ready for inspection will send pressure down through every institution, creating cultures of fear rather than of learning'
>
> Coffield, 2012:21).

Post inspection also often raises a problem for schools as pre and during the inspection staff have worked flat out, received their grade and then relaxed or were exhausted from their efforts leaving a slump in performance (a survey of 1933 schools proved a dip in GCSE grades by 0.5% after inspection) (Perryman 2010). Similarity exists in Chapman (2002) however from his findings he concluded that staff found pre inspection to be good for the school as it encouraged staff to implement necessary change yet it was the post inspection stage that had huge implications through staff energy levels dropping from exhaustion. A rise in staff absences is also evident post inspection due to either stress of the inspection or from staff feeling they are entitled to time off after the long hard days building up to the inspection (Perryman, 2010).

3.2 Results

Davis et al (2001) questions if schools have good results in SATS, GCSE's and A-levels, are they improving schools? He concludes that they are not; as we do not know how adequate the national curriculum is and tests cannot measure areas such as personal qualities. Davis et al (2001) reckons serious problems exist about how schools are held accountable for results and thinks the best way to hold them accountable is through both Ofsted and individual pupil assessment. On the other hand Winch (2001) says the problem with Ofsted is that findings are left too open to interpretation. Specific terms should hold different values depending on the social and academic background leaving teachers satisfied that expectations are realistic and related to their school circumstances (ibid). Furthermore Schagen and Weston (1998) show a correlation between socio–economic circumstances and poor Ofsted reports saying it is down to the schools social climate that builds its grade. Lefstein (2013) argues that Ofsted do not take social class or social backgrounds into consideration when making judgements and that they blame teachers and hold them accountable for underachieving students. The blame according to Fielding (2001) and Lefstein (2013) should not be moved to parents, students or social class but should be broken down and replaced by making these links stronger and not using them as scapegoats.

Similarly the BERA (2001) report says it cannot put improvements into statistics for Ofsted as the educational system changed with the introduction of the national curriculum in 1988 before Ofsted was in operation. Secondly, as Scotland does not use Ofsted as their inspection body and yet they have seen similar signs of improvement. Hood et al (1999) says inspections were justified on a basis of improving school performance with exam results being the main indicator. Ofsted's had questionable influence over teaching practices however Hood et al (1999) has failed to find consistent evidence to prove Ofsted has improved exam results. Rosenthal (2004) takes this research a step further finding that not only is there no evidence to say Ofsted has improved exam results as stated by Hood et al above but that there is a proven negative effect on exam results following an inspection.

Overall, research by Rosenthal (2004) finds a steady improvement in GCSE exam performance since the early 1990's. Ofsted argue that they are the major contributor to this by improving school procedures and management, providing incentives for schools to improve and by eradication of poor teachers and administrators (ibid). Yet with a decrease in results in the year of inspections, and no evidence to prove significant improvement the year after inspection (Shaw et al 2003), Rosenthal (2004) describes Ofsteds effect on exam results as being 'small and perverse' (p.150).

Ironically Chapman (2002) explains how Ofsted have documented the success they brought to under achieving schools by offering support and challenging schools along with more inspections, provision of resources and monitoring visits. If this is to be brought full circle to the comments in section 3.1 by Perryman (2010) about the fear of inspections, would the idea of more inspections be good for the morale of those schools that are under achieving? Further research by Chapman (2002) does in fact state that all teachers found the process of inspection negative due to the increased workload, stress and lack of job satisfaction. This is exacerbated for class teachers as they commented that the inspection had no effect on their teaching whatsoever (Plowright, 2007).

Ouston et al (1997) looks at the revision of the 1992 policy in 1996 which paid greater attention to schools individual development plan and internal evaluation. In Ouston et al (1997) some respondents said the inspection process had prevented planned developments however others said it encouraged developments earlier due to oncoming inspection. Although in a survey in 1995, 55% of schools said the Ofsted action plan coincided with their school development plan, yet just 29% in 1994 (ibid). In '94, 17% of schools had major differences between Ofsted's action plan and their own school development plan yet by '95 this had fallen to 5% indicating the importance the inspection framework was having on school priorities (ibid). McCrone et al (2009) and Cuckle (1998) look at similar areas to Ouston et al but note how staff comment that the inspection did not tell the school anything it did not already know in terms of areas of improvement. Chapman (2002) poses the question that if schools knew about these issues, were they doing anything about them? In contrast to this McCrone et al (2006) commented on schools thinking, that it is a good point to have identified the same troublesome issues as the inspection.

3.3 Leadership

A survey of 1500 senior school leaders by the National Association of Head Teachers (2010) agreed a key purpose of Ofsted should be school improvement. Yet only 16% said that inspections accelerated improvement, 38% said it was a distraction from school improvement and 12% said Ofsted actually hindered school improvement with the rest saying it had little or no impact on school improvement (ibid).

The perceptions of Ofsted appear to change depending on the level of hierarchy in any given school (Chapman, 2002). Head teachers and senior managers were the most positive about Ofsted as they saw it as a way of implementing change (ibid). However Chapman (2002) also commented on how changes were short term, high pressure changes instead of strategic planning. Showing a very different perspective closer to the classroom, one middle manager commented how Ofsted didn't identify important issues deep in the school whether good or bad (ibid).

The leadership styles adopted by different senior leaders during Ofsted vary widely but can often involve a power transition where the head wants all the power to make things right (ibid). This style according to Clarke (2005) was found to de-motivate staff and make them seem worthless. In contrast another head teacher distributed power as she was only in the school short term (5 terms) and so this encouraged staff to take responsibility (ibid).

According to a study of 10 different schools by Chapman (2002), in the face of Ofsted an autocratic leadership style and 'short termist' approach was being used even though this was not the usual style of leadership. The change of leadership style was often justified by the external pressure for immediate change after being given a poor inspection; subsequently these stress levels had a knock on effect and filtered down to the rest of the school (ibid). According to Ouston (1997) there is abundant evidence that inspection causes stress, yet he states that increased levels of stress improve performance until a point when stress deteriorates performance. This is often influenced by senior leaders whether consciously or unconsciously (ibid). Chapman (2002) comments how the little evidence available on school improvement often points to heroic leadership rather than tackling the complex issues of the school and community. The need for heroic leadership becomes more apparent as Richards (2001) indicates that class teachers can receive a 'good' if they tick the boxes set out by government initiatives such as literacy and numeracy or by a good 3 step lesson plan leaving the leadership team to shoulder the rest of the school improvement. However according to research by McCrone et al (2009) the majority of schools believed that there had been no measureable impact on the responsibility of school leaders due to inspection but instead put any changes down to a change in head teacher.

Nicolaidou (2005) shows that all schools are unique and a good leader needs to understand the culture, environment, relationships and interactions of staff instead of trying to use just one method of leadership style for all schools. This raises the point about how often LEA's bring in head teachers to schools in special measures to help turn the school around (Clarke, 2005). This can cause feelings of intimidation and insecurity as staff know the head will leave after the school is brought out of special measures (ibid). These dramatic improvements needed to turn a school around are largely down to the leadership team as inspectors are advised to report to schools about how they could improve, but they cannot say how these improvements should be made as this is the role of the governors and staff (Holmes, 2000, Clarke, 2005, Plowright, 2007).

3.4 Problems

The relationships between teachers and Ofsted inspectors was reported as a major problem as Davis et al (2001) indicates that the idea of a group of inspectors who are superior to those they inspect is fundamentally inappropriate. If inspectors are to be 'superior' to teachers then they should have knowledge and be experts in teaching, leadership, pupil progression and assessment (ibid). Richards (2001) points out that inspector's capabilities to make judgement calls on students learning are severely limited. While Winch (2001) seconds the idea, he goes on to say there is no relationship between teachers and inspectors in its current state and further suggests that teachers themselves should go to other schools to do the inspections. In contrast Heimer (1999) compares the English Ofsted system to that of the Swedish equivalent and explains how the Swedish inspectors are not even from an educational background but are seconded out to inspect schools.

The relationship and trust set out by Ofsted (1999) says inspectors should be impartial, honest and fair, accurate and reliable. This is in stark contrast to the opinions of teachers in the research by Chapman (2002) where concerns were raised regarding the variation the inspection team possess in terms of quality and quantity of formative feedback. Furthermore research by Scanlon (1999) found it was mainly schools that were placed in special measures that had concerns over Ofsteds judgement. Three-quarters of heads and teachers at non special measures schools said the judgement was fair whereas half of heads and nearly two thirds of teachers at special measure schools said it was too negative/ much too negative (ibid). Another concern raised was inconsistency where one particular school was not placed in special measures however the staff thought they should have been (Chapman, 2002).

Richards (2001) says the Ofsted language is full of ambiguities and imprecision which often results in it being re-interpreted in various ways by different parties. Richards (2001) continues to question Ofsted and their perceptions and asks whose perceptions are being judged? Does a lesson need to be inspiring to students or to the inspector? (Richards, 2001).

One head teacher argued how been given a label such as 'serious weakness' was intended as a support method for the school however the head said it lowered public perception of him and the school and therefore made the job of improving the school much harder (Chapman, 2002). These labels given to schools were also a problem for some middle leaders in underachieving schools as they said the label does not always fit across all departments and those in successful departments were branded with the same label (Chapman 2002). Moon (1995) indicates how although a poor Ofsted report leads to a government plan to help a school improve it can also seriously damage a school's reputation. This negative reputation goes further than the pride of the headteacher and can affect consumer interest in the school which in turn leads to erosion of staff morale (ibid). On another scale this label can be attached to students from the school moving into work or university with a stigma they have no control over (Moon, 1995). In contrast to the negative labels and repercussions given to schools, McCrone's (2009) research found that a number of schools who were happy with the grade they received served to motivate staff and raise morale along with making the school more popular and increasing the numbers of applicants to the school.

Section 4.0

Development in policy

Since the initial round of inspections between 1993 and 1997 the system has been reformed to improve the inspection process and relieve some of the burdens that it imposes (Rosenthal, 2004, Shaw et al 2003). In 1997 inspections were moved from one in every four years for to one in every six years (Rosenthal, 2004). After 2000, a two day inspection format began along with a change in the reduction of notice period given to alleviate the preparation time (Rosenthal, 2004, McCrone et al,

2006). This overlapped with research from Ouston et al (1997) who stated that if trends continued from the initial inspection framework his central finding was how the main impact of inspections happened before inspection and not after due to all the changes put in place for Ofsted's arrival. Contrastingly McCrone et al (2006) points out how the shorter time period spent in schools encourages Ofsted to narrow their focus and not get a true feel for a school.

Lloyd and Pratt (2012) say along with the changes to the Ofsted framework, inspectors have changed their practice also. Chapman (2002) reports teachers saying how Ofsted have become more teacher friendly by being affable and also by giving feedback to teachers. Inspectors are now allowed to discuss a lesson afterwards which staff found beneficial as previously they were not allowed (ibid).

Per Mark's (2006) article, David Bell, secretary at the Department for Education and Skills in 2006 said how one in twelve schools are failing and it is a big challenge to turn things around. The new Ofsted inspection was created by Bell while he worked as the chief inspector (Mark, 2006). Bell makes no apology for creating the harder inspection saying people demand continual improvement and that if schools follow the 1992 criteria there would be no expectations for things to improve (ibid). Furthermore Russell (2006) said how the new inspection process was setting schools up to fail and not enough praise was given for the rise in standards in recent years. John Dunford the General Secretary of the Association of School and College Leaders said in response to the new framework that school leaders do not need more pressure and continually moving goalposts (ibid). However with the revised inspection framework in 2012 James et al (2013) says that the governing body are at the focus of accountability in terms of student attainment. If student attainment is poor or shows underperformance an Ofsted inspection is often triggered (ibid). James et al (2013) reckons that with the new framework not only is the pressures of accountability strong but that the stakes are higher and the requirements have stiffened.

The new Common Inspection Framework (CIF) according to Coffield (2012) asks inspectors to make judgements which are far from precise interpretations which can have large impacts on those involved. Due to this Coffield (2012) speculates that the judgement of inspectors is influenced by their prior knowledge of performance data. An assessment of learners form is partially filled in before inspection according to Coffield (2012), and who in his opinion is going to say teaching and learning is inadequate, when their test scores are above the national average?

Coffield (2012) comments how the CIF will no longer allow management to hand pick students to try and promote the school and how inspectors will not just be focusing on grading lessons but will be meeting groups of students to review their learning and assessed work. Baxter et al (2013) says how after only six months of the new 2012 framework, change was implemented once again, this time due to the number of schools found to be coasting along as satisfactory. This move saw the grading change from 'satisfactory' to 'requires improvement' (Baxter et al 2013, Coffield, 2012). Furthermore Coffield (2012) indicates that schools graded as outstanding or good should also be labelled as requires improvement as they too are given areas in their report to improve on.

Moreover Coffield (2012) thanks Ofsted as the new CIF makes teaching and learning the first priority throughout the learning and skills sector. A consequence of this development means in order to be graded outstanding, a school must have outstanding teaching (Lloyd and Pratt, 2012). Conversely the large amounts of data that Ofsted require (even though Ofsted claim documentation is kept to a minimum (Ofsted, 2012)) means large organisations will need to employ staff to have all this data in place in preparation for the Ofsted phone call, resources which according to Coffield (2009) would be better spent on teaching and learning.

Baxter et al (2013) says the number of complaints about inspections has risen mainly from headteachers about the lack of consistency. Research from the National Association Head Teachers published in the House of Commons Education Committee (2011) found the most frequent issue regarding inspection is consistency with 61% of headteachers rating Ofsted as inadequate with regards to the inspection team and said it was luck which team turned up.

Section 5.0

Conclusion

This assignment has critically reviewed the impact that Ofsted has had since its launch in 1992. This has been achieved by gaining an understanding of the history of school inspections leading to why Ofsted was created and put into place in the 1992 Education Act. Furthermore the purpose and function of Ofsted was examined resulting in the impact that this new inspection regime has had upon schools, the stress caused for teachers, the opinions of senior leaders but more importantly on the minute effect on students' results. Within this assignment we have seen how Ofsted has developed over the past 20 years by adapting its policy and showing their intention to keep raising the standards of inspection in England and Wales (Russell, 2006). Though the evidence has appeared bleak in proving inspection has been positive on exam results (Hood et al 1999, Cuckle, 1998), some teachers and senior leaders have been optimistic about the impact Ofsted has had both on the structures and strategies of their schools (Chapman 2002). Feedback and better rapport with inspectors (Chapman 2002) along with a greater focus on teaching and learning have shown to be encouraging factors to teachers through Ofsteds development (Coffield, 2012). However the consistency of inspectors remains a significant issue among the opinions of schools (Baxter et al, 2013). Holmes (2000) states that few teachers welcome an inspection but none would object that Schools do not need to be assessed from an outside agency to help them improve. Although it is hard to see any direct impact from this research further investigation into issues such as the financial implications and cost effectiveness of Ofsted along with statistical measures of schools progressing out of special measures would add valuable interest to this work.

References

Anonymous (2012) Teachers use stress as excuse, says Ofsted chief, The Safety and Health Practitioner, June 2012, 30, (6), pp. 8.

Baxter, J. and Clarke, J. (2013) Farewell to the tick box inspector? Ofsted and the changing regime of school inspection in England, Oxford Review of Education, 39 (5), pp. 702-718.

Bevan, G. and Cornwell, J. (2006) Structure and logic of regulation and governance of quality of health care: was OFSTED a model for the Commission for Health Improvement? Health Economics, Policy and Law, 1, pp. 343-370.

Bolten, E. (1998) HMI – The Thatcher Years, Oxford Review of Education, 24 (1), pp. 45-55.

Brighouse, T. and Moon, B. (1995) School Inspection, London: Pitman.

British Educational Research Association (BERA) (2001) Research Intelligence, 75, April, pp. 12-13.

Chapman, C. (2002) Ofsted and School Improvement: Teachers' perceptions of the inspection process in school facing challenging circumstances, School Leadership & Management, 22 (3), pp. 257-272.

Coffield, F. (2009) Ofsted inspected, Adults Learning, December 2009, pp. 26-27.

Coffield, F. (2012) Ofsted re-inspected, Adults Learning, Winter 2012, pp. 20-22.

Clarke, P. (2005) Improving Schools in Difficulty, London, Continuum.

Cuckle, P., Hodgson, J. and Broadhead, P. (1998) Investigating the Relationship between Ofsted Inspections and School Development Planning, School Leadership & Management, 18 (2), pp. 271-283.

Davis, A. and White, J. (2001) Accountability and School Inspection: In Defence of Audited Self-Review, Journal of Philosophy of Education, 35 (4), pp. 667-681.

Education (Schools) Act 1992.

Fielding, M. (2001) OFSTED, Inspection and the Betrayal of Democracy, Journal of Philosophy of Education, 35 (4), pp. 695-709.

Harris, S. (2007) The Governance of Education, How neo-liberalism is transforming policy and practice, London: Continuum.

Heimer, J. (1999) Ofsted: The Swedish Version, Management in Education, 13 (4), pp. 20-21.

House of Commons Education Committee (2011) The role and performance of Ofsted, Second Report, Volume III, London: The Stationary Office.

Holmes, E. (2000) School Inspection, A teachers guide to preparing, surviving & evaluating Ofsted Inspection, London, The Stationary Office.

Fullan, M. (2001) Leading in a culture of change, San Francisco: Jossey Bass.

Hood, C., James, O., Scott, C., Jones, G. and Travers, T. (1999) Regulation Inside Government, Oxford: Oxford University Press.

James, C., Brammer, S., Connolly, M., Spicer, D.E., James, J. and Jones, J. (2013) The challenges facing school governing bodies in England: A 'perfect storm'? Management in Education, 27 (3), pp. 84-90.

Kennedy, J. (1995) The evolution of inspection and other tools for education accountability, School Inspection, London: Pitman.

Kerr, J. (1891) Inspection of Schools, Chamber's journal of popular literature, science and arts, Jan 1854 – Nov 1897, Jan 31, 1891; (8), 370; British Periodicals.

Lefstein, A. (2013) The regulation of teaching as symbolic politics: rituals of order, blame and redemption, Discourse: Studies in the Cultural Politics of Education, 34 (5), pp. 643-659.

Lloyd, D. and Pratt, A. (2012) The new Ofsted framework – implications for teaching and learning, Teaching Business and Economics.

Mark, C. (2006) Bell defends Ofsted regime as one in 12 schools 'fail', Public Finance, Nov 24, pp. 6-7.

Matthews, P. and Sammons, P. (2004) Improvement through inspection, An evaluation of the impact of Ofsted's work, HMI 2244.

McCrone, T., Coghlan, M., Wade, P. and Rudd, P. (2009) Evaluation of the Impact of Section 5 Inspection – Strand 3: Final Report for Ofsted, Slough, National Foundation for Educational Research.

McCrone, T., Rudd, P., Blenkinsop, S. And Wade, P. (2006) Impact of Section 5 inspections: maintained schools in England, Slough, National Foundation for Educational Research.

McLaughlin, T. (2001) Four Philosophical Perspectives on School Inspection: An Introduction, Journal of Philosophy of Education, 35 (4), pp. 647-654.

Nicolaidou, M. (2005) What is Special about Special Measures? Improving Schools in Difficulty, London: Continuum.

Office for Standards in Education (Ofsted) (1999) Lessons Learned from Special Measures, London:HMSO.

Ofsted (2005) School Inspection Handbook, London: Ofsted.

Ofsted (2012) School Inspection Handbook, London: Ofsted.

Ofsted (2013) School Inspection Handbook, London: Ofsted.

Ouston, J., Fidler, B. and Earley, P. (1997) What Do Schools Do after OFSTED School Inspections – or before? School Leadership & Management, 17 (1), pp. 95-104.

Perry, P. (1995) The formation of Ofsted, School Inspection, London: Pitman Publishing.

Perryman, J. (2010) Improvement after Inspection, Improving Schools, 13 (2), pp. 182-196.

Pike, C. (1999) Using Inspection for School Development, Oxford, Heinemann Educational Publishers.

Plowright, D. (2007) Self-evaluation and Ofsted Inspection: Developing an Integrative Model of School Improvement, Educational Management Administration and Leadership, 35 (3), pp. 373-394.

Richards, C. (2001) School Inspection: A Re-appraisal, Journal of Philosophy of Education, 35 (4), pp. 654-665.

Rosenthal, L. (2004) Do school inspections improve school quality? Ofsted inspections and school examination results in the UK, Economic of Education Review, 23, pp. 143-151.

Russell, V. (2006) Gap between best and worst must close, says chief inspector, Public Finance, Nov 24, pp. 6.

Schagen, I. and Weston, P. (1998) Insights into School Effectiveness from Analysis of OFSTED's School Inspection Database, 24 (3), pp. 337-344.

Shaw, I., Newton, D. P., Aitkin, M. and Darnell, R. (2003) Do Ofsted Inspections of Secondary Schools Make a Difference to GCSE Results? British Educational Research Journal, 29 (1), pp. 63-75.

Smith, G. (2000) Research and Inspection: HMI and OFSTED, 1981-1996-a commentary, Oxford Review of Education, 26 (3&4), pp. 333-352.

Scanlon, M. (1999) The Impact of OFSTED Inspections, National Foundation for Educational Research.

Winch, C. (2001) Towards a Non-Punitive School Inspection Regime, Journal of Philosophy of Education, 35 (4), pp. 683-694.

Wilcox, B. and Gray, J. (1996) Inspecting Schools, Buckingham: Open University Press.

7 SUH-LYN PARK

I am a Korean student of education at Brunel University. I came to the UK interested in developing a general understanding of education, as well as write about Gifted education, pupil voice, and person-centred teaching and learning. After my MA, I am considering a PhD program, and will one day return to Korea to work in education.

Literature Review

Evaluating the implementation of Section 176 of the 2002 Education Act

ABSTRACT

This literature review focuses on the 2002 Education Act (Section 176), which stated that schools must "listen to and involve young people" (Appendix A). This formalisation of students' as stakeholders in schools came within a series of policies encouraging young people's wider involvement in schools. Consulting students was a new direction for UK schools in the early 2000s, forming part of a drive for higher standards. The research emerging in the years following this policy explored policy documents and subsequent government guidance, and found that the policy rested on positive ideals. For example, it described the transformative potential of this simple, straightforward change it had prescribed for schools. However, its practice in schools was frequently disappointing, modest or tokenistic. This assignment discusses how this policy has been practiced, juxtaposing it alongside the positive ideals it appears to rest on. It appeared that schools have practiced this policy with limited results, and its promised transformations of schools have not materialised. The assignment goes on to illuminate a range of issues preventing its effective implementation. These include its limited impact in schools, and the lack of government guidance for its practice. It goes onto suggesting some research directions which might identify approaches for a more satisfying use of student voice.

INTRODUCTION

Policy in context

Section 176 of the 2002 Education Act (Appendix A) required schools to consult young people on decisions affecting them, providing a legal formality to a notion gathering momentum for over a decade. According to Flutter, the 1989 UN Convention on the Rights of the Child, referenced in the policy, was the "catalyst" (2007, p.345). It outlined young people's right to express themselves on matters concerning them, although it took two years for the UK to ratify. It took another ten to provide for young people's systematic contribution, firstly through creation of the Children and Young People's Unit in 2001, then through the new Citizenship curriculum in 2002 (Flutter, 2007, p.345). The 2002 Education Act, however, and its later documentation supporting implementation in schools, "Working Together, Giving Children and Young People a Say" (DfES, 2004), presented student voice as a vehicle for improving schools. For example, it depicted students at the heart of the community, working together with adults, thinking through ways to shape the school experience and contribute to a more cohesive community (*ibid*).

According to Whitty and Wisby, the next few years saw elements of student voice ever more deeply engrained into UK policy (2007, p.304). The 2004 Children Act legislated that local authorities should provide for young people's participation. This was reinforced further in Green Papers (Youth Matters, 2005; Care Matters, 2006); in the National Healthy Schools Status, an award depending on student involvement in school policy development; and in OfSTED's emphasis after 2005 on student voice in relation to teaching and learning.

Patchwork of influences

This policy, or trail of policies, was driven by several influences. One was from the EU, many of whose nations had long implemented 'voice'-led initiatives in their schools, and frequently criticized the UK for its lethargic adoption of the UN

Convention's principles (Flutter, 2007, p.345). Another was the broader knowledge-economy discourse (Ball, 2013, p.25), frequently cited in global and UK politics, which underlines the role of education as providing young people with skills, so they might contribute more usefully to the economy. This critical function of schools was further stressed in public discourse in the face of intense competition from the global economy, where imperatives for schools were frequently voiced (Ball, 2013, p.29). For example, the Prime Minister, Blair, pointed to the correlation between fast-growing cities and knowledge workers, and underlined the contribution of schools for future prosperity (2000). As suggested by Arnot and Reay, the student voice movement hid a "diverse and complex alliance of reform agendas" (2007, p.311).

Consulting students was a new direction for school improvement, although as Flutter and Rudduck point out, the state "has not necessarily supplied schools effectively in meeting the challenges" (2004, p.1). Arnot and Reay concur, suggesting a lack of guidance leads to unsatisfying practice of student voice, without focus on learning or improving the classroom experience. Accordingly, young people might "therefore become incorporated into the project of social control" (2007, p.321), adding that such voice-led initiatives only "imply social transformation when none is delivered" (2007, p.323).

This assignment evaluates this policy's practice against the positive ideals it was presented alongside, and highlights issues preventing its more fruitful implementation.

POSITIVE IDEALS

The 2008 DCSF document, "Working together: listening to the voices of children and young people" was part of the government's guidance for schools implementing student voice. This excerpt from its foreword lists several beneficial outcomes for schools practicing student voice:

Giving children and young people a say in decisions can improve engagement in learning, help develop a more inclusive school environment, and improve behaviour and attendance. Through effective pupil participation, schools give young people the opportunity to develop critical thinking, advocacy and influencing skills, helping every child to fulfil their potential

(DCSF, 2008, p.2).

These are described as "lofty ideals" (den Besten *et al*, 2008, p.207), against which this policy should be evaluated. Flutter also notes these positive ideals, suggesting the bold, prescriptive tone in official policy documents leads teachers to believe that "introducing these approaches is easy and straightforward" (2007, p.350).

The idealistic assumptions this policy rests on might be mapped out before exploring how schools have practiced it. Den Besten *et al* neatly map out this terrain, picking out how consulting students is presented as something that is possible, straightforward, a good thing, that has transformative potential, and is prescribable (2008, p.200). Flutter lists how practicing student voice might benefit students, for example, activating their metacognitive skills and improving their motivation through discussing learning and participating in school improvement (2007, p.349). Urquhart added that student voice was an opportunity for schools to move towards practicing a student-centred philosophy, suggesting it offered an "alternative to the adult-centred bureaucracy that 'cramps' much of modern schooling" (2001, p.86). The policy's benefits for teachers were similarly described as an investigative opportunity for better understanding classrooms and improving teaching and relationships (Flutter, 2007, p.344). Finally, its potential for school-wide transformation and an improved, closer teacher-student culture was described as deriving from 'voice'-led tasks (Flutter, 2007, p.345).

According to Whitty and Wisby (2007), schools that have enthusiastically adopted 'voice'-led initiatives have found a strong rationale in their potential for school improvement. Their explorative study on implementations of student voice found that schools generally expected it would contribute to school improvement gains, such as improved behaviour, trusting relationships, and raised awareness of learning. Conversely, notions of fostering citizenship or children's rights were less cited (2007, p.308), in official school discourse loosely mirroring the policy guidance literature. However, while schools described how consulting students informed and improved practice, Cremin *et al's* research into student voice participants found that schools had "neither the time nor the capacity to engage meaningfully with what young people have to say" (2010, p.598).

The next section juxtaposes these positive ideals against research findings of how this policy has been practiced in schools. Although policy guidance has idealised student voice, much research has found its practice disappointing.

POLICY IN PRACTICE

According to den Besten *et al* (2008:201), this policy's practice has not measured up to the ideals and exemplars put forward in policy documents. There is a "ladder of pupil participation" (Hart, 1997), where most schools' practice of student voice sits on the lower rungs (Flutter and Rudduck, 2004, p.16). Whitty and Wisby also cited this ladder, describing how most practice was at the "tokenistic" (2007, p.306) end of the continuum, falling considerably short of consultation. They added that less than one fifth of researched schools felt they had an effective school council (2007, p.311).

Den Besten *et al* described the policy's practice as patchy, disappointing, foreclosed, modest, and contingent (2008, p.201).

> 4. Students as full active participants and co-researchers
>
> 3. Pupils as researchers
>
> 2. Pupils as active participants
>
> 1. Listening to pupils
>
> 0. Pupils not consulted

Figure 1. Ladder of pupil participation.

Foreclosed

Given the limited time in which consultation can take place, and the sheer numbers of students in schools (den Besten *et al*, 2008, p.202), it is perhaps unsurprising that 'voice'-led initiatives only capture a limited account. Whitty and Wisby view consultation pragmatically, describing it as "unfeasible", adding that "tokenism is the only possible outcome" (2007, p.312), as the majority of students are not included. Commonly, "high-achieving" (Whitty and Wisby, 2007, p.313), "articulate" (McIntyre *et al*, 2005, p.167) and "confident" (Flutter, 2007, p.349) students populate school councils, with the remainder omitted. In addition, schools find the tokenistic consultation emerging from such heterogeneous councils quite acceptable (Arnot and Reay, 2007; Weller, 2007; Mannion, 2007), so do not seek to elicit a wider range of voices.

That investigations generally capture the perspectives of these confident students might represent a flaw in common practice of this policy. MacBeath *et al* (2003, p.42) explained this process, along with its impact, in that students more versed in the language of the school are likelier to be noticed by teachers, exacerbating feelings of disenfranchisement among those not consulted. This is ironic, given that the policy was presented as an empowerment initiative, yet in practice, it merely reflected divisions in schools rather than challenged them (*ibid*, p.42). Cremin *et al* further describe the marginalised voices in schools, suggesting the school council is just as alien to them as the head-teacher (2010, p.599). Arnot and Reay claim this effectively silences students who feel unable to legitimately contribute in such forums (2007, p.311). Other studies have similarly reached the conclusion that heterogeneous school councils serve to marginalise the majority of student perspectives (Fielding, 2007; Weller, 2007).

This research described how this partial insight into student perspectives falls short of providing meaningful feedback into what might transform the classroom experience. Cremin *et al* more directly summarise the process, claiming it is merely "putting words into young people's mouths (2010, p.601). Flutter suggests schools must begin listening to "lower-achieving, less articulate" students, as well as eliciting "the widest possible range of voices" (2007, p.350), so that the process might become suitably insightful.

Modest

The following research into 'voice'-led tasks describes their limited impact. Den Besten *et al* describe this practice as banal, modest, predictable and superficial (2008, p.203), while Whitty and Wisby's (2007) analysis of student council practice found a similar dearth of creativity, where students called for quite limited improvements, and "were almost universally concerned with 'toilets and chips' issues" (*ibid*, p.312). This falls short of the transformative vision put forward as part of this policy, although it might be only natural for young people to be comfortable with this level of consultation. In fact, these findings echo Bragg's (2007), who found her students gave superficial, unconstructive, unsatisfactory responses during consultation (*ibid*, p.510). This level of student contribution is considered disappointing (den Besten *et al*, 2008, p.201), and furthermore, its modest impact may reduce the credibility of further 'voice'-led initiatives. As Bragg

(2007, p.510) suggests, perhaps participants on both sides, teacher and student, lack the consultation skills to create the desired, transformative impact? A plausible barrier to effective practice might be the abilities of its participants. While den Besten *et al* point out that 'voice'-led initiatives are "limited by lack of understanding" (2008, p.202), McIntyre *et al* suggest that these will always be prioritized down, as "teachers are under pressure" (2005, p.167) to produce academic results first. Bragg points to the critical role of guidance for teachers implementing student voice, stating her belief that obtaining meaningful contributions from children "depends on structuring the processes" (2007, p.512). She suggests scaffolded examples, containing questions for discussion (2007, p.516), but notes how these derive from teacher creativity, and were missing from the government guidance for implementation.

Contingent

The policy's practice appears to differ depending on conditions within each school. Den Besten found that schools vary in their appetite for 'voice'-led initiatives, even finding "apathy and antipathy" (2008, p.205) towards students practicing them. Bragg pointed to the influence of critical variables, such as which students speak and which teachers listen (2007, p.509), which would produce significant variance in school council data. Meanwhile, Flutter and Rudduck conceded that schools introducing 'voice'-led initiatives often did so on "unprepared ground" (2004, p.76), lacking routines, processes, tasks or guidance for practice. This, in turn, led to "culture shock" (Flutter and Rudduck, 2004, p.77), a counter-productive outcome given that policy guidance described how adults and young people should work together to transform the school environment. Therefore, the experience of participating in consultation that did not measure up would often prove disappointing (den Besten *et al*, 2008, p.201). As Bragg (2007, p.505) suggests, perhaps teachers found that empowering students undermined their own authority? Rudduck and Flutter found teachers were anxious of "unlocking a barrage of criticism of them and their teaching" (2003, p.75). These early experiences practising this policy raised such issues, not least, how to best handle "the voices of those who might have doubts" (Bragg, 2007, p.510). In fact, a range of issues emerged during the initial years of implementing this policy.

ISSUES

Participation and consultation

The phenomena discussed above illustrate how schools practice tokenistic participation, rather than the more complicated (but potentially more transformative) consultation (see Figure 1) (Whitty and Wisby, 2007, p.306). In fact, there is evidence of fruitful consultation with students, who provided insightful input on improving classroom activities (Cooper and McIntyre, 1996; Rudduck *et al*, 1996). Similarly, McIntyre *et al* noted the constructive and consensual nature of student input during consultation, as well as a positive team spirit between teachers and students (2005, p.149). Nevertheless, as Whitty and Wisby suggest (2007), participants held back from the more risky, potentially destabilizing practice of consultation. This widespread tokenistic practice is described as potentially alienating the young people who participate, who might naturally conclude that the process is a sham (Whitty and Wisby, 2007, p.304).

The movement towards participation (and occasionally consultation) is also described as serving the neo-liberal agenda for education, which positions students as consumers, responsible for their own choices (Whitty and Wisby, 2007, p.304). More specifically, school issues, hitherto the responsibility of the state, might one day be considered as falling within the domain of the individual if schools would further this responsibilization agenda (Whitty and Wisby, 2007, p.314). As such, student voice initiatives might be seen as an exercise in young subjects exercising power over themselves. This fits into a national context in which parents are increasingly positioned as consumers, choosing schools to send their children to, which in turn flourish or struggle depending on these choices (*ibid,* p315). Accordingly, by increasing the perceived choices of families, citizens might come to be defined as consumers, with the state's role becoming narrower over time (Whitty and Powers, 1997, p.220).

Minimal encouragement from government

According to Rudduck and McIntyre (2007), the government documentation supporting schools implementing this policy served more as cheerleading than as guidance, although the lower status of student voice is unsurprising given the national performance agenda. This is somewhat ironic, given that the policy documentation claims that consultation helps achievement. Nonetheless, the minimal support from policy-makers was echoed in schools, content to practice a minimal form of student voice. This is described as allowing important questions about the purpose of 'voice'-led activities to be avoided (Whitty and Wisby, 2007, p.303).

This is also described as withholding a critical factor for successful practice. Promoting participation and engagement among young people requires "top-down leadership" (Bragg, 2007, p.511). Den Besten *et al* suggested a range of guidance, conspicuous by its absence, such as having qualified staff to facilitate the process, publishing explicit, step-by-step guidance on involving students, and leading a research agenda into its practice (2008, p.208).

This top-down ambiguity surrounding this official endorsement trickled down into schools, who remained unclear on how to implement the day-to-day practice of student voice (Flutter, 2007, p.343). This proved contentious, because as Whitty and Wisby note, schools rarely considered student voice as an opportunity to empower students, or acclimatized their participants to the role of consulting over teaching and learning (2007, p.311). For example, schools did not evaluate the output of school councils, or provide success criteria for their practice; neither did they tend to provide status for them in the form of meetings with the head, or time out of lessons to attend (*ibid*, 2007, p.312). Accordingly, this lack of clarity ran throughout practice of student voice (Rudduck and McIntyre, 2007), from the policy-makers, through to school leaders, and ultimately to the young people attempting to have a say in the decision-making affecting their lives.

Consultation and citizenship

Some literature paired the twin announcement of this policy with the Citizenship curriculum, suggesting both merely engaged young people with politics without offering opportunity to practice it (Rudduck and McIntyre, 2007, p.1). Arnot and Reay claim this is social control by design (2007, p.230), while Whitty and Wisby claim it is a means of incorporation, where student voice is merely appropriated to legitimize the policies of school leaders (2007, p.314).

Social control through bounded pedagogic events

Arnot and Reay's examination of student voice illuminated the machinations of this social control (2007, p.321). They claim schools are environments which confirm the place of marginalized children, who come to learn their place through interactions in adult-led processes. This derives from these students not processing sufficient communication skills to operate successfully in a school context that requires verbal negotiation with adults (*ibid*, 2007, p.316). They suggest that students generally succeed due to their linguistic competency, which enables them to communicate their perspectives and needs to teachers, and therefore acquire the support which brings about their success (*ibid*, 2007, p.321). They argue that the school council context resembles any other within a school, where the needs most clearly expressed are likeliest to elicit responses from teachers. These needs, in councils comprised of high-achieving students using appropriate language forms, might not align with those of marginalised students (*ibid*, 2007, p.322). Therefore, if pedagogical practices are reshaped, they are likelier to derive from motions put forward by the above-mentioned articulate speakers. Such confident, focused voices come across as independently constructed, and indeed echo those of the ideal student in government literature, although as Arnot and Reay (2007, p.321) point out, they represent a smoothly-run, manageable type of participation that continues to marginalise the majority.

The implications of Arnot and Reay's argument are that social control can be exerted over 'voice'-led initiatives, the opportunities for higher-level thinking and self-direction notwithstanding. Arnot and Reay state how consulting young people in a democratic effort is, in fact, "a bounded pedagogic event" (2007, p.322) that merely appears democratic, and which hides the social hierarchy within the school. They take issue with how school leaders and policy-makers might readily use 'voice'-led initiatives "to imply social transformation when none is delivered" (2007, p.323). Cremin *et al* (2010) dig deeper, questioning the will of politicians and education professionals to listen to young people. They also question the means to act on any input emerging from school councils, and ultimately, they question the ethics of claiming to involve young people in the design, delivery and evolution of educational practice (2010, p.586).

Some teacher resistance

There is ample research evidence of teacher resistance to 'voice'-led initiatives (Cremin *et al*, 2010; Bragg, 2010). Cremin *et al* believe that teachers see through the formalised rhetoric about consulting young people, and merely disregard their students' perspectives on their day-to-day practice (2010, p.587). Bragg, meanwhile, sees teachers as critical enablers of student voice's short-term success and its longer-term sustainability, although she notes (and empathises with) their minimal input (*ibid*, 2007, p.505). She explains how enabling student voice alters the professional relationship between the expert adult and the young learner, and finds in their lukewarm reactions to this policy a telling account of the complexities of implementing it.

Legitimate concerns leading to limited practice

Bragg's (2007) research was a formal attempt to understand the legitimate concerns of teachers, who she considered critical drivers of student voice in schools. She highlighted a range of issues voiced by teachers, for example, that it takes too long to successfully implement – one school council alone would need to follow extensive consultation of students in all year groups beforehand to identify issues, then feature a meeting with senior leaders to report and negotiate on these issues, followed up by a range of assembly visits to present the outcomes to the school. Furthermore, she highlighted how teachers felt that the policy merely presented existing good practice as a formal directive – teachers claimed that they already consulted their students, listened to and were in tune with their needs, and therefore the policy was not a departure. In addition, she highlighted how teachers felt the policy's unsophisticated, whole-school practice only blurred issues, as inexperienced participants worked with overgeneralized, coarse data on their peers' perspectives (*ibid*, 2007, p.516). These concerns contained the sceptical position that mis-managed consultation risks exacerbating the existing tensions and divisions in schools (2007, p.516). The concerns also covered the imbalance caused by prioritizing student perspectives, while ignoring those of teachers, whose voices were not "respected or considered" (2007, p.508).

According to Bragg (2007), these concerns about the questionable input of young people influenced teachers' management of student voice, and ultimately limited its effectiveness. Teachers were, in some cases, wary of students making unrealistic, ill thought-through requests, such as the teacher Bragg interviewed who "was upset because she received a report card on her performance as a teacher from one of her pupils – complete with targets" (*ibid*, 2007, p.512). Bragg suggested a range of teacher doubts (*ibid*, 2007, p.512): whether young people were competent enough to make valid judgements about their work; whether students possessed the maturity to keep the content of their consultation confidential; and whether their reductionist perspectives on school would boil complex situations down to lowest common denominator 'voice'. These concerns would be exacerbated during consultation with students who did not have positive relationships with teachers (*ibid*, 2007, p.513). These concerns explain the resistance of many teachers to 'voice'-led activities, and just as tellingly, why so many schools "take the easier option of training up outstanding but acquiescent pupils" (Bragg, 2007, p.512) whose sensible, smooth, trustworthy participation in student voice would prove less traumatic all round.

Bragg's (2007) discussion of teacher resistance illuminates a central argument on which practice of this policy rests. On one hand, practicing student voice disrupts the balance between teacher and student, yet it also promises an improved, mutually supportive teacher-student relationship. Whitty and Wisby underline this tension, describing student voice as, at best, "an element in establishing a collaborative professionalism", while expressing concerns that it is "part of a neo-liberal concern to challenge teachers' authority and cement a managerial model of professionalism" (*ibid*, 2007, p.304). In fact, working closer with young people to co-create an improved learning environment holds much in store for those teachers who manage it. The following section suggests that teachers might come to see collaborating with students as contributing to a more progressive professionalism (Whitty and Wisby, 2007, p.314).

Some insights for development

Student voice remains an initiative that may hold positive transformation for the students, teachers and schools practicing it. McIntyre *et al* underline the issue emerging from the wider research when they note that it is not so much students' 'voice'-led ideas, but rather "teachers' responsiveness to them that is important" (2005, p.151). Accordingly, the realisation of students' 'voice'-derived contributions to improving their learning environments depends on teachers' "wholehearted support for and belief in the potential for student voice" (Martin *et al*, 2005, p.7). This chimes with Bragg's (2007, p.506) position that student voice rests on teachers' and school leaders' belief in it (along with finding a way to alleviate their legitimate reservations). For more teachers to begin to champion student voice, they would need to perceive it as a means to "serve collaborative rather than managerial practice" (Whitty and Wisby, 2007, p.303), and indeed, seize the opportunity to ensure that it does so. McIntyre *et al*'s (2005) interviews with student voice co-ordinators contain sufficient findings that record mature practice of consulting students to improve teaching and learning, which may light the way forward. Although expressed as student (i.e. teenage or younger) voice, once paraphrased, these, echo some well-known pedagogical best practices. Namely, students requested more interactive lessons, so that they might come to a group understanding through shared dialogue (*ibid,* p.153). They also requested learning to be placed within real world contexts, so they might understand how classroom tasks fit into their own experiences (*ibid,* p.153). They also requested that teachers would arrange learners into groups, so they might approach difficult tasks collaboratively and think them through together (2005, p.153). One teacher interviewed expressed their surprise that students "were generally, in a polite, nice way, good at criticizing the lessons" (2005, p.156). McIntyre *et al* (2005) suggest teachers should come to view this process as an opportunity rather than a threat. They maintain that the positives, now that listening to young people has become policy, outweigh the drawbacks (*ibid*, 2005, p156). One is that, once collaboration is initiated, and co-ordinated to provide useful perspectives on the classroom, it is a constructive, consensual experience (*ibid*, 2005, p166). Another is that the classroom is a shared experience, therefore students' and teachers' perspectives will commonly overlap (*ibid*, 2005, p166). Another still is that students tend to describe what they like about school, and often see consultation as an opportunity to build on it (*ibid*, 2005, p166). However, the majority of teachers engage with student voice on a minimal level, and must see past their concerns in order to focus on bringing about its rewards (*ibid*, 2005, p167).

CONCLUSIONS & SUGGESTIONS

Several recommendations for more effective practice of this policy emerge from the research literature. These begin with seemingly trivial, localised instances of good practice, for example, Bragg's suggestion of having students investigate the make-up of a good teacher (2007, p.514). Although this one 'voice'-led initiative has a narrow application, it might prompt shared reflections on the human qualities and categories of pedagogical practice which enable learning, as well as create an opportunity for teachers to listen to young people when they present their findings. In fact, recommendations for instances of practice might serve as a useful focus for future research on this policy. Teaching is, after all, a significant commitment, and 'voice'-led initiatives which improve teaching and learning have much to contribute; a worthy aim of future research might be to facilitate this.Such educational applications, rather than addressing canteen and facilities issues, might be a fruitful direction for student voice. Flutter and Rudduck (2004) argue this point, that student voice needs to be grounded in educational principles throughout their book on consulting students. This policy has made this practice compulsory in schools, although to address the disappointing drift towards tokenistic participation, future research should aim to facilitate its application to genuinely improving what happens in classrooms. These research aims are articulated by Bragg, who believes the place of research should be to identify strategies to support consultation about teaching and learning, and to gather evidence of the positive impact of this consultation (2007, p.506). Teachers have emerged from this review of literature as key drivers of this policy (Bragg, 2007), yet also requiring practical support for how to practice it. Flutter (2007) takes this position, describing teachers as shackled by habit and needing insight into the factors that make a difference to their students. Accordingly, she articulates the role of research as identifying consultation which has improved practice such as assessment, use of success criteria, creation of classroom groups, sustaining of engagement, and interactions which build motivation (*ibid*, 2007, p.352). Research into such narrow applications might take the form of teacher-led action research, as this would potentially profit from its closeness to the participants, who might illuminate how its practice played out in their classrooms. Flutter and Rudduck suggest some useful approaches, such as using student voice to spotlight issues, monitor new strategies, support individuals, and so on (2004, p.25). If teacher-led projects entered into the wider research on student voice, they might come together as part of an emerging toolkit for its practice. According to Bragg (2007), research will enhance practice of this policy if it explores effective processes to embed within schools. She articulates this need, calling for "ways of building consultation into the organisational structure of schools" (*ibid*, 2007, p.506). This would inform co-ordination of student voice so that it does not exclude some voices while privileging others. A process for consulting every student in a school needs developing, one in which every student's perspective is elicited, collected, processed, prioritized, and presented to senior leaders, whose considered response is presented to all students. Flutter and Rudduck (2004) reduce this process into steps, where schools consider their students' readiness for consultation, the issues to spotlight before initiating consultation, practical issues such as the number of participants and the timescale for consultation, how to gather and analyse its data, how to use and communicate its findings, and how to monitor any resulting actions (*ibid*, 2004, p.24). This review has highlighted how such pervasive consultation is not common practice. However, if research developed effective working processes, it might automate teachers' and schools' implementations of this policy, thus helping establish more democratic school systems.

REFERENCES

Arnot, M. and Reay, D., 2007. 'A sociology of pedagogic voice: power, inequality and pupil consultation', *Discourse: studies in the cultural politics of education*, vol. 28, no. 3, pp. 311-325.

Ball, S.J., 2013. *The Education Debate (Policy and Politics in the Twenty-first Century)*, Bristol: The Policy Press.

Blair, T., 2000. 'Knowledge 2000', *Conference on the knowledge-driven economy*, 7 March. Available: www.number-10.gov.uk.

Bragg, S., 2007. "But I listen to children anyway!' – teacher perspectives on pupil voice', *Educational Action Research*, vol. 15, no. 4, pp. 505-518.

Cooper, P. and McIntyre, D., 1996. *Effective Teaching and Learning: Teachers' and Pupils' Perspectives*, Buckingham: Open University Press.

Cremin, H., Mason, C. and Busher, H., 2010. 'Problematising pupil voice using visual methods: findings from a study of engaged and disaffected pupils in an urban secondary school', *British Educational Research Journal*, vol. 37, no. 4, pp. 585-603.

Den Besten, O., Horton, J. and Kraftl, P., 2008. 'Pupil involvement in school (re)design: participation in policy and practice', *CoDesign*, vol. 4, no. 4, pp. 197-210.

DfES., 2004. *Working together: giving children and young people a say*, London, DfES.

DfES., 2005. *Youth matters*, Green Paper, Norwich: HMSO.

DfES., 2006. *Care matters*, Green Paper, Norwich: HMSO.

DfES., 2008. *Working together: listening to the voices of children and young people*, London: DfES.

DfE., 2012. *Listening to and involving children and young people*, London: DfE. Available: http://www.education.gov.uk/aboutdfe/statutory/g00206160/listening-to-and-involving-children-and-young-people [27th December, 2013.]

Fielding, M., 2007. 'Beyond 'voice': new roles, relations and contexts in researching with young people', *Discourse: Studies in the Cultural Politics of Education*, vol. 28, no. 3, pp. 301-310.

Flutter, J. and Rudduck, J., 2004. *Consulting Pupils: What's in it for Schools?* Abingdon: Routledge.

Flutter, J., 2007. 'Teacher development and pupil voice', *The Curriculum Journal*, vol. 18, no. 3, pp. 343-354.

Hart, R.A., 1997. *Children's Participation. The Theory and Practice of Involving Young Citizens in Community Development and Environmental Care,* London: Earthscan Publications.

MacBeath, J., Demetriou, H., Rudduck, J. and Myers, K., 2003. *Consulting Pupils: a Toolkit for Teachers,* Cambridge: Pearson Publishing.

Mannion, G., 2007. 'Going spatial, going relational: why 'listening' to children and children's participation needs reframing', *Discourse: Studies in the Cultural Politics of Education*, vol. 28, no. 3, pp. 405-420.

Martin, N., Worrall, N. and Dutson-Steinfeld, A., 2005. 'Student voice: Pandora's box or philosopher's stone?' Paper presented at the *International Congress for School Effectiveness and Improvement (ICSEI)*, Barcelona, Spain, 2-5 January. Available: http://networkedlearning.ncsl.org.uk/knowledge-base/conference-papers/icsei-05-student-voice-v2.doc [2nd January, 2014].

McIntyre, D., Pedder, D. and Rudduck, J., 2005. 'Pupil voice: comfortable and uncomfortable learnings for teachers', *Research Papers in Education*, vol. 20, no. 2, pp. 149-168.

Rudduck, J., Chaplain, R. and Wallace, G., 1996. *School Improvement: What can Pupils Tell us?* London: David Fulton.

Rudduck, J. and Flutter, J., 2003. *How to Improve your School: Giving Pupils a Voice*, London: Continuum Press.

Rudduck, J. and McIntyre, D., 2007. *Improving Learning through Consulting Pupils*, Abingdon: Routledge.

Urquhart, I., 2001. ''Walking on air'?: pupil voice and school choice', *Forum*, vol. 43, no. 2, pp. 83-86.

Weller, S., 2007. *Teenage Citizenship: experiences and education,* London: Routledge.

Whitty, G. and Powers, S., 1997. 'Quasi-markets and curriculum control: making sense of recent education reform in England and Wales', *Educational Administration Quarterly*, vol. 33, no. 2, pp. 219-240.

Whitty, G. and Wisby, E., 2007. 'Whose voice? An exploration of the current policy interest in pupil involvement in school decision-making', *International Studies in Sociology of Education,* vol. 17, no. 3, pp. 303-319.

8 USMAN AHMED CHOUDHURY

Are we educating for the knowledge-driven economy?

A review of policy and literature

Abstract

This assignment focuses on a critical review of significant matters arising in the knowledge-driven economy through policy and literature. It begins with a definition of the knowledge economy and an outline of the policy topic. It examines the meaning and significance of the knowledge economy and describes how the nature of work has been transformed in many different ways. This paper describes how knowledge and innovation are hallmarks of a global skills race. This asserts that the most developed economies can counter issues regarding economic efficiency through a high-skilled, high-wage workforce. This paper intends to illustrate how the competitive advantage of developed countries relies upon the knowledge, skills and experience of individuals.

Introduction

A recurring theme in recent governments is the correlation between education policy to the wishes of the state and the economy. Policy is a notion that advocates progress. It concerns imperfections of the past and present to a future ideal. The education sector plays a fundamental role as a producer of knowledge and skills in response to global competition to achieve economic growth.

This paper will highlight the role of the UK government in the global skills race of the future. The key challenge is to outsmart other national economies by unlocking all of the talents of all the people in the 'knowledge wars' of the future. This will lead to personal and national benefits. Individuals will benefit as they seek to gain knowledge in order to gain better jobs. The more qualified an individual becomes, the greater the chance of career progression. This, in turn, will lead to a higher net income and more likely a higher standard of living. The end goal from an individual perspective is to lead a better quality of life. There are many benefits for employers such as an increased productivity of the workforce which should keep costs down. The wider community will also benefit as the nation becomes a 'magnet' economy; will attract highly skilled individuals to the country (Brown, 2008).

This assignment will examine the rise of the knowledge economy, explaining that transnational companies have much more scope to compete on a global scale, as they have greater access to global markets (Department for Trade and Industry, 1998). Employability is increasingly seen as an advantage as a nation's economic success is dependent on gaining the required knowledge and experience of the workforce (Brown and Lauder, 2001).

There is a definitive social relationship between the government and individuals. The state provides the educational opportunities and are counting upon the individuals to be independent learners and gain the higher qualifications so that they can secure the best jobs. Brown et al (2011) equates the government-individual relationship as a realisation of social justice.

Context

In the UK's White Paper *'Our competitive future: Building the knowledge driven economy'* (Department for Trade and Industry, 1998) the role of the state is outlined to enable individuals and firms to make full use of the possibilities of the digital age. The aim of the New Labour government is to increase productivity levels, granting firms a clearer access to global markets. The government has set out a framework that it wants to follow to improve the UK's economic standing. The concept of a 'knowledge economy' can best be described as:

> 'the idea that knowledge and education can be treated as a business product, and that educational and innovative intellectual products and services, as productive assets, can be exported for a high-value return
>
> (Ball, 2008: 19)

Education reform began to take shape in the Conservative governments during 1979-1997. Whitty and Power (1997) have developed the idea that the reforms introduced by the Thatcher and Major governments in Britain have led to quasi-markets in education. It was argued (ibid.) that the creation of a quasi-market would only widen the existing inequalities that exist in society. Gamble (1998), however, argues that the reforms in education were part of a New Right agenda to develop a free economy and a strong state. When New Labour came into power in 1997, they placed a major emphasis on the economic role of education.

The term 'knowledge economy' was first named by Drucker (1969) and differs with the concept that industrialisation is the most contributing factor to creating wealth. It is said that higher education policies are adopted from three key terms – the 'network society', the 'information society' and the 'knowledge economy' (Bastalich, 2010). As a result, higher education policies regarding the knowledge economy are firmly settled on universities and their affinity with other producers of knowledge (ibid.).

Powell and Snellman (2004) highlight a key concept of a knowledge-based economy which involves a dependence on intellectual competencies rather than a reliance on natural resources or labour input. The term, 'knowledge economy' roots from three different research angles. Firstly, in the last few decades, the increasing number of science-based industries has played a pivotal role in economic growth. A sharp rise in employment numbers in this sector has been observed by Stanback (1979) and Noyelle (1990). Indeed, Bell (1973) was one of the first to suggest that knowledge on a theoretical level can be a source of innovation. Secondly, the amplification of knowledge-intensive industries coupled with a great increase in productivity levels has led many individuals, including Kochan and Barley (1999) to suggest that work, on an organisational front, has changed. Thirdly, continuous innovation and proactive learning in industries has led to an increase in the production of knowledge (Nonaka and Takeuchi, 1995).
The knowledge economy has transformed the nature of work in many different ways. It is argued that knowledge workers are no longer as dependent on firms for career progression. Previously, one had to show a long-term loyalty to a firm in order to progress up the career ladder. At present, capitalism has changed as individuals themselves own the knowledge that they have gained and they can take this knowledge with them if they move onto another firm. Employers now need to

find ways to not only attract talent but to also retain their knowledge workers (Burton-Jones, 1999; Cortada, 1998).

In economically developed countries such as Australia, Neumann (2002) observes that Australia's interpretation of the knowledge economy has led to a confinement of research activity to definitive areas within the sciences. Economic activity is characterised by networks on a global stage (ibid.). Bastalich (2010) and Thompson (2004) oppose this view, stating that in the business domain, information and communication technology has not led to global networks.

It is interesting to note that there is not always a definite link between research and growth. This has been apparent after the global crisis swept through the financial world. Indeed, France and the United States have the highest proportional spend on the field of research and development yet have been hardest hit by the global financial crisis (Cutler, 2008). Lyon (1995) takes the stance that the knowledge economy is not always beneficial for the individuals in research and development. One major factor is the exploitation of doctoral researchers, who have very little power within a research partnership.

Studies have shown a positive correlation between increased investment in technology and increased growth in labour productivity (Oliner and Sichel, 2000). There is an acceptance from many experts that information and communication technology (ICT) investment have led to an increase in productivity levels (Powell and Snellman, 2004). Typically, economic growth is seen as a combination of growth in labour productivity and in labour supply. Those individuals who support the theory of the knowledge economy state that technological investment is the driving factor behind economic growth (ibid.).

Brown et al (2011) describe the social relationship between individuals and the government. The state government are responsible for the provision of educational opportunities for all, whilst it is up to the individuals to study hard and secure the highly paid jobs. Brown et al (2011) even went as far to say that 'learning equals earning'. The aim of the government is to become globally competitive on an economic scale and to realise social justice. Bastalich (2010) describes a perceived knowledge economy as a drive to increase the number of 'knowledge workers.' The state makes the assumption that knowledge is at the forefront of economic competitiveness. It was believed that the knowledge economy would lead to a greater number of knowledge workers; increasing numbers of individuals in well-paid jobs. Rizvi and Lingard (2010) described the key role that education has to play in society as it is embedded in everyday ideas and practices.

Friedman (2005) shares the view of many authors that nations must compete with one another to succeed in the labour market and goes as far to say that knowledge and innovation are the two hallmarks of this. In a knowledge-based economy, innovation is an oft-repeated term. Innovation, by and large, can have many benefits. Firstly, innovation can lead to a reduction of costs for goods and services but most importantly, the primary focus is to develop new goods and services (Powell and Snellman, 2004).

There are substantial arguments from some quarters (Meyer et al, 1992; Schofer and Meyer, 2005) that national education systems are concentrating at a global level to ensure a structured model of education is in place throughout the world. If similar subjects are taught with similar critical analysis, individuals across the world will receive similar degrees that carry a global weight. However, Alexander (2001) has carried out a comparative study which shows that each nation varies in the way they set out a curriculum.

Prior to the recession, Blair and Brown's Labour government spoke proudly of their intention that fifty percent of students from each age group would attend university. When the new coalition government formed in 2010, approximately 210,000 eligible students were refused funding for university places (Lauder et al, 2012). Despite the increased number of individuals entering tertiary education, Rothstein (2010) explains how the demand for skilled graduates isn't increasing as expected. The most worrying indicator is that in the United States, of all the new graduates looking for jobs, only 20% can find a job that is applicable to their education.

Currently, many young people enter tertiary education as a degree grants the most realistic possibility for a job. This is in the face of rising tuition fees. Tuition fees in the UK have now risen to £9,000 a year, almost treble the previous amount. In effect, individuals enter an opportunity trap as they are left with little other choice. They need to weigh up a cost-benefit analysis of spending a minimum of three years at university to come out with a qualification which may or may not open up doors to a specific career path. It must be noted that this will probably not apply to students who attend the most elite universities (ibid.).

Critical Review of Policy and Literature
In the United Kingdom (UK), there is not much statistical evidence to conclude that increased numbers entering higher education has led to significant returns for the economy (Mayhew, Deer and Dua, 2004). This is despite the fact that those who enter higher education, the 'knowledge workers', will receive numerous benefits compared with those who do not enter university. In fact, Strathdee (2005) highlights that an increase in qualifications has led to an excess supply of graduates for skilled jobs. Yet, the demand for a skilled labour force has remained the same. Employers do not solely rely on academic qualifications. When searching for

workers, employers look at many attributes such as inferred knowledge and a potential for innovation (ibid.).

Being highly educated doesn't necessarily ensure that an individual will be an effective contributor to the labour market. Kemp (1999) states that research programmes can sometimes be too theoretical and specialised; leading to graduates whose interpersonal skills need additional development. Graduates who study very narrow research degrees could lack the required communication and leadership skills needed in the industrial field. Another concern is the potential cultural gap between researchers in the academic field and workers in the field of industry (ibid.). Contrastingly, Barnacle and Usher (2003) point to the fact that a large percentage of doctoral students are secure in their profession. The research carried out by Barnacle and Usher (2003), Barnacle (2004) and Kendall (2002) highlight how many research students come to university with the aim to take in the new knowledge and expertise gained from study and put this into practice in the professional work setting. Kendall (2002) further argues that the majority of PhD graduates are extremely educated and skilled; when they enter the work field, they have the ability to revolutionise the nature of their jobs. One convincing argument is that research students enter university and become reflective practitioners (Barnacle, 2004).

Despite this, Bastalich (2010) explains that one of the key problems with knowledge economy discourse is the commitment to instil certain attributes in graduates. A degree educational programme is meant to introduce dispositions in individuals. Such examples are the ability to solve problems, to work independently as well as cooperatively and to be creative thinkers. The idea is to build up transferable employment skills in all graduates so that they can be knowledge workers in any field of employment (Craswell, 2007). Individuals are viewed as a product of education. It is these individuals who gain knowledge as a result of gaining experience in the education sector who go on to change their behaviour in a positive way, for the benefit of society (Holmes, 2003). Arguably, a skillset gained in certain conditions may not be transferable to another context as it is difficult to illustrate this empirically. Moore (2004) argues that certain skills gained in higher education are useful only if individuals remain in similar settings in the workplace; developing the skill that an individual gained through experience.

Holmes (2003) and Bastalich (2010) convincingly put across the argument that there is such a spotlight on how the education system can produce a certain calibre of student that there is a diversion from a much-needed emphasis on addressing curriculum and pedagogy. Now, there is a greater consideration on self-directed learners who can manage their own learning. This, in effect, marginalises the role of teachers leading to academics being solely 'facilitators' of learning (Holmes, 2003). Not placing enough consideration on the curriculum and pedagogy because of the idea of the experiential learner will hinder individuals undertaking a research degree. This will lead to limited structured direction on the expectations of a research student (ibid.). This view is opposed by Johnson, Lee and Green (2000) who take up the Oxbridge tradition that independent learners are more likely to be innovators and pioneers in their respective fields of research.

Bastalich (2010) argues that universities are bound by policies that are set by the state with a nation's economic principles in mind. It is made clear that government policy to enhance levels of innovation; leading to economic growth and progress is naïve. It is very difficult to impartially weigh up the benefits of such new ideas (ibid.).

The knowledge economy can lead to distributional consequences. It is known that an imbalance exists between an individual's skillset and the job the individual holds. In a knowledge economy, greater discrepancy in income has led to income inequalities and unemployment levels that are noticeable. Wage inequality is ever-increasing and the development of technology is usually depicted as a cause for this (Morris & Western, 1999). Technological development has brought about an increased demand for a highly-skilled labour workforce; adding to the wage differentials observed. Skill-based technological advancements have led to a greater demand of workers who possess the required skills and knowledge of a specific type of technology. In essence, there has been an upshot in demand for knowledge-based workers. Consequently, the constant advancements in technology have also led to a decrease in the demand for low-skilled positions to be filled. Thus, changes in technology have led to an increased need for educated workers and a decreased wish for less educated workers (ibid).

Policymakers explain that individuals need to attain the key competencies and skills in order to attract potential employers in a knowledge-based economy (DfEE, 2000). Individuals who are easily employable are assumed to have an advantage over others as economic growth and prosperity of a nation is dependent upon the knowledge, skills and enthusiasm of society (Brown and Lauder, 2001). In this respect, employability can be seen as the solution. If education standards are raised, the state can entice a greater number of highly skilled workers in high waged jobs.

The global knowledge-driven economy is believed to help remove conflict between different countries. Rosecrance (1999) explains that there is now a shift between a 'bloody war' to a 'knowledge war.' Across the globe, there is a rivalry for ideas, skills and knowledge in order to ascertain an economic advantage. Workers face competition to show their insights in the job market. Reich (1991) gives evidence to address the issue of increasing wage inequalities. Reich argues that it is a failure of the education system in enabling a greater percentage of the workforce to compete for high-skilled work that will deliver higher wages. In effect, there is a global 'auction' for both low-skilled and high-skilled jobs. Low-wage economies, for example countries such as Bangladesh and Thailand, will receive a supply of low-skilled jobs that have migrated to a less economically developed country on the basis of price. In contrast, on the basis of quality, the highest-skilled jobs will attract the highest wages. This will lead to the more economically developed countries becoming 'magnet economies.' Countries such as the UK or the United States will appeal to the high-skilled jobs, enticing the greatest share to these countries (Brown and Lauder, 2001).

Those nations that have the potential to become magnet economies will be able to attract the greatest number of foreign workers to cater for the requirements of the domestic economy (Robertson et al, 2002). This means that the most developed economies are competing on two fronts – for the highest skilled jobs and for the most talented knowledge workers. The United States is just one example of a nation that competes in this way in an endeavour to address skill shortages (Alarcon, 1999). Brown and Lauder (2006) would argue that the magnet economy is a myth as there is little evidence to support an increase in the demand for highly skilled individuals. In fact, (ibid.) there is a large proportion of highly educated individuals in jobs for which they are overqualified. Consequently, the greatest hurdle for the government to address is not a lack of skills or knowledge of graduates, but there is a worrying trend that highly skilled individuals will not have their skills employed. Put simply, there is a shortage of highly-skilled jobs available. An accelerated expansion of higher education in emerging economies such as India and China has resulted in a substantial supply of high-skilled knowledge workers. Transnational companies can make use of the global supply of highly qualified Indian and Chinese workers who offer similar skills to graduates from more developed countries but at a far cheaper premium. A global rise in mass higher education will lead to increased competition for high-skilled jobs (Schofer and Meyer, 2005). Nonetheless, Brown and Lauder (2006) make a valid point that developing economies have now entered the pool for high-skilled employment which may in fact have a negative effect on the demand for existing highly-skilled workers in developed nations.

An assumption of the knowledge economy is that allocation of high-skilled employment would be between the most developed countries in the world. Reich (1991) states how low-skilled work will be undertaken in developing economies. However, as a result of the 'global skills race', Brown (2008) explains that developing economies such as India, China and Malaysia are becoming much more competitive for high-skilled work positions. This closing of the quality gap could, in the near future, bind the high-skilled knowledge workers in more developed economies to price competition. As a result, many jobs tackled by university graduates in the UK could be done at a far lower cost in another part of the world. All firms seek to reduce overall costs whilst attempting to improve the quality of a service or product. Previously, the supply of a high-skilled labour workforce was bound by the global supply of talent. In recent years, there has been a significant tightening of the productivity and quality gap that was apparent in emerging economies. Global competition is based on quality and cost and now the quality and price revolution is leading to a rapid improvement in quality standards across the globe. The performance gap is slimming at a fast pace, however there still remains a substantial difference in labour costs between developed and less developed economies (Lauder et al, 2012).

The war for talent has seen transnational companies look further afield to recruit outstanding knowledge workers to lead these global companies. Many transnational companies only recruit individuals from the global elite of universities as they are perceived to have the most intelligent students. The world-leading universities promote this notion; ensuring that higher education itself has become a global enterprise. The Skill Bias Theory stipulates that when there is a depleted supply of a skilled labour workforce, the recognition of skilled graduates will rise (Goldin and Katz, 2008).

The Human Capital Theory, stated by Lauder et al (2012), can be simplified as a large educational investment which will lead to a productive contribution from the workforce; differential incomes will be acquired. In essence, the better educated an individual, the increased chance of productiveness that they will exhibit; the individual will earn a higher wage. If these assumptions are true, the theory predicts that there will be a positive correlation between the education level of an individual and the personal income and national income for the state. One such assumption is that employers will invest in new technology to profit on the productive potential of their knowledge workers. However, Brown et al (2001) debate some of the assumptions made as theoretically, employers may not have the means to invest in new technology.

The majority of new graduates finish university with a large amount of financial debt and enter the labour market. Even with tuition fees rising in recent times, it is the opinion of most that the idea of a significant debt is not too much of an anxiety. Many individuals believe that they can earn a better paid job compared to those without a formal university education (Hesketh, 1999; Purcell and Pitcher, 1996).

A graduate premium goes a long way to answering a pivotal question – is it worth attending university in order to gain a higher income? Unfortunately, the immediate outlook for the UK employment market has been hampered by the global recession. A number of graduates are finding it difficult to secure a job that they are not overqualified for. The notion of a graduate premium goes hand-in-hand with the theory of the knowledge economy. Yet, the graduate premium cannot inform us of the demand for university graduates in the workforce. The graduate premium could result because of a fall in wages of a non-graduate worker or if a university graduate was in employment in a role that a non-graduate worker previously occupied (Pryor and Schaffer, 2000).

A criticism of the knowledge economy and its associated policies is that it depicts a narrow approach to the economics behind the knowledge discourse. Social values are effectively erased as a result of labelling knowledge as a commodity and students as customers (Slater and Tonkiss, 2001). An assumption is made that a degree is merely something that can be used as leverage to gain a high-skilled job rather than an intellectual experience that can define an individual's life. Keep (1997) illustrates that there is very little empirical evidence that the knowledge economy is at all significant. In fact, the key areas of economic growth are in service employment, rather than knowledge (ibid.).

Conclusion and recommendations for future research

Worldwide, there are hundreds of polytechnic institutions that have changed their name to include the word 'university' in the title. A simple name change confirms the importance of universities in the knowledge economy. A fundamental measure of the knowledge economy is a dependence on intelligence rather than physical labour or natural resources. In today's society, integral sectors of the economy are more dependent on the gaining of knowledge than ever before.

Over the past thirty years, there has been a steady shift from a manufacturing-based to a services-based economy. It is clear that knowledge can be incorporated in goods and services. Technological change is often shown as a determining factor of increased wage inequality. It has been recognised that technology can lead to a lower demand for low-skilled workers as technological advancements substitute the jobs of these workers.

Morris and Western (1999) have shown that many new jobs that are created are knowledge-based and so leading to a demand for higher skilled workers.

Brown and Lauder, (2006) mention that the full potential of mass education has not been realised. Employers should be more enterprising to fulfil the promise for greater levels of productivity and growth. An unintentional consequence could develop if students discover that their degree does not afford them the luxury they thought they deserved. This could mean that employers will have a high number of overqualified graduates. Expansion of tertiary education can lead to labour market congestion as a direct result of positional competition (Brown et al, 2003).

Looking ahead, the next few years will be crucial as policymakers have the daunting challenge to raise the number of job opportunities for highly-skilled graduates to aspire to. With a steady increase in the number of students going to university, the state must act quickly to ensure an efficient allocation of resources otherwise there is likely to be a surplus of highly trained graduates looking for a small number of highly paid jobs. In the United States, some states have taken action to safeguard public sector employment at a domestic level (Brown and Lauder, 2006). This is an idea that could perhaps be trialled in the UK.

References

Alarcon, R. (1999) 'Recruitment processes among foreign-born engineers and scientists in Silicon Valley', *American Behavioural Scientist*, 42(9): 1381-1397.

Alexander, R.J. (2001) *Culture & Pedagogy: International Comparisons in Primary Education*, Oxford: Blackwell.

Ball, S.J. (2008) *The Education Debate*, Bristol: The Policy Press.

Barnacle, R. (2004) 'A critical ethic in a knowledge economy: Research degree candidates in the workplace', *Studies in Continuing Education*, 26(3): 355-367.

Barnacle, R. and Usher, R. (2003) 'Assessing the quality of research training: The case of part-time candidates in full-time professional work', *Higher Education Research and Development*, 22(3): 345-358.

Bastalich, W. (2010) 'Knowledge economy and research innovation', *Studies in Higher Education*, 35(7): 845-857.

Bell, D. (1973) *The Coming of Post-Industrial Society*, New York: Basic Books.

Brown, G. (2008) 'We'll use our schools to break down class barriers', The Observer, February 10. http://www.guardian.co.uk/commentisfree/2008/feb/10/gordonbrown.education

Brown, P., Green, A. and Lauder, H. (2001) *High Skills: Globalization, Skill Formation and Competitiveness*, Oxford: Oxford University Press.

Brown, P., Hesketh, A. and Williams, S. (2003) 'Employability in a knowledge-driven economy', *Journal of Education and Work*, 16(2): 107-126.

Brown, P. and Lauder, H. (2001) *Capitalism and Social Progress: The Future of Society in a Global Economy*, Basingstoke: Palgrave.

Brown, P. and Lauder, H. (2006) 'Globalisation, knowledge and the myth of the magnet economy', *Globalisation, Societies and Education*, 4(1): 25-57.

Brown, P., Lauder, H. and Ashton, D. (2011) *The Global Auction: The Broken Promises of Opportunities, Jobs and Rewards*, New York: Oxford University Press.

Burton-Jones, A. (1999) *Knowledge Capitalism*, Oxford: Oxford University Press.

Cortada, J.W. (1998) *Rise of the Knowledge Worker*, Oxford: Butterworth-Heinemann.

Craswell, G. (2007) 'Deconstructing the skills training debate in doctoral education', *Higher Education Research and Development*, 26(4): 377-391.

Cutler, T. (2008) *Venturous Australia: Building Strength in Innovation*, North Melbourne: Cutler & Company.

Department of Education and Employment (DfEE). (2000) *Final Report of the National Skills Task Force*, London: DfEE.

Department of Trade and Industry (DTI). (1998) *Our Competitive Future: Building the Knowledge Driven Economy*, London: DTI. (www.dti.gov.uk/comp/competitive/wh_int1.htm)

Drucker, P. (1969) *The Age of Discontinuity: Guidelines to our Changing Society*, New York: Harper & Row.

Friedman, T. (2005) *The World is Flat: The Globalized World in the Twenty First Century*, New York: Penguin.

Gamble, A. (1998) *The Free Economy and the Strong State*, London: Macmillan.

Goldin, C. and Katz, L. (2008) *The Race Between Education and Technology*, Cambridge, MA: Harvard University Press.

Hesketh, A. (1999) 'Towards an economic sociology of the student financial experience of higher education', *Journal of Education Policy*, 14(4): 385-410.

Holmes, L. (2003) 'The learning turn in education and training: Liberatory paradigm or oppressive ideology', Paper presented at *Critique and inclusivity: opening agenda* 3rd International Critical Management Studies Conference, July 2003, in Manchester.

Johnson, L., Lee, A. and Green, B. (2000) 'The PhD and the autonomous self: Gender, rationality and postgraduate pedagogy', *Studies in Higher Education*, 25(2): 135-147.

Keep, E. (1997) '"There's no such thing as society...":some problems with an individual approach to creating a learning society', *Journal of Education Policy*, 12: 457-471.

Kemp, D. (1999) *Knowledge and Innovation: A Policy Statement on Research and Research Training*, Canberra: Australian Government Publishing Service.

Kendall, G. (2002) 'The crisis in doctoral education: A sociological diagnosis', *Higher Education Research and Development*, 21(2): 131-141.

Kochan, T. and Barley, S. (1999) *The Changing Nature of Work and Its Implications for Occupational Analysis*, Washington DC: Natl. Res. Counc.

Lauder, H., Young, M., Daniels, H., Balarin, M. and Lowe, J. (2012) *Educating For The Knowledge Economy? Critical perspectives*, London: Routledge.

Lyon, E.S. (1995) 'Dilemmas of power in post-graduate practice: A comment on research training', *Sociology*, 29(3): 531-540.

Mayhew, K., Deer, C. and Dua, M. (2004) 'The move to mass higher education in the UK: Many questions and some answers', *Oxford Review of Education*, 30(1): 65-82.

Meyer, J., Kamens, D. and Benavot, A. (1992) *School knowledge for the Masses: World Models and National Primary Curricular Categories for the Twentieth Century*, Brighton: Falmer Press.

Moore, T. (2004) 'The critical thinking debate: How general are general thinking skills?' *Higher Education Research and Development* 23(1): 3-18.

Morris, M. and Western, B. (1999) 'Inequality in earnings at the close of the twentieth century', *Annual Review of Sociology*, 25: 623-657.

Neumann, R. (2002) 'Diversity, doctoral education and policy', *Higher Education Research and Development*, 21(2): 167-178.

Nonaka, I. and Takeuchi, H. (1995) *The Knowledge-Creating Company*, New York: Oxford University Press.

Noyelle, T. (1990) *Skills, Wages, and Productivity in the Service Sector*, Boulder: Westview.

Oliner, S. and Sichel, D. (2000) 'The resurgence of growth in the late 1990s: Is information technology the story?' *J. Econ. Perspect.* 14: 3-22.

Powell, W. and Snellman, K. (2004) 'The knowledge economy', *Annual Review of Sociology*, 30: 199-220.

Purcell, K. and Pitcher, J. (1996) *Great Expectations: The New Diversity of Graduate Skills and Aspirations*, Manchester: CSU.

Reich, R. (1991) *The Work of Nations*, London: Simon and Schuster.

Rizvi, F. and Lingard, B. (2010) *Globalizing Education Policy*, London: Routledge.

Robertson, S., Bonal, X. and Dale, R. (2002) 'GATS and the education service industry', Comparative Education Review, 46(4): 472-497.

Rosecrance, R. (1999) *The Rise of the Virtual State*, New York: Basic Books.

Rothstein, R. (2010) *Is Education on the Wrong Track?* Washington: Economic Policy Institute, 24 March.

Schofer, E. and Meyer, J. (2005) 'The worldwide expansion of higher education in the twentieth century', *American Sociological Review*, 70 (Dec): 898-920.

Slater, D. and Tonkiss, F. (2001) *Market Society*, Cambridge: Polity Press.

Stanback, T.M. (1979) *Understanding the Service Economy: Employment, Productivity, Location*, Baltimore, MD: Johns Hopkins University Press.

Strathdee, R. (2005) 'Globalization, innovation, and the declining significance of qualifications led social and economic change', *Journal of Education Policy*, 20(4): 437-456.

Thompson, G.F. (2004) 'Getting to know the knowledge economy: ICTs, networks and governance', *Economy and Society*, 33(4): 562-81.

Whitty, G. and Power, S. (1997) 'Quasi-markets and curriculum control: making sense of recent education reform in England and Wales', *Educational Administration Quarterly*, 33(2): 219-240.

Wilby, P. (2012) 'Can we believe the international league tables?', *Forum*, 54(2): 341-344.

9 MARIAM KHOKER

The changing role and effectiveness of partnerships following the 1988 Education Reform Act.

Mariam Khokar graduated from Kingston University with a B.A. Honours degree in Primary Education, specialising in History. She has gone on to teach with distinction across the primary phase in a number of school settings. Mariam has worked in conjunction with Local Authorities as a Lead Teacher and NQT mentor.

An impassioned commentator on Primary Education, she currently teaches at Botwell House Catholic School, where she is Year Leader and member of the Senior Leadership Team.

Abstract

This essay shall begin by looking at reforms prior to the 1988 Educational Reform Act (ERA), particularly the 1944 Education Act, with a focus on the reasons why confidence in teachers and LEAs became so eroded that legislative changes to LEAs were deemed necessary. The second part discusses the main provisions of the 1988 ERA in relation to partnerships between the 'tripartite' system and discusses the changing nature and responsibilities of LEAs. The third part focuses on developments in local educational administration and alternative models under the New Labour government of 1997 with the emergence of a 'Third Way'. This essay concludes by suggesting there are few markets, in any field, which operate freely away from government control, regulation and funding, Chitty, (2008). Education is no exception and so a partnership between central government and LEAs will continue albeit imbalanced.

Introduction

The 1988 Education Reform Act (ERA) represented one of the most influential and long lasting governmental initiatives in education since 1944, (Bash and Coulby, 1989). Local Educational Authorities (LEAs) had previously been key features of educational administration, (Riddell, 2003; Reay and Ball, 1998). Both Morris, (2001) and Maden, (2001) contend they acted as central government's main partner in the operational functions of the British education system. Tipple, (1998) supports this view in describing LEAs as a fundamental feature of the educational landscape of Britain. He describes the contributions made by LEAs as both distinctive, positive and practical. However, by the late 1970s and early 1980s dissatisfaction with the products of the education system and the incremental increase in unemployment, led to intense criticism of educational organisations and standards, (Sharp, 2002; Lupton, 2005). Callaghan's Ruskin speech of 1976 suggested a 'fallacious and facile link between education and unemployment', (Bash et. al., 1985, p. 7) which pointed towards the national system of education and those responsible for its local administration. Both Batteson, (1997) and Chitty, (2009), further this, suggesting it was unavoidable that education would become the culprit of such failings.

Thus, the speech (according to Bailey, (1995) and the ensuing Great Debate (described by Gibbons et. al., (2006), was the beginning of an effort to establish a new educational consensus constructed around greater central control and the role of LEAs. Both Chitty, (1989) and Simon, (1991) categorise the speech as a significant point, implying the end of consensual, interventionist actions and the beginning of a critical momentum.

The tripartite partnership leading up to 1988 ERA

Strain and Simkins, (2008, p. 155), describe LEAs as one of the three pillars in the education cooperative of central and local government and schools. This is a view supported by Sinclair et. al., (1994) who argue the wide range and level of services facilitated by LEAs in collaboration with other agencies. As LEAs have been a feature of the educational landscape for more than a century, (Wilcox and Gray, 1996; Tough and Brooks, 2007), it is necessary to look at reforms prior to that being debated, particularly the 1944 Education Act and the effects these reforms had on shaping LEAs leading to the 1988 ERA.

According to Bash and Coulby, (1989); Bennett et. al., (2004) and Whitty, (2008), whether deliberate or incidental, the 1944 Education Reform Act established balance and coherency between the many facets of education. A tripartite system between the LEAs, the Department of Education and Science (DES) and the teachers arose, with each taking responsibility for specific areas of the education system, (Bash and Coulby, ibid). Bennett, et. al., (ibid) go further to describe the code of practice created under the system and responsibilities discharged by each, as both substantial and progressive. Bash and Coulby, (ibid) suggest they sought to homogeneously implement programmes and policies. However, Leonard (1988, p. vi) describes the role of central government, particularly that of the Secretary of State, as one which was 'often left fuming on the touchline'. This is supported by Fisher, (2008, p. 255), who describes a political consensus prior to the 1988 ERA as a 'non-interventionists approach'. This tripartite system would eventually become the tipping point for reformation changes focused around management and control, (Bennett et. al., 2004). Riley et. al. (1999), contend that as LEAs were the creation of central government, without constitutional rights to exist, they would inevitably be at the disposal of centralised forces.

However, the tripartite system, (Rao, 1990) continued for some time with the strong will and relative independence of LEAs continuing as the 1944 framework did not enable the DES to micro-manage the education system through Circulars, (Bash and Coulby, 1989). Ranson, (2008) goes further describing the customised powers of LEAs in direct conflict with national regulations and accountability. Therefore, if governments were determined to implement educational reforms they would need to take account of recalcitrant LEAs, (Ball, 2008).

Richards, (1992) describes obstreperous and defiant LEAs through the example of the 1976 Tameside LEA embattlement with the then Labour-controlled DES, in which Tameside LEA fought to prevent the scheme of comprehensivisation by means of a Circular, (Bash and Coulby, 1989). Their victory in 1976 demonstrated that the power of LEAs under the 1944 Act was something which would need to be confronted, if not abolished, if any government wished to coherently and succinctly implement national changes in education, (Bull, 1989).

Radical changes in partnerships

Thus the passing of the 1988 ERA dramatically severed this equilibrium and shifted huge areas of power and control over educational institutions to the Secretary of State at the DES, (Richards, 1992; Machin et. al., 2007). The amount of central power given by the Act to the Secretary of State was unparalleled, (Bash and Coulby, 1989). Ranson, (2008, p. 201) supports this view in describing the passing of ERA as 'the most radical reconstitution of the governance of education since the Second World War'.

Sharp, (2002), goes further to suggest Conservative legislation moved towards increasing the powers of central government and at a local level, those of schools and parents; thus severing the 'close administrative partnership between central and local government', Sharp, (2002, p. 197). Tipple, (1998) supports this, describing how LEAs were rendered powerless through their reduced administrative functions and later unable to amend localised injustice and inequalities created by the Act.

Since 1988, the existence of LEAs has been widely debated amongst differing political parties, with a general consensus being they must, 'earn their place', DfEE (1997, p. 66). According to Sharp, (2002, p. 200) 1988 ERA was the beginning of LEAs moving towards greater 'control and direction' under the Minster of Education. Levacic, (1992) affirms this view as she describes the curtailing of the controls of LEAs as leaders of local education services, owing to the organisational and centralising changes of ERA.

It is argued here that the period during the late 1940s and up to the 1960s was witness to the LEAs 'golden age', (Simmons, 2008; Dent, 1969; Kogan et. al., 1984). However, at an administrative level, concerns arose surrounding the size and resources of LEAs, with some concerned that educational opportunities were far too dependent upon locality, (Sharp, 2002). Strain and Simkins, (2008, p. 157), describe this as the threat of polarisation between 'gentrified' and 'ghettoized' communities. This saw a number of local government reorganisations during the 1970s, which resulted in reduced number of LEAs and an increase in the size of others, (Levacic, 1992). This had the unforeseen result of many interested parties, including parents and industries, believing local educational administrations were failing to effectively serve their communities, (Abbott et. al, 2013).

Concern also began to develop around local government's involvement in education and whether or not this was too dominant, coupled with their organisational effectiveness, (Radford, 1988). The Hillgate Group (1986: 7, 10), was influential in shaping public opinion on decentralisation, stating that 'schools should be self-governing', arguing for a more marketable partnership. Consequently, an emphasis was developing around 'corporate management' Sharp, (2002, p. 200). Abbott et. al., (2013), describe this as the emergence of educational policies which sought to improve the national economy. Walford, (1990, p. 129), concurs with this view in describing the major changes and administrative revolution brought about as an 'ideological commitment to privatization', marginalising any pre-existing partnerships. However, Radford, (1988, p. 747) challenges this view in suggesting 'local authorities have always been empowered to contract with the private sector for the provision of services.' He argues it was widely accepted, by central and local government, that it was the most proficient way to deliver public amenities and that in itself created a partnership between not only central and local government, but across parties as well (Radford, ibid).

Sharp, (2002, p. 200) indicates that further dissatisfaction evolved around the perception LEAs prohibited schools from developing their own character and prevented parents from partaking in the work of their children's schools. This perspective is continued by Doe, (1999, p. 335) who describes this as weakening education, with LEAs being held responsible 'for a decline (or inadequate rise) in standards'.

This developing negativity surrounding the functionality of LEAs and the education system in general, lead to cynicism of the central government at that time, (Tipple, 1998). Sharp, (2002) suggests the 'impressive powers of the Minister of Education, now Secretary of State...appeared to promise more than they could deliver' and furthermore, questioned 'which parts of the education system did the minister actually control?' Sharp, (2002, p. 201).

Tomlinson, (1992), an eminent academic and former chief education officer, provides a perspective on partnerships from those working in LEAs at the time of ERA. He contrasts the role of education officers with that of the Secretary of State for Education describing it as being mismatched, disproportionate and often vilified. McLean, (1989, p. 237) goes further to describe the relegation of 'local authority official to little more than consultants whose advice had little sanction.' Tipple, (1998) claims many of the effects of the 1988 ERA resulted in an arduous and unsuitable partnership at local level and national level. However, Marchington et. al., (2004), suggest arrangements at local levels were a 'best fit', suggesting fewer alternatives would have been equally successful.

It was these concerns coupled with growing dissatisfaction and failed attempts to rectify the role and responsibility of LEAS which eventually paved the way for the 1988 ERA and the diminished role and altered partnerships with LEAs, (Walford, 1990; Ball, 2008; Batteson, 1997; Gillard, (2011).

The 1988 Education Reform Act and its impact upon partnerships in education

Leonard, (1988) argues the conception of the 1988 ERA lacked the through consultation and debate with educational professionals which previous acts had so effectively done. The response from schools and LEAs which should have been 'thorough, measured and above all-far sighted', Leonard, (1988, p. vi), was instead far from monolithic with schools and LEAs responding 'to the Act quite differently,' Airasian and Gregory, (1997, p. 311). Radford, (1988, p. 750) describes this resilience as a 'marked reluctance to submit more of their services'. This strained the evolving partnership, with considerable hostility and resentment by LEAs towards central government, (McCulloch, 2002). Sharp and Dunfold, (1990, p. 39) suggest this was a product of the mounting 'power-down system'. A view echoed by Maclure, (1998) and Airasian and Gregory, (1997) who describe the Act as having ruthlessly reduced authorities' educational function and all but eradicated their strategic role.

LEAs were seen to be stifling schools abilities to innovate and respond effectively to the needs of parents, pupils and those of the wider society. A view intensified by media commentators; 'We recommend the eventual abolition of local education authorities...because their role is withering away and the ground must be cleared.' Independent, (1991) as cited by Riley et. al., (1999, p. 29). Thus LEAs were regarded as having engineered and maintained a 'dull uniformity to the system and levelling down of standards', Whitty, (2008, p. 166). Bennett et. al. (2004, p. 218) label this as the perceived 'progressive weakening' of schools.

Central government regarded the 1988 ERA as the means by which to combat this issue and re-establish partnerships with parents to increase their power and influence in the tripartite system (Sexton, 1998). Doe, (1999, p. 336) claims the new parental partnership or 'parent power', focused not only around greater choice of schooling, but elevating parent's voices in school management. The terms 'consumer' and 'producers' (Whitty 2008, p. 166) concurred by Levacic, (1995), were introduced ending the coercive partnership between LEAs, central government and schools, whilst marking the beginning of greater parental choice and school autonomy, (Strain and Simkins, 2008).

However, Whitty, (2008) describes how the Conservative government enacting ERA, although eager to make schools receptive to parents' wishes, were not willing to surrender control over the outcomes that schools should strive to achieve. Both Riley et. al. (1999) and Gamble, (1988) describe this as the emergence of a stronger state with a shift in the way the public sector was managed and controlled by central government. Whitty, (2008, p. 166) describes this as 'steering at a distance'. However, Tipple, (1998) contradicts this view in suggesting that power and influence did shift towards the centre, but this was not a direct consequence of the 1988 ERA, rather an evolved process for which the Act served as a catalyst. Naturally, as political agendas change in line with social and economic changes, so do the administrative functions, role and partnerships of LEAs (Ball, 2008).

Whilst the process of devolving powers to schools and parents appeared to mark the beginning of a more levelled partnership (Kelly, 2006), central government retained overall strategic control by setting the outputs to achieve and publishing theses. Neave, (1988); Whitty et. al., (1998); Jones, (1990) all contest the view that central government and LEAs were in partnership. Instead, they developed a thorough case study of a power struggle as in the Labour-controlled county borough of Swansea. Kerckhoff et. al., (1996, p. 117) support this view in stating that 'few LEAs were bold enough to contemplate dissent from the orthodoxy...' This suggests a climate of fear and apprehension rather than the emergence of a levelled partnership, (McCulloch, 2002).

Central government were now the key player who would be happy to encourage and develop certain partnerships whilst others would be side-lined and marginalised, (Levacic, 1995). One major partnership strengthened and evolved would be that between parents and schools, (Airasian and Gregory, 1997).

Parental choice, or 'parent power', Doe, (1999, p. 336), evolved to a degree that had previously been unmatched, (Haydn, 2004; Ranson, 2008). Pierson, (1998, p. 132) describes this as the 'transfer of power from the producers (members of the 'educational establishment') to the consumers (in this context parents, at other times, employers; never, of course, pupils themselves)'. Parents as 'consumers', Whitty, (2008, p. 166) were now encouraged to be more selective of which school their child should attend, resulting in greater competition between schools. To help parents in selecting a school, LEAs were obliged to provide parents with key information about their schools, including examination results, (Whitty, 2008; Strain and Simkins, 2008). Levacic, (1992) portrays the benefits of this new partnership as one which would allow parents to make judgements on the basis of more thorough factors.

At the same time, the schools were given the option to 'opt-out' of their LEA and establish themselves as grant-maintained schools, receiving funding directly from central government, (Doe, 1998; Richards, 1992; McLean, 1989). In this capacity, the partnership between schools and central government was strengthened as schools would be working more closely with central government, (Ball, 2008). However, research carried out by Riley et. al., (1999), typically describes very few schools having adopted this model, with many negative connotations for those which had.

The 1988 ERA sought to enable schools to manage their resources. Mercer, (1989) depicts this as a positive move towards greater autonomy and self-governance. Conversely, Levacic, (1992, p. 19) questions the benefits of this new function, describing LEAs as simply 'banker to the school'. According to both Walford, (1990) and Leonard, (1988, p. 61), the key motivations behind this was to ensure those involved in the management of schools were able to make key decisions to ensure the 'optimum use of these resources'. Central government anticipated schools would make greater 'efficiency savings', Leonard, (1988, ibid), as they would be better placed to manage funding rather than the distant administrative LEA.

However, Leonard, (1988) suggests although this left plenty of scope for a school to greatly benefit, it also gave way for inequalities and biases that previously had not existed. Meredith, (1989, p. 221) affirms this, suggesting that as the devolved school budget was related to pupil numbers, schools would 'be driven to compete directly with each other for pupils and, thus, for money.' This suggests that inter-school partnerships were at risk as schools within the same LEA would potentially have considerably different budgets and therefore resources (Richards, 1992; Ball, 2008).

Airasian and Gregory, (1997) and Mercer, (1989) both describe 1988 ERA as forcefully adapting partnerships in education.

The introduction of Local Management of Schools (LMS) forced schools to yield yet more control over their finances and day-to-day administration, (Whitty, 2008). 85% of LEAs' school budget was handed over to schools to manage and distribute, an unprecedented amount, (Whitty, 2008). Tipple, (1998, p. 37) describes this as the creation of a 'financial straightjacket' for LEAs.

Riley, et. al., (1992), suggest this led to a more obvious and equalled partnership between LEAs and parents as there was greater fiscal transparency. Whilst Fisher, (2008, p. 257) goes further to describe the consequences as 'hostile to elected local education authorities, and allowed them only a limited administrative function'. Under Clause 33 of the Act, LEAs were required to hand over control of their 'budget share', ERA (1988, Section 36), to schools which was determined on a per capita basis, a distinct centralised steering mechanism, (Whitty, 2008).

The introduction of per capita funding created a 'virtual voucher' system, Sexton, (1987, p. 168) in which schools were now not only responsible for managing resources and funding but to a certain extent, determining the quantity of such fiscal resources. 80% of the total decentralised budget was determined directly by the amount and ages of a school's pupils, (Shleifer, 1998). Schools attempted to remedy the per-capita limitations and disadvantages through the 'recoupment process', Tipple, (1998, p. 38), in which schools taking pupils from a neighbouring LEA (owing to greater parental choice) could charge the pupil's home LEA at an agreed rate. However, in a further attempt to weaken LEA's fiscal power, central government abolished this process putting further strain on LEAs and their ability to financially govern themselves, (Lister, 1991). Tipple, (1998, p. 38), proclaims how 'locally it resulted in severe injustice' and resulted in LEAs having to make expenditure cuts. In turn, this resulted in negative public opinion and doubts about the benefits of many aspects of local management of schools, (Walford, 1990;

Tomlinson, 1992).

At the same time, the introduction of open enrolment removed numerical restrictions schools had previously faced from LEAs, (Ball et. al., 1997). It allowed the most popular schools to attract the greatest possible number of students up to the school's physical capacity (Doe, 1999). Subsequently, schools could no longer rely upon the LEA to fill places and therefore had to be more proactive in attracting and retaining pupil numbers, (Ranson, 2008; Riley, 1994). This echoes Whitty's, (2008, p. 166) description of the partnerships between the historic tripartite system as one of growing 'consumer' and 'producer' with a move towards greater 'marketisation', Whitty, (2008, p. 169). However, McKenzie, (1995) as cited by Whitty, (2008, p. 169) describes this as 'merely a superficial and symbolic movement towards consumer sovereignty.'

Following the 1988 ERA the traditional distribution of roles and partnerships within the tripartite structure of central government, LEAs and school/teacher had been considerably restructured with far-reaching changes to the structure and content of schooling, Whitty, (2008). New Labour continued many of these structural and content changes, (Riley, 1997; Ball, 2003).

LEAs under New Labour

New Labour's time in government saw the continuation of themes and reforms in a step away from their traditional political ideology, (Lawton, 2005); adjusting Conservative policies to fit their own remit, (Whitty, 2008). According to Barber, (1996), the 1997 New Labour government marked the beginning of a period of greater evidence based reforms and the emergence of the 'Third Way', Whitty, (2008, p. 170). This may have led some to believe the resurrection of LEA power and control to that of pre-ERA, however, New Labour pledged a commitment to creating and maintaining greater social fairness, (Blair, 1998) through greater challenge and support, (DfEE, 1997) rather than simply returning to previous models, (Barber, 1996).

Conversely, Haydn, (2004), argues it was unrealistic and idealistic at best to believe inequality could be removed from a system which so intrinsically created 'winners' and 'losers' through systems such as the per-capita funding arrangement. Bailey, (1995), describes this as the continued friction between so-called popular and unpopular schools.

Power and Whitty, (1999), go further by arguing that New Labour did not present a new or radical direction in educational reform policy, instead they sought to amend rather than replace the legacy of ERA. Hargreaves et. al., (2010), support this in arguing that whilst devolved control appeared to create a new partnership with equal power, central government retained overall control by setting specific outcomes which schools, teachers and LEAs had to achieve.

Partnerships under New Labour

Ranson, (2008, p. 202) describes how New Labour 'did not alter, but rather accentuated' finance autonomy between schools and LEAs, introducing further devolved fiscal power to schools; a view shared by Levacic, (1992) and Sexton, (1998).

In 1998, Educational Action Zones (EAZs) distributed £750,000 between groups of under-performing schools with those participating in the programme given the freedom to decide rates of pay for staff and the focus of their provisions, (Gewirtz et. al., 2005). Bailey, (1995, p. 480) defines this as 'individualised and fragmented.' Although Whitty, (2008), depicts this as widening partnerships between schools themselves.

Gerwirtz et. al., (2005, p. 652) criticises the programme, arguing it lacked the partnership with parents with which it had been intended, describing it as a 'contradiction between working on parents and working with them'.

New Labour's desire to forge partnerships between schools was evident in the 1999 'Excellence in Cities' programme, in which the highest performing schools were encouraged to serve as a developmental adviser to schools in their locality, (Kendall et. al., 2005). The emphasis of such programmes was on multi-agencies working together in partnership, (Gewirtz, 1999). This suggests a move towards localised solutions; a belief that educational provisions could be made better not by schools competing against one another, but by localised solutions stemming from school to school collaboration, (Commission on Social Justice, 1994; Blair, 2002). Whitty, (2008), furthers this suggesting, this approach focused on improving standards through schools rather than their operational context. This would mark the beginning of a new partnership, one between schools themselves, (Gerwirtz et. al., 2005). However, Thrupp and Lupton, (2006 p. 215), critically describe this emergent partnership process as one which demonstrated central government's desire to attribute blame for poor standards as it was firmly rooted in the belief that '...quality differences between schools are primarily the responsibility of schools themselves'; rather than the beginning of a fair and even partnership.

Under New Labour, school partnerships were extended through various partnered programmes such as 'London Challenge', which Whitty, (2008, p. 172), describes as 'a partnership between government, schools and boroughs to raise standards'. Kendall et. al., (2005), argue that such schemes forged under new partnerships had benefits to combat educational achievement in ways previous mandates had failed. This suggests New Labour sought to move towards greater collaboration following a previously divisive and competitive system, (Smith and Noble, 1995; Sexton, 1998). Tomlinson, (2003, p. 195) suggests the development of an ethical perspective on partnerships demonstrates 'New Labour was ideologically committed to returning a measure of social justice and equality.' In contrast, Machin et. al., (2007), argues there were very limited developments and gains through this partnered approach, making it harder to discriminate between the old and new parties enactment of ERA Tomlinson, (2004).

This led to New Labour's belief that LEAs should seek to improve standards through monitoring and target setting, within the 'triangular partnership', (Barber, 1996; Reynolds, 2008). New Labour sought to modify the existing strategies to focus on traits which would deliver on targets and raise standards, (Beecham, 2006). In this regard, LEAs would be working alongside rather than directing, (Reynolds, 1995; Sammons et. al., 1997; Teddlie and Reynolds, 2002). However, this focus merely continued the recommendations of the Audit Commission Report, (1989), rather than introduce a new concept, in which LEAs had been encouraged to adopt more of an Ofsted role, (Evans and Penney, 1994).

'Successful' schools, those which achieved government targets and succeeded in school inspections, were then rewarded with new freedoms, (Whitty, 2008). This clearly shows that autonomy was still regarded as a reward to be earned. Furthermore, these 'successful' schools were actively encouraged to expand their intake, whilst in contrast; 'failing' schools were subjected to stringent measures and targeted 'support', (Gorard, 2005).

This shift in the partnership saw the emergent role of the LEA as a 'scapegoat', (Tomlinson, 1992). In this capacity, Tippple, (1998), views the LEA as a now meek and 'browbeaten' commodity, the 'scapegoat' for matters which they have little or no control over. For example, LEAs were regarded as the employers, however, this responsibility in reality, rested with the governors, (Young, 1989; Adams and Punter, 2008). Thus, important decisions regarding the quality of the teaching force fell outside their physical control. Tipple, (1998, p. 37) supports this, in describing it as a 'grinding and remorseless process which did much to reduce the vitality of local decision making.'

Under the 2005 schools White Paper, Department for Education and Skills (DfES), (2005), schools were encouraged to tailor their educational provisions to meet the needs of each pupil, including various catch-up programmes. In this way, schools sought to forge a closer partnership with pupils themselves, (Burnitt and Gunter,

2013; Whitty, 2008). However, Kelly, (2006: 1) proposes New Labour failed in their attempt to do so as such partnerships only had a 'slight' positive effect. Plewis and Goldstein, (1998) and Kelly, (2005) question the ability of schools to manage such programmes, casting doubts over the ability of central government to manage educational partnerships in the absence of LEAs, (Radford, 1988; Levacic, 1992; Nightingale, 1990).

New Labour's education and political partnerships were made clearer during a 2006 speech made by the then Prime Minister Tony Blair:

> "At first we put a lot of faith in centrally driven improvements in performance...But over time I shifted from saying "it's standards, not structures" to realising that school structures could affect standards."
>
> Blair, (2006)

This would suggest a belated recognition and acceptance of contributions made by the differing partnerships and the need for productive collegiality among these partnerships (Reynolds, 2008). However, Adnett and Davies, (2003), argue that collegiality is unobtainable in a system where schools and LEAs are operating on different legal and budgetary positions.

Education policy across both Conservative and New Labour administrations has been strong and sequential, (Ball, 2008). Connolly et. al., (2008) argue throughout this period there has been increased centralisation of services within the constraints of increasingly detailed target-setting and monitoring objectives set by central government. While the 'Third Way' did not return to the historic partnerships of pre-1988 ERA and take LEAs back to their former glory days, New Labour did seek to create a new partnership, one between schools and pupils themselves, (Newman, 2001; Hollingshead, 2005; Driver, and Martell, 1999).

Conclusion

Both Tomlinson, (1992) and Tipple, (1998) suggest in light of the 1988 ERA, LEAs have had to adopt a more business-like operational structure; under this model, LEAs have worked with a wider range of agencies and practitioners. Ball, (2008) and Riley et. al., (1999) indicate this to be an area for future research in relation to partnerships as they contend the distinct differences between the priorities of educators, parents, central and local government is likely to continue effecting their partnership as each strives to priorities further their own cause, (Wilby, 2007).

McKenzie, (1995) suggests that as ERA arose from economic and social difficulties at a specific time, partnerships inevitably evolved and changed adapting with the process. Tipple, (1998) argues as political imperatives changed, so did the urgency and the lack of consultation. This is true for the repercussions of the 1988 ERA, which brought about an avalanche of changes with seemingly little consultation, (Bennett et. al., 2004). However, as these central imperatives have remained, so to, have the everlasting effects of the ERA, significantly the evolution of partnerships within the education system, (Whitfield, 2006; Riley, 1997). This would suggest changing and evolving partnerships should be regarded as a natural process, although not always well received, (Ball, 1999; Gould, 1998). Walford, (1990) suggests governments have continued to work more closely with LEAs forging a deeper partnership. Through this alliance they have exerted greater force and influence over the education system; although, Meredith, (1989, p. 216) views this as an 'elective dictatorship'. It would be naive to imagine an education system totally separate from the political system, (Ball, 2008; Abbott et. al, 2013). Governments, irrespective of the political party, will always need LEAs for administrative and practical purposes, given the geographical restraints of centralised power, (Caldwell, 2008). The metaphor used by Kenneth Baker (1993), the Secretary of State for Education responsible for the Act, was of a wheel with himself in the centre and self-governing schools at the fringe; even this model depicted a partnership at the most contentious time, one which has weathered both changes to governments and to political agendas, (Doe, 1997). It is clear that this need for LEAs will see them survive political changes and actually result in closer partnerships, between the key stakeholders in the education system as change brings about great opportunity, (Whitty, 2008; Tipple, 1998).

References

Abbott, I., Rathbone, M., Whitehead, P. (2013) *Education policy.* SAGE, Los Angeles, California.

Adams, J., Punter, A. (2008) *Finding (and keeping) school governors: The work of the School Governors' One-Stop Shop.* Management in Education, vol. 22, no. 4, pp. 14-17.

Airasian, P.W., Gregory, K.D. (1997) *The Education Reform Act of 1988.* Taylor & Francis Ltd, Abingdon.

Audit Commission. (1989) *Losing an Empire, Finding a Role: the LEA of the future.* (London, HMSO).

Ball, S.J. (2008) *The education debate,* Policy, Bristol.

Ball S.J. (1999) Labour, learning and the economy: a policy sociology perspective. *Cambridge Journal of Education* 29(2): 195–206.

Ball, S.J., Vincent, C. & Radnor, H. (1997), Into confusion: LEAs, accountability and democracy. *Journal of Education Policy*, vol. 12, no. 3, pp. 147-163.

Bash, L., Coulby, D. & Jones, C. (1985) *Urban Schooling: Theory and Practice.* London: Cassell.

Bash, L. & Coulby, D. (1989) *The Education Reform Act: competition and control.* Cassell, London.

Batteson, C. (1997) 'A Review of Politics of Education in the 'Moment of 1976' *British Journal of Educational Studies*, vol. 45, no. 4, pp. 363-377.

Bailey, L. (1995) 'The Correspondence Principle and the 1988 Education Reform Act', *British Journal of Sociology of Education,* vol. 16, no. 4, pp. 479-494.

Baker, K. (1993) *The Turbulent Years*. London: Faber and Faber.

Barber, M. (1996) *The learning game- arguments for an education revolution* (London, Victor Gallancz).

Beecham, J. (2006) *Beyond boundaries: citizen centred local services for Wales* (Cardiff, WAG).

Bennett, N., Harvey, J., Anderson, L. 'Control, Autonomy and Partnership in Local Education: Views from Six Chief Education Officers', (2004), *Educational Management Administration & Leadership,* vol. 32, no. 2, pp. 217-235.

Blair, T. (1998) *The Third Way: new politics for the new century* (London, The Fabian Society).

Blair, T. (2002) *The courage of our convictions: why reform of the public services is the route to social justice* (London, The Fabian Society).

Blair, T. (2006) *'Education is the most Precious Gift'*, Speech at Specialist Schools and Academies Trust Conference, November. Available at: http://www.number10.gov.uk/ output/Page10514.asp

Board of Education. (1944) *Principles of Government in Maintained Secondary Schools* (London, HMSO).

Bull, D. (1987), 'Tameside Revisited: Prospectively "Reasonable'; Retrospective 'Maladministration', *The Modern Law Review,* vol. 50, no. 3, pp. 307-344.

Burnitt, M., Gunter, H. (2013) 'Primary school councils: Organization, composition and head teacher perceptions and values', *Management in Education*, vol. 27, no. 2, pp. 56-62.

Caldwell, B.J. (2008) "Reconceptualizing the Self-managing School", Educational Management Administration & Leadership, vol. 36, no. 2, pp. 235-252.

Chitty, C. (1989) *Towards a New Education system: The Victory of the New Right?* (Lewes, The Falmer Press).

Chitty, C. (6th November, 2009). *Ruskin's Legacy*. Available: http://www.tes.co.uk/article.aspx?storycode=19668. Last accessed 8th Dec 2013.

Commission on Social Justice. (1994) *Social justice strategies for national renewal.*

(London, Vintage).

Connolly, C., Martin, G., Wall, A. (2008), "Education, Education, Education: The Third Way and PFI", *Public Administration*, vol. 86, no. 4, pp. 951-968.

Dent, H.C. (1969) *The Educational System of England and Wales* (4th edn) (London, University Press).

Department of Education and Science (1944) *Education Reform Act*, (London, HMSO).

Department of Education and Science (2001) *Education Bill*, (London, HMSO).

Department of Education and Science (1985) Better Schools (London, HMSO); *Education Reform Act*, 1988.

Department for Education and Employment (1997) *Excellence in Schools* (London, HMSO).

Department for Education and Employment (2005) *Higher Standards, Better Schools for All.* London: TSO.

Doe, B. (1999) 'The Role of the Media in the Reform of School Management', *Educational Management & Administration,* vol. 27, no. 3, pp. 335-343.

Driver, S. and L. Martell . (1999) 'New Labour: Culture and Economy' , in L. Ray and A. Sayer (eds), *Culture and Economy: After the Cultural Turn* . London : Sage .

Evans, J., and Penney, D. (1994) Whatever happened to good advice? Service and inspection after the Education Reform Act. *British Educational Research Journal*, 20, 5, pp. 519-583.

Fisher, T. (2008) "The Era of Centralisation: The 1988 Education Reform Act and Its Consequences", *FORUM: for promoting 3-19 comprehensive education,* vol. 50, no. 2, pp. 255-261.

Gamble, A. (1988) *The Free Economy and the Strong State.* London: Macmillan.

Gewirtz, S. (1999) Education Action Zones: emblems of the third way? in: H. Dean & R. Woods(Eds) *Social Policy Review 11* (Luton, Social Policy Association).

Gewirtz, S., Dickson, M., Power, S., Halpin, D. & Whitty, G. (2005) "The Deployment of Social Capital Theory in Educational Policy and Provision: The Case of Education

Action Zones in England", *British Educational Research Journal*, vol. 31, no. 6, pp. 651-673

Gibbons, S., Machin, S. and Silva, O. (2006) *Competition, Choice and Pupil Achievement.* London: LSE/CEE.

Gillard, D. (2011) *Education in England: a brief history.* Available at: www.educationengland.org.uk/history. Last accessed 8th Dec 2013.

Gorard, S. (2005) 'Academies as the "Future of Schooling": Is this an Evidence-based Policy?', *Journal of Education Policy* 20(3): 369–77.

Gould P. (1998). *The Unfinished Revolution: How the Modernisers Saved the Labour Party.* Little Brown: London.

Haydn, T. (2004) 'The Strange Death of the Comprehensive School in England and Wales, 1965–2002', *Research Papers in Education* 19(4): 415–32.

Hillgate Group (1986) *Whose Schools? A Radical Manifesto.* London: Imediaprint.

Hollingshead , I. (2005) *Whatever happened to the third way?,* The Guardian , 29 October.

Jones, G.E. (1990) *1944 and all that, History of Education*, 19, 3, pp. 235-50.

Kelly, R. (2005) 'Education and Social Progress'. Keynote speech, Institute of Public Policy Research, July. Available at:http://www.dcsf.gov.uk/speeches/speech.cfm?SpeechID=242

Kelly, R. (2006) 'Education and Social Mobility: Progress for All'. Speech to the Institute of Public Policy Research, April.

Kendall, L., O'Donnell, L., Golden, S., Ridley, K., Machin, S., Rutt, S., McNally, S., Schagen, I., Meghir, C., Stoney, S., Morris, M., West A. and Noden, P. (2005) *'Excellence in Cities: the National Evaluation of a Policy to raise Standards in Urban Schools 2000–03'.* Research Report RR675A. Available at:http://www.dfes.gov.uk/research/data/uploadfiles/RR675a.pdf

Kerckhoff, A., Fogelman, K., Crook, D. & Reeder, D. (1996) *Going Comprehensive in England and Wales: a study of uneven change* (London, Woburn).

Kogan M (ed), Johnson D, Packwood T and Whitaker T (1984) *School governing bodies* London: Heinemann Educational Books.

Lawton, D. (2005) Education and Labour Party Ideologies—1900–2001 and Beyond. Abingdon: RoutledgeFalmer.

Leonard, M. (1988), *The 1988 Education Act: a tactical guide for schools,* Blackwell Education, Oxford.

Levacic, R. (1992), "Local Management of Schools: Aims, Scope, and Impact", *Educational Management and Administration,* vol. 20, no. 1, pp. 16-29.

Lister, E. (1991) *LEAs-Old and New. A View from Wandsworth* (London, Centre for Policy Studies).

Lupton, R. (2005) 'Social justice and School Improvement: Improving the Quality of Schooling in the Poorest Neighbourhoods', *British Educational Research Journal* 31(5): 589–604.

Machin, S., McNally, S. and Meghir, C. (2007) Resources and Standards in Urban Schools. London: Centre for the Economics of Education.

Maclure, S. (1998), "Through the Revolution and out the Other Side", *Oxford Review of Education*, vol. 24, no. 1, pp. 5-24.

Maden, M., ed. (2001) *Success Against the Odds Five Years On.* London: RoutledgeFalmer.

Marchington, L., Earnshaw, J., Torrington, D. & Ritchie, E. (2004) "The local education authority's role in operating teacher capability procedures", *Educational Management Administration & Leadership,* vol. 32, no. 1, pp. 25.

McCulloch, G. (2002) "Local Education Authorities and the Organisation of Secondary Education, 1943-1950", *Oxford Review of Education*, vol. 28, no. 2/3, pp. 235-246.

McKenzie, J. (1995) 'Education as a Private Problem or a Public Issue?', in S. Edgell, S. Walklate and G. Williams (eds) *Debating the Future of the Public Sphere.* Aldershot: Avebury.

McLean, M. (1989) "Populist" Centralism: The 1988 Education Reform Act in England and Wales", *Educational Policy,* vol. 3, no. 3, pp. 233-244.

Mercer, R. (1989) "And Now for the Soaring Turkeys: Managing the Implementation of the 1988 Education Reform Act", *Educational Management Administration & Leadership*, vol. 17, no. 2, pp. 55 62.

Meredith, P. (1989) "Educational Reform", *The Modern Law Review*, vol. 52, no. 2, pp. 215-231.

Morris, E. (2001) 'We need your help to make a Difference', *Education Review* 15(1): 4.

Neave, G. (1988) 'On the Cultivation of Quality, Efficiency and Enterprise: An Overview of Recent Trends in Higher Education in Western Europe, 1968–88', *European Journal of Education* 23(1/2): 7–23.

Newman J. (2001) Modernising Governance: New Labour, Policy and Society . *London: Sage*.

Nightingale, D. (1990) Local Management of Schools at Work in the Prirmary School, Falmer Press: Basingstoke.

Pierson, C. (1998) "The New Governance of Education: The Conservatives and Education 1988-1997", *Oxford Review of Education*, vol. 24, no. 1, pp. 131-142.

Plewis, I. and Goldstein, H. (1998) 'Excellence in Schools—A Failure of Standards', *British Journal of Curriculum and Assessment* 8(1): 17–20.

Power, S. and Whitty, G. (1999) 'New Labour's Education Policy: First, Second or Third way?', *Research Papers in Education* 14(5): 535–46.

Radford, M. (1988) "Competition Rules: The Local Government Act 1988", *The Modern Law Review,* vol. 51, no. 6, pp. 747-767.

Ranson, S. (2008) "The Changing Governance of Education", *Educational Management Administration & Leadership,* vol. 36, no. 2, pp. 201-219.

Rao, N. & Joseph Rowntree Foundation (1990) *Educational change and local government: the impact of the Education Reform Act,* Joseph Rowntree Foundation, York.

Reay, D. and Ball, S. (1998) 'Making Their Minds Up: Family Dynamics and School Choice', *British Educational Research Journal* 24: 431–48.

Reynolds, D. (1995) The effective school: an inaugural lecture, *Evaluation and Research in Education*, 9 (2), 57–73.

Reynolds, D. (2008) It boils down to money, *Times Educational Supplement* Cymru, 25 July, p. 21.

Richards, S. (1992) "The School Budget, Power and Responsibility in Grant-Maintained Schools", *Educational Management & Administration,* vol. 20, no. 4, pp. 249-57.

Riddell, R. (2003) *Schools for Our Cities: Urban Learning in the 21st Century.* Stoke on Trent: Trentham Books.

Riley, K.A. (1994) *Quality and Equality: Promoting Opportunities with Schools.* London: Cassell.

Riley, K.A. (1997) 'Changes in Local Governance—Collaboration Through Networks: A Post-16 Case Study', *Education Management & Administration* 25(2): 155–7.

Riley, K.A., Docking, J., Rowles, D. "Can Local Education Authorities Make a Difference?: The Perceptions of Users and Providers", (1999), *Educational Management & Administration,* vol. 27, no. 1, pp. 29-44.

Sammons, P., Mortimore, P., Thomas, S. (1997) *Forging limits: effective schools and effective departments* (London, Paul Chapman).

Sharp, P. (2002), "Surviving, Not Thriving: LEAs since the Education Reform Act of 1988", *Oxford Review of Education,* vol. 28, no. 2/3, pp. 197-215.

Sharp, P.R., Dunford, J.R. (1990) *The Education System in England and Wales* (London, Longmans).

Sexton, S. (1987) *Our Schools—A Radical Policy*. London: Institute of Economic Affairs, Education Unit.

Sexton, S. (1998) "The profession of teaching", *Education* 3-13, vol. 26, no. 1, pp. 17-19.

Simmons, R. (2008) "Golden Years? Further Education Colleges under Local Authority Control", *Journal of Further and Higher Education,* vol. 32, no. 4, pp. 359-371.

Simon, B. (1991) *Education and the Social Order 1940-1990* (London, Lawrence and Wishart).

Sinclair, R., Grimshaw, R., Garnett, L. (1994) "The Education of Children in Need: The Impact of the Education Reform Act 1988, the Education Act 1993 and the Children Act 1989", *Oxford Review of Education,* vol. 20, no. 3, pp. 281-292.

Smith T., Noble, M. (1995) Education Divides: Poverty and Schooling in the 1990s. *Child Poverty Action Group*: London.

Strain, M., Simkins, T. (2008) "Continuity, Change and Educational Reform-Questioning the Legacy of the Education Reform Act 1988", *Educational Management Administration & Leadership,* vol. 36, no. 2, pp. 155-163.

Teddlie, C., Reynolds, D. (2002) *The international handbook of school effectiveness research* (London, RoutledgeFalmer).

Tipple, C. (1998) "Tracking the Phoenix: The fall and rise of the local education authority", *Oxford Review of Education,* vol. 24, no. 1, pp. 35-43.

Thrupp, M., Lupton, R. (2006) 'Taking School Contexts More Seriously: The Social Justice Challenge', British Journal of Educational Studies 54(3): 308–28.

Tomlinson, J. (1992) The case for an LEA or comparable body, in: Education, Putting the Record Straight, various authors (*Network Education Press*).

Tomlinson, S. (2003) "New Labour and Education", *Children and Society*, vol. 17, no. 3, pp. 195-204.

Walford, G. (1990) "The 1988 Education Reform Act for England and Wales: Paths to Privatization", *Educational Policy,* vol. 4, no. 2, pp. 127-144.

Whitty, G. (2008) "Twenty Years of Progress?", *Educational Management Administration & Leadership,* vol. 36, no. 2, pp. 165.

Whitty, G., Power, S. and Halpin, D. (1998) *Devolution and Choice in Education: The School, the State and the Market.* Buckingham: Open University Press.

Whitfield, D. (2006) 'The Marketisation of Teaching' , *The PFI Journal* , 52 , March , 92 – 3.

Wilby, P. (2007) 'Why Education Remains the Priority', *New Statesman,* 14 May.

Wilcox, B., Gray, J. (1996) *Inspecting Schools: Holding Schools to Account and Helping Schools to Improve.* Buckingham: Open University Press.

Young, H. (1989) *One of us* (London, Macmillan).

10 DANICA HINES

Now what can I say about myself? Well I've been teaching for 7 years and have been a form tutor, KS3 coordinator of English and I am currently KS5 coordinator of English.

An Investigation into the Impact of the Local Management of Schools Policy Established in the 1988 Education Reform Act and The Critical Comparison to the 2010 Academy Act.

Abstract

This assignment will consider the impact of the Local Management of Schools policy launched in the 1988 Education Reform Act in comparison to the 2010 Academy Act. The outline of each policy is explored and compared employing a plethora of theoretical perspectives. The impact of Neo-liberalism in education and the establishment and operation of academies are investigated at a time of institutional disengagement from social necessities and an emphasis on economic improvement.

Introduction

This essay critically evaluates the emergence of the Local Management of Schools (LMS) policy launched in the 1988 Education Reform Act. The outline and aim of the policy is investigated where the impacts of cream-skimming, as a result of quasi-markets, are assessed and the LMS policy is compared to the 2010 Academy Act as the effect of both are synonymous (Cave and Wilkinson, 1990; Bhattacharya, 2013).

Findings are subsequently supported by the critical review of the literature where the LMS policy is analysed from a number of theoretical perspectives. The success of the policy is considered from the viewpoint of stakeholders as the disparities between social classes are examined. Next, Neo-liberalism in education is investigated and the impact of privatisation of education, which the LMS policy can be considered to be the first step (McMahon and Bolam, 1990; McGregor, 2009). Money was invested into education with the expectation that the knowledgeable contribute economically (Davies and Bansel, 2007). Critical opinions of the marketisation of education are compared and contrasted.

The essay will then examine the establishment of academies and the government's aim when implementing this scheme. Government support and University and college opposition are explored and the different types of sponsors are investigated (Wrigley, 2009; Curtis, 2009). Similarities between the LMS policy and the 2010 Academy Act are considered (Cave and Wilkinson, 1990). The schools intake is examined and the economical effect on education is scrutinized inspecting the impact on the social purpose of education (Ball, 2007; Wrigley, 2009; Bhattacharya, 2013). Lastly changes to the curriculum and the success of academies are re-examined with the use of evidence and theoretical perspectives (Wrigley, 2009; Bhattacharya, 2013).

Outline and Aim of the Policy in Context.

The 1988 Education Reform Act devolved money and responsibility to schools directly in a bid to empower institutions and give them additional freedom in regards to their budget and day to day management (McMahon and Bolam, 1990). As a result LEAs (Local Education Authorities) would become redundant and consequently schools would gain further autonomy (Hill, 1989; Cave and Wilkinson, 1990). The aim was to give schools direct funding inclusive of teachers salaries which was the most contentious part of the legislation; however the amount of the funding given would be dependent upon the number of school pupils and their ages (Cave and Wilkinson, 1990; Hill, 1989; Edwards, Ezzamel, Robson and Taylor, 1995). The intention was for Head teachers to take responsibility for the general management of the school's operation with the overall objective being to raise standards nationally and subsequently improve economic growth (Whitty and Power, 2008).

In 2008 the labour Prime Minister Gordon Brown stressed in one of his speeches:

> "The challenge this century is a global skills race and that is why we need to push ahead faster with our reforms to extend education opportunities for all."
>
> Whitty and Power, 2008, p5

It can be argued that the government believe a knowledge based economy is essential to global competitiveness (Whitty and Power, 2008), as the more people whom are educated would possibly rely less on government funding. Therefore these individuals would be able to aid the economy to develop and flourish (Peters, 1999). According to data Asia continuously produce highly qualified people, more so than Europe and the USA (Whitty and Power, 2008). The UK government perhaps feel pressurised to remain competitive (Gamble, 1994). In addition, the movement towards reorganisation of public service funding for education is not a new element in public policy as this has been ascertained globally for example: Scandinavia, New Zealand and the United States (Bhattacharya, 2013); therefore the emergence of the local management policy is not innovative. However Ball disagrees with Brown stating 'the influence of policies between nations must be addressed with care' (Ball, 2008 p. 19) instead of rapid reform changes. Policies must be thoroughly researched in order to be successful and any reform must consider the variation of practices, conflict and change in perception (Ball, 2008).

The local management of schools policy had another drawback as the local management of schools led to cream-skimming due to quasi-markets (Gamble, 1994; Whitty and Power, 2008). According to Whitty and Power schools begun to compete and 'seek students who were 'able', 'gifted', 'motivated and committed,' and 'middle class' (Whitty and Power, 2008 p 89) creating a huge disparity between the social classes (Whitty and Power, 2008). Thus, schools debatably started to have an elitist view due to the demands of the league tables (McGregor, 2009; Meyland-Smith and Evans, 2009). Though the aim of the policy was to raise standards and narrow the attainment gap, there had not been any proof at this time that the local management of schools had in fact improved teaching and learning (Levacic, 1998). The initiative was conceivably very similar to the Academy Act of 2010 where schools were given the opportunity to transform into academies (Bhattacharya, 2013; DfES, 2007; West and Bailey, 2013). Improving standards is a government priority; principally improving literacy and numeracy (HMI, 1992). The Leitch Review of skills (2006) and The Moser Report (1999) were a couple of initiatives to try to solve the problem hitherto improvement is yet to be seen.

Critical Review of the Literature

This assignment has considered the proposed aims and will now investigate the positive and negative impact of the policy. The Conservative government decentralised management to a local level for schools under the 1988 Education Reform Act and as a result led to many positive outcomes and negative repercussions affecting stakeholders (Cave and Wilkinson, 1990; Hill 1989). The local management of schools was labelled a 'system of resource allocations' (Levacic, 1995, p.189) where costing could become more efficient and effective due to the schools new found independence. Though, the model was firstly taken from a general model entitled School-based Management (SBM) (Levacic, 1998; Hill, 1989) and later the Coopers and Lybrand Report introduced the term 'Local Management of Schools' (Edwards, Ezzamel, Robson and Taylor, 1995). The main elements of the SBM were to share the decision-making amongst parents, pupils, the community and the head teacher consequently empowering individuals (Levacic, 1998). Secondly, the responsibility for the decisions regarding the curriculum, resources and teaching could also be shared (Levacic, 1998; Hill, 1989). In fact placing head teachers and governing bodies under more pressure for their culpability is to arguably gain better standards as they respond to that pressure (DfE 1992). Hence the introduction of league tables used to inform parents has also enhanced the pressure put upon those in charge (Meyland-Smith and Evans, 2009). Nevertheless Loeb in Bhattacharya argues for the necessity of the league tables as parents/carers can then make an informed decision about where they want to send their child/children (Bhattacharya, 2013). In a bid to achieve reform and improve standards, whilst reducing state intervention, school opposition and parental choice are possible ways to achieve this (Ball, 1993; Bhattacharya, 2013).

In 1994 the Conservative government made a statement about the requirement for the local management of schools stating the purpose of the change in the management of the funds was to enable more cognizant and effective use to be made of the resources accessible for teaching and learning (DfE 2007). In addition, the policy also encompassed social factors of repression, discrimination and poverty (Ball, 2008). Conversely Levacic argues that the Conservative government may not have considered the negative implications and repercussions of the policy as the local management of schools led to the development of dual labour markets resulting in an increase of temporary contracts being given to teachers (Levacic, 1995; HMI, 1992). Debatably the local management of schools may have also contributed to the number of teachers leaving the profession resulting in an unstable labour force in age and experience which is in opposition to the actual purpose of the policy (Wrigley, 2009). Levacic (1995) questions and raises concerns on whether the emphasis of the policy is on cost rather than quality of the workforce as the major stakeholders arguably seem unaffected by the periodic changes (Levacic, 1995; Cave and Wilkinson, 1990). Moreover, the local management of schools policy encourages receptiveness to societal needs as parents are empowered, yet the limitation of the policy impinge on teachers professional needs (Edwards, Ezzamel, Robson and Taylor, 1995).

On the contrary, the local management of schools is notably regarded as a successful policy (Levacic, 1994; Hill, 1989; HMI, 1992). In addition, Ball argues 'good policies will produce fairer outcomes by raising the achievement of all pupils' (Ball, 2008 p.153). According to a study carried out in 1997 ninety percent of Head teachers in 160 schools 'welcomed the responsibility and flexibility of local management schools' (Bullock and Thomas, 1997 p. 336). Nevertheless, the positive reception to the changes may perhaps be due to the annual budget increase schools would receive as part of the reform (Audit Commission, 1989).

Furthermore there have been reports stating that the implementation of the local management of schools has been connected to the improvement of pupils' learning (Levacic, 1998). According to a survey conducted in 1993 47 percent of primary Head teachers and 80 percent of secondary Head teachers agreed that children's education had improved from the local management of schools policy (Levacic, 1998). However, there was a clear correlation with the positive assessment by Head teachers whom had gained an enhancement in their budget as a result of local management schools (Levacic, 1998). Hence, smaller schools that did not receive a substantial increase in their budget were less ardent about the initiative (Levacic, 1998; Bullock and Thomas, 1997). The findings may be of a concern to the government as the purpose of the policy and the actual impact do not seem to correlate (McGregor, 2009).

Viewpoints about the success of the policy differ vastly depending on the role of the person in question as teachers tend to view the policy negatively whereas Head teachers and governors seem to be in favour (Cave and Wilkinson, 1990; McGregor, 2009). Nonetheless the management of the finances were not the only aspects to change from the policy (Levacic, 1998). Arguably, the disparity between the class systems widened with the working class children being left short-staffed and with inadequate resources (Bhattacharya, 2013). The evidence suggests failing schools in general neither close nor improve (Bullock and Thomas, 1994; Levacic, 1995). Though in order to incentivise parents to send their children to a particular school, Head teachers would seemingly readily permanently exclude disruptive pupils (Bhattacharya, 2013). Consequently there was an increase in the number of exclusions which was a clear repercussion of the local management of schools policy (Levacic, 1998). On the other hand some may view this as a positive aspect of the policy because if there are less disruptive children in the classroom the learning of the students cannot be hindered (Levacic, 1998; Bhattacharya, 2013; West and Bailey, 2013). Furthermore another problem and concern in regards to the policy is that as a consequence of local management evidence suggests disadvantaged pupils have gained the least (Levacic, 1998; Maychell, 1994). Possibly as a result of the dual labour markets and the cream-cropping schools partake in order to remain competitive (Cave and Wilkinson, 1990; Levacic, 1998). Considering the aim of the policy was to improve standards in education the evidence would suggest the Conservative government may have lacked the prowess necessary and inadvertently created other problems (Wrigley, 2009). However, the positive impact and outcomes cannot be discredited (West and Bailey, 2013).

Neo-liberalism in Education

This assignment has identified, analysed and investigated the positive and negative impact, concerns and repercussions of the implementation of the local management of schools policy employed in the 1988 Education Act. The assignment will now investigate the reasoning behind the political movement of Neo-liberalism in accordance to the policy which was introduced to advance economic growth (Ball, 2008).

Neo-liberalism was a political group which began approximately during the 1960s with the sole purpose of creating economic growth (Davies and Bansel, 2007). It has materialized in many semblances over the years with the view that to maximise profit and efficiency, trade between nations must be simpler (McGregor, 2009). In order to achieve this privatisation must occur with the removal of various controls for example: tax; regulatory measures, laws, and restrictions on capital flow and assets (Davies and Bansel, 2007). However not everyone agreed as economist John Maynard Keynes' views led to a 'Keynesian' model of development as he suggested rules and regulations are indeed needed in order to provide more equity (Davies and Bansel, 2007).

Moreover, education was almost immediately targeted for the same neoliberal philosophy (Davies and Bansel, 2007). To remain competitive globally the government invested munificent funding into education institutions in the belief that knowledge and edification were important to the country to ensure all members were able to partake and contribute (Davies and Bansel, 2007; Whitty and Power, 2008). Therefore developing people as a national resource is considered fundamental to achieving a competitive international advantage (McGregor, 2009). Similar to the local management of schools policy where it is believed that giving schools autonomy would result in the raising of standards in Education and ultimately benefit the economy with an influx of highly educated and capable individuals whom contribute economically (Maychell, 1994; Whitty and Power, 2008; McGregor, 2009).

There are differing opinions in regards to neo-liberalism in education; Adam Smith was completely against the idea; however Margaret Thatcher, leader of the Conservative government (1979-1997) disagreed (Matinson, 2011). Thatcher arguably felt that the marketisation and privatisation of education would improve standards ensuing in more competition amongst education institutions and parental choice (Hannan, 2011; Matinson, 2011); consequentially resulting in freedom of individualism and the removal of the state in the market place. Likewise the implementation of the local management of schools would reduce the control and influence of the Local Education Authorities (LEAS) and thus creating competition between increasingly diversified types of schools (McMahon and Bolam, 1990; Cave and Wilkinson, 1990). A further impact of the implementation of the local management of schools is the greater focus on school inspection which possibly affects morale amongst teachers working in pressurised conditions (Levacic, 1995) and Head teachers being given more authority over decisions regarding budgeting (Whitty and Power, 2008; McGregor, 2009). Nevertheless the DES (Department for Education) suggests inspection; monitoring and advisory services from the LEA are a benefit to schools which should be maintained if possible (Audit Commission, 1989).

Nonetheless, economic growth may perhaps stem from the possible transformation of education into a product that can be purchased rather than simply an outcome of government investment in education (Davies and Bansel, 2007). Peters concurs stating:

> 'There is nothing distinctive or special about Education or health; they are services and products like any other, to be traded in the market place.'
>
> Peters, 1999 p.2

Arguably Margaret Thatcher was in agreement with Peters' view as the Conservative government ideals' are still prevalent in twenty-first century education establishments (Matinson, 2011). For example the local management of schools (a policy introduced by the Conservative government) is a step towards privatisation as it gives school leaders the autonomy and control to make their own decisions without having to rely on the Local Education Authority (Hill, 1989; McMahon and Bolam, 1990; Cave and Wilkinson, 1990). Education was perhaps viewed as a product or service when the 1988 Education Reform Act was introduced as the privatisation had many facets of neo-liberalism (Davies and Bansel, 2007). The removal of an authoritative figure (LEA) led to competition and opposition between schools all vying to surpass the other (McGregor, 2009).

Furthermore, developing individuals to have the ability to contribute economically to society is practical. However a concern may be that schools focus too much on people being used as resources economically and as a result young people in Education are perhaps being failed by the education institutions (McGregor, 2009). McGregor states:

> 'It is time for schools to resist systematic impulses to make them producers of human capital and claim their role as transformative institutions of human possibility'.

> McGregor, 2009 p. 21

McGregor disagrees with Peters and Margaret Thatcher's views as the success of young people in education is questioned. Ibid to oppose the 'systematic impulses' (McGregor, 2009 p. 21) is to disregard the policies put into place with the aim to solely expand economic growth (McGregor, 2009). McGregor (2009) proclaims education institutions' focus should be on developing young people personally as well as academically. Consequentially at variance with the local management of schools initiative as the purpose of the policy was to give responsibility and independence directly to schools by way of funding (Cave and Wilkinson, 1990; McGregor, 2009). Subsequently with ample financial support standards in education would have been expected to improve (Hill, 1989; Cave and Wilkinson, 1990). Yet McGregor states that it would be more beneficial for young people if the education institutions broaden their aspirations and develop young people in all areas (McGregor, 2009). Indeed success in exams provide stakeholders with useful information, however they are not indicative of the whole picture (Audit

Commission, 1989).

Policies introduced before the 1988 Education Reform Act were generally viewed as having minimal impact on practice (Powers, 1992) as the Act was viewed as a 'ground zero in the history of education' (Ball, 2008 p.18). Yet to achieve improvement and progression the evidence suggests it is wise to compare the effects of the pre and post 1988 policies (Ball, 2008). Only then can the impact of the local management of schools' policy be analysed effectively (Cave and Wilkinson, 1990). On the other hand, policies, whether pre or post 1988, can cause problems for stakeholders as policymakers may perhaps assume any problems encountered will be from a breakdown on the part of teachers or schools (Ball, 2008). Policies are implemented to provide solutions to problems, therefore they can not have fault, which would subsequently lead to teachers and policymakers blaming one another (Ball, 2008). This would be unproductive for all involved (Ball, 2008). Though policies are generally replicated and reworked over time when gauging the full impact it must be considered that it is a process: unbalanced, incomplete, continuous and interactional (Ball, 2007). For that reason, there cannot be an expectation for faultlessness (Ball, 2007).

Academies

This assignment further discusses and investigates the impact of the privatisation of education which stemmed from the local management of schools policy which commenced in the 1988 Education Reform Act. The objective of the policy, otherwise known as the 'new public management' model (Ferlie, Ashburner, Fitzgerald and Pettigrew, 1996) was to tackle societies' educational needs (Chubb and Moe, 1988). Proving to be a difficult task schools were later given the opportunity to become academies, a principle synonymous with the local management of schools ideals and standard (Bhattacharya, 2013).

The Academies Aims

Academies were expected to be the answer to failing schools with the focus on deprivation and narrowing the attainment gap (Wrigley, 2009). The idea initially emerged from charter schools, namely in America, and City Technology Colleges (CTC) launched in 1990 by Tony Blair's Labour government and later transformed under the Conservative-Liberal Democrat coalition government (Bhattacharya, 2013). It became part of the 2010 Academy Act yet the objective remained the same: elevate achievement in under-performing schools in underprivileged areas (Wrigley, 2009; Bhattacharya, 2013). Wrigley (2009) had criticize the policy for being repetitive and outmoded as it is arguably lacking innovation, yet the government were resolute to raise attainment (Bhattacharya, 2013; Wrigley, 2009).

Moreover, the government originally set out to open 200 academies by 2010, yet later amplified the target to 400 without a timeframe (BBC News, 2006). However, they soon found the limitation to this decision as the government became desperate for enough sponsors to replace LEAs (Wrigley, 2009). A lack of sponsors was possibly due to the primary requirement to provide two million pounds in sponsorship, hence when the judgment was removed more sponsors came forward (Curtis, 2009). The academies focal point was on diversity and as the number extended into rustic areas city academies became recognized as academies (Bhattacharya, 2013).

In 2005 the labour government declared their support for Academies in their manifesto (West and Bailey, 2013) yet critics may argue the emergence of academies has led to market-based alternatives to education. The alternatives are inclusive of: grammar, comprehensives, voluntary, religious schools etc which provide additional choice for parents and as a consequence increases competition between schools (Bhattacharya, 2013). Milton Friedman commended strong competition and he argued the quality of education would improve as a result

(Chubb and Moe, 1988). However Ball (2008) and McGregor (2009) disagree as the focus of educating children can be lost in the midst of rivalry and opposition. The ideal is identical to the local management of schools policy as the responsibility of budgeting has led to education institutions vying against one another (Bhattacharya, 2013).

The Autonomy of Academy Sponsors

Although the Academy programme had a plethora of government support there was also an abundance of resistance from schools and colleges (Wrigley, 2009). Renowned universities such as Cambridge and Oxford refused to sponsor the programme; the Universities and Colleges Union (UCU) contested and local campaign groups formed the Anti-Academies Alliance (Wrigley, 2009). The educational institutes debatably did not agree with the government's vision as privatisation is generally viewed to be about control and ownership, therefore these prestige educational institutions did not want to be associated with the programme as it is economical rather than educational (Wrigley, 2009; Ball, 2007).

In addition, funding from educational institutes is minute in comparison to the amount from entrepreneurs (Curtis, 2009). Though according to Ball the wealthy sponsors represent new labours values as the individuals accomplish success even though possibly coming from humble beginnings (Ball, 2007). Thus, these successes should inspire young people (Ball, 2007). On the other hand, critics may disagree as the sources of the sponsorship tend to influence the selection of school specialism (Curtis, 2009). Therefore the choice of school specialism is not reflective of or necessarily beneficial to the local intake, but is made purely to please the schools financer which is in opposition to the principle objective (Curtis, 2009).

The 2010 Academy Act is similar to the local management of schools policy where a strategy is implemented yet there is no uniformity in the distribution (Wrigley,

2009). In fact it can be argued the 2010 Academy Act is a transformation of the Local Management of Schools policy established in the 1988 Reform Act as both initiatives set out to empower parents and ultimately improve attainment in education (Chubb and Moe, 1988; West and Bailey, 2013).

Yet, in academies there are huge differences in the intake and achievement as sponsors have the authority to hire, fire, exclude and admit whomever whether pupil or member of staff (Wrigley, 2009). Even though Ed Balls (Labour party politician) argues there is no requirement for academies to have fair admissions (West and Bailey, 2013) the DfES is of a different opinion declaring the schools admission criteria should be reasonable and unambiguous. As long as schools have adequate capacity for children they should be admitted (DfES, 2007). Additionally critics have highlighted a flaw in the selection procedure as sponsors have the freedom to decide on their own admissions policy (Wrigley, 2009). Consequently the ability to change the intake is remarkable as expensive school uniforms and school necessities such as access to the internet will disadvantage children from deprived areas which is in opposition to the government's objective (Wrigley, 2009). Notably, there have been fewer free school meal (FSM) pupils registered in academies recently. According to an independent body in 2002 there were 42 percent of FSM pupils in academies and in 2008 this percentage had fallen to 35 percent (PwC, 2008). The autonomy given to schools and academies by means of local management or direct sponsorship has not had the desired impact, when put into practice, to narrow the attainment gap and improve standards in education (Wrigley, 2009; Bhattacharya, 2013). Thus the type of children being taught has changed due to the modification of the intake (Wrigley, 2009).

Concerns and Repercussions

The concerns and repercussions of the local management of schools policy and the 2010 Academy Act are synonymous (Cave and Wilkinson, 1990). Education is considered economically since there is a stress on competitiveness and the social purpose of education is being disregarded (Ball, 2008). Wilby concurs affirming academies are political, rather than didactic and enlightening (Wilby, 2009). When a school becomes an academy the sponsor is given ultimate authority and the Education Law, which protects stakeholders (staff, pupils and parents) is eradicated (Wrigley, 2009). The 2006 Education Act presented further changes to the curriculum which coincide with Wilby and Ball's views as 11-13 year olds were entitled to a broad and balanced curriculum whereas 14-16 year olds' curriculum had a stronger focus on English and Maths (Wrigley, 2009). Thus pupils are being prepared for the world of work for economic gain and their social needs are debatably being neglected (Bhattacharya, 2013).

Though Gove (2008) argues academies improve standards in education (West and Bailey, 2013) pupils are not viewed as well-read and skilled outside of Europe (Wrigley, 2009). Furthermore in 2002-2007 there was only a 4% improvement in academies' school results in comparison to the predecessors (Wrigley, 2009). Considering the cost of the school equipment and construction of new buildings the government may have to review the impact and expenditure of academies and possibly examine other avenues (Wrigley, 2009; Bhattacharya, 2013). In addition when successful schools become academies for monetary incentives the original objective is disregarded (Curtis, 2009). Another concern stemmed from the 2010 Academy Act is the sponsors (Wrigley, 2009).

Rich sponsors giving back to the community may inspire children; however some may exploit the poor and accordingly become richer (Wrigley, 2009). Notably poor children still achieve less in academies, yet the government and sponsors arguably do not make failure a focal point (McGregor, 2009; Wrigley, 2009). As a result in September 2012 it was recorded that 2,309 academies were functioning in England (Bhattacharya, 2013). On the other hand it can be argued that the government continue to raise standards for schools as a new measure was ascertained in 2006 for all students to achieve 5 GCSEs including English and Maths (Wrigley, 2009). Consequently the published results will increase competition between schools with the ultimate aim to narrow the attainment gap and advance education standards (Ball, 1993; Levacic, 1998).

Markedly in November 2008 the government bespoke an independent body (Pricewaterhouse Coopers) to assess the success of the academies programme (Wrigley, 2009). Pricewaterhouse Coopers stated the performance of the academies as a representation for school advancement was inconclusive (Wrigley, 2009; Bhattacharya, 2013). Therefore the impact of the local management of schools policy and the 2010 Academy Act cannot be proven as successful initiatives (Levacic, 1998). A concern is the amount spent on the policies as the results do not correlate and a repercussion is arguably the neglect to pupils' social needs (McGregor, 2009).

Conclusion

This essay has critically evaluated the emergence of the Local Management of Schools (LMS) policy launched in the 1988 Education Reform Act. The outline and aim of the policy has been investigated where the impacts of cream-skimming, as a result of quasi-markets, were assessed and the LMS policy was compared to the 2010 Academy Act as the effect of both are synonymous (Cave and Wilkinson, 1990; Bhattacharya, 2013).

Subsequently findings were supported by the critical review of the literature where the LMS policy was analysed from a number of theoretical perspectives. The success of the policy was considered and the results for the performance of academies were inconclusive (Wrigley, 2009). In addition the gain in percentage points acquired by academies in comparison to its predecessor revealed very little impact (Wrigley, 2009). Next, Neo-liberalism in education was investigated and the impact of privatisation of education, which the LMS policy can be considered to be the first step (McMahon and Bolam, 1990; McGregor, 2009). Money was invested into education as knowledge was viewed as a social commodity (Davies and Bansel, 2007) even though social purposes were neglected (Ball, 2008). Critical opinions of the marketisation of education have been compared and contrasted.

Next the essay examined the establishment of academies and the government's aim when implementing this scheme. Government support and University and college opposition were explored and the different types of sponsors investigated (Wrigley, 2009; Curtis, 2009). Similarities between the LMS policy and the 2010 Academy Act were considered (Cave and Wilkinson, 1990). The schools intake was examined and the economical effect on education was scrutinized inspecting the impact on the social purpose of education (Ball, 2007; Wrigley, 2009; Bhattacharya, 2013). Lastly changes to the curriculum and the success of academies were re-examined only to find the government have not achieved their target of narrowing the gap and raising attainment for FSM pupils (Levacic, 1998). Ball (2008) suggests a need for vigorous examination and analysis of policies pre and post the 1988 Reform Act to recognize the weaknesses and acknowledge the possible development necessary to improve standards in education (Wrigley, 2009; Bhattacharya, 2013).

References

Audit Commission. Assuring Quality in Education. The Role of the Local Education Authority Inspectors and Advisers. 1989

Ball, S. 2008. *The Education Debate*, Bristol: The Policy Press.

Ball, S. 1993. *Education Markets, Choice and Social Class: the market as a class strategy in the UK and the USA.* Volume 14, Issue 1

Ball, S. 2007 *Education plc: Understanding Private Sector Participation in Public Sector Education,* London: Routledge.

BBC News. November 30 2006. *Blair wants another 200 academies* November 30, Retrieved January 14, 2013, fromwww.news.bbc.co.uk/1/hi/education/6157435.stm

Bhattacharya, B. 2013. Academy Schools in England. Volume 89, Issue 2.

Bullock and Thomas, 1997. *The Impact of Local Management on Schools*. (Birmingham: National Assocociation of Headteachers and University of Birmingham.

Cave, E and Wilkinson, C. 1990. *Local Management of Schools. Some Practical Issues*. Routledge

Chubb, J. E. and Moe, T. M. 1988. Politics, markets, and the organization of

schools. *American Political Science Review*, 82(4): 1065–1087.

Curtis, A. 2009. *Academies and School Diversity*. British Educational Leadership, Management and Administration Society (BELMAS), Volume 23, issue 3.

Davies, B and Bansel, P. 2007. *Neoliberalism and Education. International Journal of Qualitative Studies in Education.* Issue 3, Volume 20.
Department for Education and Skills. 2007. *School admissions code* London, , England:

Edwards, P, Ezzamel, M, Robson,K and Taylor M. 1995. *The Development of Local Management of Schools' Budgets, Accountability and Educational Impact*. Routledge

Ferlie, E., Ashburner, L., Fitzgerald, L. and Pettigrew, A. 1996. *The new public management in action* Oxford, , England: Oxford University Press.

Gamble, A. 1994. *The Free Economy and the Strong State: The Politics of Thatcherism,* New York: MacMillan.

Hannan, D. 2011. *Margaret Thatcher*. Volume 67. Issue 40.

Hill, D. 1989. *Management in Education: Local Management of Schools*, Industrial Society Press.

HMI, 1992. *The Implementation of Local Management of Schools*. A Report by HM

Inspectorate 1989-92. Department for Education. (London: HMSO)

Levacic, R. 1995. *Local Management of Schools: Analysis and Practice*. Volume 7, Issue 2.

Levacic, R. 1998. *Local Management of Schools in England: Results after Six Years*. Volume 13, Issue 3 Published online 2006.

Matinson, D. 2011. Margaret Thatcher. Volume 140 Issue 5073.

Maychell, 1994. *Counting the Cost: The Impact of Local Management of Schools on School
Pattern of Spending.* (NFER: Slough)

McGregor, G. 2009. *Educating for (Whose) Success? Schooling in an Age of Neo-Liberalism*. Volume 30, Issue 3.

McMahon, A and Bolam, R. 1990. *A Handbook for LEAS*. Second Edition National Development Centre for Educatrional Management and Policy. Paul Chapman Publishing.

Meyland-Smith, D. and Evans, N. 2009. *A guide to school choice reforms* London, , England: Policy Exchange.. Retrieved January 10, 2013.

Peters, M. 1999. *Neoliberalism in the Encyclopedia of Philosophy of Education.* PricewaterhouseCoopers. November 2008. *Academies evaluation: 5th annual

report* November, Annesley, , England: DCSF Publications.

Power, S. 1992. *Researching the Impact of Education Policy: Difficulties and Discontinuities.* Journal of Education Policy. Volume 7, Issue 5.

West, A and Bailey, E. 2013. *The Development of the Academies Programme: Privatising School-Based Education in England 1986-2013*

Whitty, G and Power, S. 2008. *Quasi-Markets and curriculum control: making sense of recent education reform in England and Wales, Educational Administration Quarterly.*

Wilby, P. 2009 *The Real Problem With Academies*. Education Guardian, 10th February

Wrigley, T. 2009. *Academies: Privatising England's Schools*. Publisher Lawrence Wishart. Volume 13

11 ALEXANDER PETROVIC

My name is Alexander Petrovic and my working background is one in Information Communication Technology and its implementation in the workplace. Taking the MA Education course has helped me to better understand the British education system, and helped me specialise in my field so I am able to research in, and contribute to, the emerging field of Cloud Computing in the sphere of British education.

Education Attainment and the Education Reform Act 1988

Abstract:

This review outlines what existing literature has to say about the Education Reform Act 1988 and the introduction of the National Curriculum. Matters of social class, ethnicity and gender parity are identified as issues of policy. Section 1 describes the aims of this Literature Review. The concept of Education Attainment as the policy field is introduced in section 2. Section 3 introduces and contextualises the objectives of the ERA, and challenges the National Curriculum had faced. Section 4 bands together policy issues of social class, ethnicity and gender parity. Section 5 concludes by suggesting that future education policy should focus on formative assessment methods to bridge attainment gaps in social class, ethnicity, and gender. Multiple future research directions arising from this literature review are suggested as part of the conclusion.

Section 1: Introduction

1.1 Literature Review Aims

The aim of this assignment is to produce a comprehensive literature review of reliable and academic research on the relationship between the Education Reform Act 1988 (ERA) and Education Attainment. The review covers the period of 1980 to 2007 and limits its research to academic journals and literature that focus on issues of Education Attainment. After defining education attainment, the review will pursue ERA effectiveness on the following policy issues:

- Education Attainment and whether it has been achieved through the implementation of the National Curriculum and subsequent initiatives
- The gap between high and low attainers across social classes
- The academic results gap between boys and girls
- Educational attainment across all ethnicities

This review will then attempt to compile the main findings of academic research to draw conclusions from the literature, analysing and synthesising their arguments. This review will commence upon this task by drawing from a wide body of literature on these key issues. This review examines some of reasons and theories which experts and researchers have put forward as to both the effective and ineffective implementation of the ERA on tackling these policy issues. It will conclude by mentioning possible future research directions.

Section 2:   What is educational attainment?

While there is no generally acknowledged definition of what education attainment is, Sandars (2012) notes two indicators which may be used to achieve education attainment; firstly the simple communication of educational information to students, and secondly inspiring students to think critically and communicate coherently with the taught information, both requirements in order to solve problems and succeed in given assessments. According to Sandars (2012), there has been a progressive shift in Curriculum delivery from a summative approach that provided large amounts of information to be absorbed by the learner, to a more formative approach that is based on inspiring individual and group activity and thought in the classroom. Stanton in Burke (1989) offers a differing and historical opinion, expressing concern that defining education standards in a narrow way through maintaining standardised education assessments may have detrimental effects on critical thinking, problem solving and later life skills in the workplace. Stanton in Burke (ibid.) further hypothesises that the ERA would lead to a more systematic approach overly focussed on information delivery and assessments. This historical analysis could be explained by the then widespread concern of the implementation of a nationwide curriculum which was quite revolutionary. Therefore one could argue that the ERA has not impacted as negatively on the field of education attainment as was initially thought.

Section 3: **Background to the Education Reform Act 1988**

3.1 The Education Reform Act 1988

Before the introduction of the ERA, educational attainment was largely defined through college and university entry requirements (McNeil, 2008). However, causes for concern over a lack of curriculum existed as early as 1980. This was spurred on in part by low pass rates; according to the House of Educational Statistics (2012), in 1953-54 the pass rate of five or more GCE O levels at schools in England and Wales was only 10.7%. According to the same study, 5.5% of the relevant age group had managed to pass one or more GCE A level. Moreover, participation in education prior to the ERA was remarkably low; in 1950 30% of 15 year olds, 14% of 16 year olds and 7% of 17 year olds were in full-time education in England and Wales (2012: ibid). Academics such as Coleman (1968) conveyed one reason for this; the intellectual rigour of the 11-Plus examination was quite unfair to learners as the results of the examinations would shape the majority of their formative education by being used as the basis for whether they would attend prestigious grammar schools.

To combat this trend, a report by Her Majesty's Inspectorate (HMI, 1980) entitled 'A View of a Curriculum' had suggested that a curriculum would need to be a government priority to increase education attainment through standardised assessments. A 1985 Government White Paper (DES, 1985) supported these claims, stating that regular assessments on mathematics, science, and geography would provide a positive boost to learner academic attainment. Not long after these recommendations, the ERA was introduced, signalling a nationwide curriculum for primary and secondary state schools in England, Wales and Northern Ireland. School assessments were separated into 'Key Stages' at the ages of 7, 11, and 14 years, giving both parents and teachers an insight into learner academic progress at each school. Kenneth Baker, the then Secretary of State for Education under Margaret Thatcher's Conservative Government had in 1988 pledged to tackle issues surrounding education attainment; namely improving educational attainment for all learners through a wider and compulsory taught subject curriculum.

3.2 Objectives of the Education Reform Act 1988

The general objectives of the Education Reform Act 1988 were twofold; improving the educational attainment across the British Education system, and introducing summative assessments at staged levels of a learner's education. Harlen (1992 p. 365) defines summative assessments as placing emphasis on traditional examination results as a marker for educational attainment, and argues that this assessment type was the primary foundation for the ERA's National Curriculum Assessments (NCA). Essentially, Harlen defines the goal of summative assessment as *measuring student learning* at the end of an academic year by comparing their results against the national average.

The first and second objectives were met through the introduction of NCA. Certainly, the ERA had succeeded in increasing education attainment in the British Education system; in 2010/11 79.6% of pupils in their last year of compulsory education in the UK achieved 5 or more GCSE grades A*-C or equivalent (House of Educational Statistics, 2012). This indicates a sharp rise in education attainment as a direct result of the ERA's initiatives. Additionally, at the end of 2010 88% of 16 year olds and 76% of 17 year olds in England were in full-time education (ibid). The objectives of the Education Reform Act had for the most part, achieved wider participation and attainment. However, academics such as Donald (1992) and Gillborn (1997) agree that these statistics do not accurately depict educational attainment across the British Education system. Donald argues that these statistics, while impressive, do not hide the attempted diminishing of the multicultural aspect of education. Gillborn shares a similar viewpoint, stating that the ERA masks issues with social class, social class, and ethnicity. These three policy issues in particular will be addressed further in the coming sections.

3.3 Challenges of the Education Reform Act 1988

The introduction of the Education Reform Act did not come without its challenges; its fiercest opponents were among those of the political Left of government, alongside non-Christian educational sociologists, who had expressed concern over the religious affiliation of those Black and Ethnic Minority (BME) learners who would feel left out of the Christian-centric aspect of the ERA. This is reflected through the research of David Miliband (2000), the then Head of Labour Policy, who notes that despite the ERA's ambition, '75 percent of 16 year olds will not be suitable for further academic education' in 2000 (p. 23), which would have an uninspiring impact on younger age groups. Miliband argues that the ERA had failed to address issues on social class, BME learners and gender parity (ibid). Non-Christian educational sociologists like Mabud (2006) similarly argued that a lack of provision towards Muslim students had 'negative effects on both Muslim parents and pupils in State schools' (p. 76), driving down educational attainment for Muslim groups. In both cases, it can be argued that the ERA had overlooked educational attainment across all groups. This could be explained by the lack of provisions the ERA has towards these groups, and the overtly summative nature of the implemented National Curriculum.

Section 4:   Policy Analysis

4.1 Social Class

One of the major issues surrounding the ERA's implementation was the success of nationwide educational attainment across all social classes. The 11 plus examination introduced by the Education Act 1944 (Butler Act) was seen by experts such as Jones (2003) as unfairly distinguishing between children's abilities at a young age. Jones (2003) argued that children from significantly wealthier economic circumstances were more likely to enter grammar schools than those of working class as a result of the 1944 Education Act. She determines that this is one of the main reasons why working class children were more commonly categorised as low-attainers. Alison Ekins in her research 'Understanding and Tackling Underachievement' (2010) argues similarly to Jones, concluding that the often disadvantaged economic conditions typical of working class backgrounds detriment the educational attainment of these learners. Gazeley and Dunne in Ekins (2010) also view social class as the greatest indicator of educational attainment and establish a causal link between underachievement and social disadvantage, stating that 'deficit views of working class children and their parents are deeply ingrained in the British Education system' (p. 253). Alison Ekins (2010) adds to this by arguing that the personal, social and economic circumstances greatly influence a child's level of motivation to achieve and the child's ability to learn and improve their literacy skills, whilst identifying a need to 'examine existing systems... so as not to perpetuate existing stereotyped notions of low attainment for those from socially disadvantaged backgrounds' (p. 263). What Ekins is effectively arguing for is greater formative education and assessment so as to reduce the education attainment gap between low-attainers of disadvantaged economic circumstances and high-attainers.

Furlong (2002) however, provides a different and historical analysis for this view. Furlong argues that children from working-class backgrounds are heavily influenced by their parents' life choices which in turn influences their educational involvement and choice. He argues that they place less emphasis on formal education as a means to personal achievement as they see 'less worth in continuing school beyond leaving age as their parents did' (p. 122) He concluded that this was one of the main reasons why working class children historically underperformed in the 11 plus examination, and were not frequent candidates for grammar-school education unlike their middle-class peers (ibid.). Additionally, children of working class background were found to lack vital middle-class values which had prohibited them from becoming high-attainers (ibid.). However, Galor (2005) disagrees with this point, arguing that wider curricular public education for the masses would 'trigger the demise of the existing class structure' (p. 85).' Galor suggests that the ERA has in fact bridged the gap between social classes; a compulsory nationwide curriculum offering equal educational allows working-class children to adopt middle-class values and eventually climb the social class ladder. Whilst it is true that children of all backgrounds tend to be influenced by their parents and kin, it must also be noted that a wide compulsory education at least on paper offers these learners the same opportunity for success.

In 2008, a report entitled Ending Child Poverty: Everybody's Business (HM Treasury, 2008) was published, emphasising the association between poverty and educational attainment. The report stated that primary social experience can determine the later life chances of a pupil. Studies done within this report show those children who scored highly on tests at the age of 22 months from low socio-economic backgrounds were overtaken by children with lower scores from higher socio-economic backgrounds by the time they get to primary school. One explanation for this is that low-income families are less likely to receive the essential access to the resources necessary for educational success (Bailey, 1978). Furthermore, the report argues that these differences persisted even until GCSE level where 35.5% of children eligible for free school meals are able to attain five or more good GCSEs whilst 62.8% of the other children are able to achieve five or more good GCSEs (ibid.).

Whilst it is evident that there is a relationship between educational attainment and the socio-economic background of a pupil, it is imperative to remember that social class is but one of various factors that can affect the educational attainment of a pupil As the next sections of this review will highlight, gender and ethnicity play important roles.

4.2 Gender Disparity

Gender parity in the British Education system is of utmost concern to experts and researchers in the field of education, primarily as it is quite a similar issue to low socio-economic disadvantage. The proportion of pupils achieving five or more good grades has increased in each year since the introduction of the GCSE and reached exceeded 80% 2011/12 (House of Educational Statistics 2012 p.11). Girls' performance on this indicator was seven percentage points higher than boys in the same year and the gap has closed somewhat over the past 10-15 years (ibid.). Female enrolment in pre-school, primary and secondary education was between approximately 49 and 52 percent of total enrolments in 2001 (DfES, 2002: 26). The introduction of the National Curriculum can therefore be seen to have reinforced greater gender parity. Educational sociologist Sharpe (1994) corroborates this with her own qualitative research, undertaken through a sample of fifty working-class secondary schoolgirls in London in 1976 and another equal sample in 1994. She found that their primary focus had changed from relationships to career over the 18 year period; demonstrating a clear increase in career determinations throughout this research period. Skelton (2001) takes the view that educational success from summative assessments taken over multiple stages benefits both genders. Skelton postulates that regular assessments increase the female focus towards education. The problem with Skelton's argument is that it does not take into account the pressures of regular assessment, and in some learners this could be a demotivating factor in their education attainment.

However, Arnot (1999) disagrees with Sue Sharpe's qualitative research conclusions, arguing that it is difficult to prove a connection between the accomplishment of gender parity in education and the ERA, even if these emerge simultaneously. In other words, Arnot rejects a positive correlation between policy introduction and change in gender parity. However, it is quite likely the ERA had some effect on improving gender parity, as according to the Equal Opportunities Commission in 1998 there had existed wider gender differences in the proportion of males and females studying particular subjects prior to the ERA (EOC: Gender and Differential Achievement in Education). The ERA could essentially be argued to have reinforced gender parity by ensuring a level playing field, in that through a wide compulsory curriculum males are forced to take subjects traditionally taken by females and vice-versa.

4.2.1 The Perceived Feminisation of School Environments

Educational sociologist Theo Cox (2002) expands upon the idea of gender disparity by arguing that the ERA did little to help existing issues that had inhibited gender parity in the field of educational attainment. Cox (2002, p.39) argues that boys are at a disadvantage in the early stages of education due to increasingly feminised school environments which fosters female accomplishment (ibid). Cox argues that literacy become heavily implicated as a result of the ERA. In other words, Cox argues that the wide compulsory curriculum can cause male learners to form uncooperative attitudes towards the English subject which damages their educational attainment through uncooperative attitudes towards certain 'feminine' subjects (p. 40). Shaw (1995) mirrors Cox's argument, stating that the knowledge associated with literacy and the subject of English in particular can be regarded by both genders as feminine. Shaw (1995) consequently argues that boys will be at an educational shortcoming because 'reading and writing have traditionally been viewed as 'feminine and passive by both genders' (p. 74). Shaw argues that because the ERA's emphasis on a wider compulsory curriculum had made it compulsory for boys to study modern languages and for girls to study mathematics, science and technology, boys had found it hard to adapt to typically masculine identity (p.86), reducing their motivation for learning and negatively affecting their education attainment. Moreover, it could be argued that the ERA had reinforced gender parity; summative assessments could cause problems for boys in school environments where masculinity is traditionally associated with success and dominance. However, other commentators such as Skelton (2001: p. 116) believe that schools have retained their masculinity through rigorous emphasis on testing and assessment as introduced by the ERA. Skelton addresses this issue by noting that the increasing use of incentives in the British Education system to hire male teachers in a predominantly female environment after the implementation of the National Curriculum can help to stem and reverse declining male educational achievement through a more effective formative experience. Male learners tend to identify more with male classroom teachers (p. 118). The literature seems to suggest that steps should be taken to ensure provisions are made to safeguard both genders to keep gender equality in educational attainment consistent.

4.3 Ethnicity

Whilst the ERA was successful in introducing a wide-ranging curriculum to the British Education system, controversy remained over the 'Christian-centred' ethos of the ERA which had alienated the newer settlers and non-religious families in Britain (Gilborn, 1989). Gilborn purports that Asian and Black communities in particular were left out of the ERA's provision for fairness and equality. (p. 484) He concludes that the normalising of the Christian ethos in British state schools has privileged white interests above other learners (p. 486). This could in turn have negative consequences for educational attainment, as Black and Minority Ethnic (BME) children could disconnect to the values of their school due to not sharing the same religion and thus values of their school. This mirrors Sugarman's (1973) earlier mentioned research that a child was more likely to perform well in school if they had felt a closer connection to the values of their school. However, Troyna (1998) argues that the mere existence of a national curriculum serves to 'discourage overt instances of discrimination and to facilitate access for all pupils' (p. 403). One could argue from these expert opinions that the ERA has essentially reformed education attainment superficially; encouraging access for all regardless of ethnicity, but reducing attainment for BME students and disengaging them from their schools through the Christian-centred ethos of the ERA which lacks complete and comprehensive inclusivity. Gillborn (1989) further notes that the white British student population enjoyed consistent yearly improvement since the inception of the ERA in comparison to Black and Ethnic Minority students. In fact, he notes, the proportion of whites attaining the 'benchmark' level (at least five higher grade passes) rises from 30% in 1989 to 55% in 2004 (Gillborn 1989: DfES, 2005, Table A). Gillborn argues that differences between white British and BME students seems to have amplified with the burden of performance-oriented schooling reinforced by the ERA, and social class differences in educational achievement are being intensified. Given these figures it is quite possible to argue that the ERA reforms have inadvertently discriminated against Black and Ethnic Minority students in practice. Broadfoot (1992) in her review entitled 'Policy Issues in National Assessment' agrees with Gillborn's position, stating that it is when assessments become the central factor in summative education that education quality, and thereby attainment, is compromised. Broadfoot (1992) found that when standards are set beyond the reach of learners, the label of failure can depress learner motivation. However, Scott (2001) partially disagrees with Broadfoot's argument, stating that a combination of both formative and summative assessments do more to help BME than white British respectively by improving classroom interaction and promoting inclusive classroom behaviour.

4.3.1 The Hidden Curriculum

Myles (2004) describes the hidden curriculum as "the set of rules or guidelines that are often not directly taught but are assumed to be known" (p 6.). According to Myles (2004) schools and their communities have their own hidden curriculum which is essentially the "unwritten culture of the school" (p 12). Gaine and George (1998) conclude that the hidden curriculum is built on traditionally Christian values that put learners from ethnic minority backgrounds at a disadvantage as they lack these Christian values which are necessary to enable them to conform to the school's hidden curriculum. As a result of this, learners from ethnic minority backgrounds might struggle to follow to the hidden curriculum and this may be the cause of their lack of educational attainment (p. 66).

4.4 Summative and Formative Assessments

Academics and education experts for the most part agree that the introduction of a standardised curriculum can greatly improve the quality of education for both learners and teachers alike. According to Lawn, the idea of wide-reaching compulsory education is context-based and defined by the governments in power (1990: p. 64) Lawn argues that each new policy addresses its own definition of education quality; and points to the passing of these policies to legitimise and solidify these definitions of quality of education. Lawn identifies that most of these education assessment policies introduce novel summative assessments, leaving formative assessments as merely an option in the classroom (ibid). This view is echoed by American education sociologists Yager and McCormack, (1989, p. 46), who commenced qualitative research in the form of a questionnaire to young science students which had shown a significant gap between what is imparted in school education and the information students essentially absorb. Yager additionally noted that formative modes of education, in other words, what students really learn, is more closely associated to their direct personal experiences in the real world and not like the interpretations and understanding advanced in typical schooling (ibid.). Taras (2011) takes the opinion that formative assessment is in fact summative assessment plus feedback which is used by the learner (p. 468). It can be argued that the contribution of formative education assessments to the field of education attainment is as significant as the summative. In other words, educational attainment is at its highest when policies of formative and summative are introduced simultaneously.

4.5 Education Reform Act and Home Learning Experiences

Many experts and researchers have put across theories as to the overall importance of the National Curriculum on educational attainment. One recent and prominent theory is that Home Learning Experiences (HLE) is the primary defining factor of a learner's education attainment. Brown (2006) postulates the British

Education system is entering a 'third wave' of socio-historical development, characterised by mass-schooling and the reduction of the social classes in education. Parents were viewed as greater decision-makers in not only the choice of school for their children, but in their children's educational attainment. (p. 81). The research of Blatchford et al. (2003) corroborates this view; undertaking research to determine the success of Effective Pre-School, Primary and Secondary Education (EPPSE) learners. The ongoing research of 3000+ participants had utilised quantitative trajectory analysis alongside qualitative questions asked to the sample when they had reached the age of 16. The main focus for EPPSE has been the extent to which pre-school, compulsory education and children's HLE could reduce inequality. Blatchford (2003) finds that children who 'succeed against the odds' manage to adapt very well to educational processes, and that it was HLE which was the primary causation factor. Moreover, Blatchford notes that social class of participants was far less important than HLE, concluding that in the homes of children surpassing their plotted trajectory pathways, HLE practices were of utmost importance (p.8) These parents 'engaged their young children in learning processes, for instance by reading with them, providing them with educational games and materials, talking with them about school and learning or and regular extracurricular activities' (p. 10). The most successful HLE continued this involvement throughout the child's learning life-course (ibid.). One reason for the reduced influence of the ERA in comparison to HLE on Educational Attainment could be that parents spend more time with their children, particularly on the weekend where they are able to communicate their own 'formative' education which has been argued by academics and experts to be a more effective form of education than summative assessments.

4.5.1   *Social Class and Home Learning Experiences*

Kyriacou (1997) weighs in to this HLE debate by suggesting that it is possible for working class-homes to possess the ideal HLE characteristics that may even be absent in middle-class homes. In other words, working class families that possess the ideal HLE through supportive parents and a supportive educational infrastructure promoting educational attainment stand a real chance at improved educational attainment (p.64). Kyriacou addresses the ideal HLE as possessing the culture and values necessary for educational success such as parental reassurance, high ambitions, respectable accommodation and the delivery by the parents of all the resources necessary for educational achievement (p.63). Kyriacou (1997) further argues that although social class may affect educational attainment, there are a number of factors which can influence a pupil's educational attainment including enthusiasm and aptitude for education, irrespective of the quality of educational infrastructure. Kyriacou demonstrates that a well delivered HLE simultaneously addresses the policy issues of gender, social class and ethnicity and notes a positive correlation between addressing these issues and progressive education attainment. Kyriacou concludes by determining that social class, ethnicity and gender are not as important as the educational infrastructure foundation of their HLE experience (ibid). Brown's (2006) conclusion that the social class system in education is decreasing is in disagreement with Blatchford's qualitative and quantitative (2003) research. Kyriacou intermediates both arguments by concluding that social class, ethnicity and gender still very much hold disparity in education attainment, formative education and the HLE experience hold more importance.

4.6 Government initiatives after the ERA

It can be argued that policy and government initiatives launched since the ERA have had significant HLE and formative assessment content. This serves as a reminder that HLE is a relatively novel concept with considerable growing importance in learner educational attainment (Avis, 2007 p. 264). One example of an HLE-influenced policy is the 'Sure Start' campaign (Avis, ibid). Sure Start was initiated in an attempt by the New Labour government to improve the educational attainment of children from disadvantaged backgrounds. The initiative launched with the purpose of giving learners the best start in life through health and family support, and early years childcare development (Glass, 1999). Approximately 250 Sure Start Local Programmes (SSLPs) were launched, reaching up to 150,000 children in areas of deprivation. Sure Start local programmes were spearheaded in part by local parents, ensuring local participation. Avis (2007) suggests that one of the key and most distinguishing features of Sure Start was a commitment to community consultation involving local parents in organising and shaping new services (p. 86). Avis concludes that recent policies such as Sure Start are shifting focus toward incentivising HLE and parent involvement in education (p. 88.). In other words, successive governments are recognising the boost to educational attainment that formative education and HLE offered through their policies. In 2004, New Labour had endeavoured to diminish social disparity in the British education system through the introduction of Every Child Matters scheme. This too was seen as a scheme to boost HLE, which would in turn improve educational attainment. One of the key purposes of this policy was to eliminate working-class poverty, which would thus escalate the HLE through a safer infrastructure more suited towards education (Simon, 2008 p. 64). The scheme also deliberated concept of 'socio-economic groups' in relation to issues such as material deprivation and the ways in which it affects educational attainment. The idea behind the Every Child Matters policy was to tackle long-term deprivation through the reframing of the association between the child's achievement and schooling. The policy made the supposition that the family of the pupil should be supported so to enhance 'family learning'. In order to support the pupil, the policy presents a number of facilities such as after school clubs, mealtime clubs, childcare contribution and healthcare and social care services on the school premises. The objective of these services was to offer an 'enabling hand' which would work to benefit the families that were in need of assistance or who were found to be wanting. It could be argued that this 'enabling hand' encouraged parents to provide home learning experiences for their children, which would in turn boost education attainment.

Section 5: Conclusion

5.1 What Does The Literature Reveal?

The National Curriculum Assessments are primarily seen by theorists such as Harlen (1992) as overtly summative in nature. This literature review had found that many theorists commenting on the issue of social class, gender parity and ethnicity, had expressed interest in formative education policy. Subsequent academic research has also proven that HLE is not entirely dissimilar to formative education of which nature theorists such as Avis (2007) have suggested will be the focus of future policy. This is corroborated through subsequent policy implementation after the ERA, in particular Sure Start, which had emphasis on HLE and formative education. On issues relating to social class, theorists such as Kyriacou suggest that it is possible for working class-homes to possess the ideal HLE characteristics that may even be absent in middle-class homes. The consensus of literature in this review is that educational institutions should undertake activities which cover a wide range of cultural and educative interests so to ensure that the needs of the working class pupils and minority ethnic groups are met.

5.2 Future Research Directions

The scope of this literature review allows for multiple research directions. One direction could possibly focus on formative-led policy changes and their effect on social class, ethnicity and gender education attainment, and compare their outcomes to summative approaches of the National Curriculum. In particular, it would be of interest to determine the extent to which formative and HLE-focussed research in the vein of Blatchford's (2003) qualitative and quantitative data comes to dominate future policy initiatives. Comparative research towards Finland and their unique education model, which possesses formative assessments as a large part of its education system, is another potential research direction.

REFERENCES:

Arnot, M., David, M. and Weiner, G (l996) *Educational Reforms and Gender Equality in Schools,* Manchester, Equal Opportunities Commission, Research Discussion Series No. 17.

Arora, D. (2005 p. 38) *Race and Ethnicity in Education.* London: Ashgate Publishing.

Avis M, Leighton P, and Schneider, J. (2007) *Supporting Children and Families: Lessons from Sure Start for Evidence-Based Practice in Health, Social Care and Education.* Jessica Kingsley Publishers

Bailey, J. (1979) *Implicit Moral Education in Secondary Schools.* Journal of Moral Education Volume 8, Issue 1, 1978.

Blatchford-Siraj I, Mayo A, Melhuish E, Taggart B, Sammons P, Sylva K (2010) *Performing against the odds: developmental trajectories of children in the EPPSE 3-16 Study.* DfE 2010

Blouin RA, Riffee WH, Robinson ET, et al. *Roles of innovation in education delivery.* American Journal of Pharmaceutical Education. 2009;73(8):Article 154.

Bolton, P. (2012 p. 4) *Social and General Statistics.* Education: Historical statistics SN/SG/4252.

Broadfoot, P. (1993: p. 2) *Policy Issues in National Assessment.* Multilingual Matters, 1993 Education.

Brown, P. (1990 p.66) *The 'Third Wave': education and the ideology of parentocracy.* British Journal of Sociology of Education Volume 11, Issue 1 Page 65-86.

Brundrett, M, Bottery, M, Silcock, P, Webb, R, Burton, N, Duncan, D, Zhang, (2013:

p. 294) *Education 3-13.* London: Open University Press.

Burke, J. (1989: p. 6) *Competency Based Education and Training.* Routledge, 30 Sep 1989.

Coleman, S. (1968 p.21), *Equity & Excellence in Education.* Vol 6, Issue 5, 19:28

Cox, T. (2002) *Combating Educational Disadvantage: Meeting the Needs of Vulnerable Children.* Routledge Publishing.

David, T. (1999: p.21) *Young Children Learning.* London: SAGE Publishing.

Department of Education and Science (1985) *Better Schools - A Summary.* London: Her Majesty's Stationery Office 1985.

Department for Education and Skills (2005) *Youth cohort study: the activities and experiences of 16-year-olds: England and Wales* (London, DfES).

Donald J, Rattansi, A. (1972 p. 41) *Race, Culture and Difference.* SAGE, 21 Apr 1992.

Ekins, A. (2010 p.250-253) *Understanding and Tackling Underachievement: Whole-school Strategies to Meet the Needs of Vulnerable Children in Primary Schools.* Optimus Education Publishing.

Equal Opportunities Commission (EOC) (1998) *Gender and Differential Achievement in Education and Training: a Research Review.*

Furlong, J and Phillip, R. (2002 p.233) *Education, Reform and the State: Twenty Five Years of Politics, Policy and Practice.* Psychology Press Publishing.

Gaine C, George R. (1998) *Gender, 'Race' and Class in Schooling: A New Introduction.* Routledge Publishing.

Galor, O and Moav, O. (2005) *Das Human-Kapital: A Theory of the Demise of the Class Structure: Review of Economic Studies* (2006) 73 (1): 85-117.

Gillborn. D (1997 p.376) *Ethnicity and educational performance in the United Kingdom: Racism, ethnicity, and variability in achievement.* Anthropology & Education Quarterly, 1997.

Gillborn, D (2005) *Education policy as an act of white supremacy: whiteness, critical race theory and education reform*, Journal of Education Policy, 20:4, 485-505.

Glass N (1999) *Sure Start: The Development of an Early Intervention Programme for Young Children in the United Kingdom.* Children & Society vol 13 pp 257-264

Her Majesty's Inspectorate Series: Matters for Discussion No. 11 (1980) *A View of the Curriculum.* London: Her Majesty's Stationery Office 1980.

Her Majesty's Treasury: Ending Child Poverty: Everybody's Business (2008)

Jones M, Lowe, R. (2002: p.53) *From Beveridge to Blair: The First Fifty Years of Britain's Welfare State.* Manchester University Press.

Kyriacou, C. *(1997) Effective teaching in schools: theory and practice.* Nelson Thornes Publishing.

Lawn, M and Grace, R. (1989) *Teacher Supply and Teacher Quality: Issues for the 1990s.* London: Multilingual Matters Publishing.

Lovat T, Clement N and Toomey R. (2010) *International Research Handbook on Values Education and Student Wellbeing.* Springer, 5 Aug 2010.

Mabud, S. (1992 p. 74) *A Muslim Response to the Education Reform Act 1988.* British Journal of Religious Education Volume 14, Issue 2, 74:98.

McNeil, J D. (2008 p. 263) *Contemporary Curriculum: In Thought and Action: Seventh Edition.* John Wiley & Sons Publishing.

Miliband, D. (1991: p. 23) *Markets, Politics and Education: Beyond the Education Reform Act.* Institute for Public Policy Research.

Myles, B, Trautman, M and Schelvan, R. (2004) *The Hidden Curriculum: Practical Solutions for Understanding Unstated Rules in Social Situations.*

Sandars, J 2012, 'Technology and the delivery of the curriculum of the future: Opportunities and challenges', Medical Teacher, 34, 7, pp. 534-538.

Scott, D. (2001 p. 2) *Curriculum and Assessment.* London: Greenwood Publishing Group.

Sharpe, S. (1994 p. 117) *Just Like a Girl: How Girls Learn to be Women - From the Seventies to the Nineties.* Penguin Books Ltd; 2nd revised edition.

Shaw, J. (1995 p.24-25) *Education, Gender, and Society.* Taylor & Francis, 3 Nov 1995.

Silvernail, D. (1996) *The Impact of England's National Curriculum and Assessment Reformers.* Educational Policy 1996 10: 46.

Simon, C and Ward, S. (2010) *Does Every Child Matter? Understanding New Labour's Social Reforms.* Routledge Publishing.

Skelton, C. (2001 p. 5) *Schooling the Boys: Masculinities and Primary Education.* Open University Press. 1:199.

Strain, M and Simkins, T. (2008) *Continuity, Change, and Educational Reform; Questioning the Legacy of the Education Reform Act 1988.* Educational Management Administration & Leadership 2008 36: 155.

Taras, M. (2005) *Assessment – Summative and Formative – Some Theoretical Reflections.* Volume 53, Issue 4, pages 466–478.

Troyna, B. *Reform or deform? The 1988 education reform act and racial equality in Britain.* Journal of Ethnic and Migration Studies (Impact Factor: 1.03). 04/1990; 16:403-416.

UNESCO International Bureau of Education; DfES, 2002: 26.

Wynne, H. (1997) *Assessment in Education: Principles, Policy & Practice* Volume 4, Issue 3, 1997 365:379.

Yager, R and McCormack, A. (1989) *Assessing teaching/learning successes in multiple domains of science and science education.* Volume 73, Issue 1, pages 45–58, January 1989.

12 MOHD SYAFIQ AIMAN MAT NOOR

Bio data

Mohd Syafiq Aiman Mat Noor taught Science in Malaysia primary schools before continuing his postgraduate level in Brunel University. His focus of interest is pedagogy in the teaching and learning of science at improving student understanding of the nature of scientific inquiry. He is very active in action research and believes that every teacher must expert in that research methodology to improve pedagogy in the classroom. His previous research is 'Improving the Quality of Pupils Response in Science Inquiry Teaching: A Participatory Action Research' and has been presented in the 6th World Conference of Education Sciences. Currently, he is doing collaborative action research to developing scientific inquiry teaching in Malaysia rural schools.

Scientific Enquiry and its Place in the National Curriculum

Abstract

This study examines scientific enquiry and encompass the statutory orders of the National Curriculum, which embraces quite different model during the decades of the twentieth century. It traces the historical moves behind the curriculum and reviews some of the reasons for this change. A particular focus is the impact of good practice and effective pedagogy, and also the initial impact of this scientific enquiry on student achievement, and attitudes towards scientific enquiry for their motivation and learning. The main purpose of this study is to examine how changes to a radically altered curriculum – particularly how scientific enquiry – have been translated into practices in schools, as seen through the statutory orders of the National Curriculum.

Keywords; scientific enquiry, National Curriculum.

Introduction

"It is, in fact, nothing short of a miracle that the modern methods of instruction have not yet entirely strangled the holy curiosity of inquiry; for this delicate little plant, aside from stimulation, stands mainly in need of freedom. Without this it goes to wrack and ruin without fail."
- Albert Einstein

This well-known adages signifies the value of engaging the learner in a task as a more meaningful way to learn. Philosophers as early as Spinoza in the 17th century purported that knowledge is found in the manipulation of ideas rather than the transmission of facts (Rachel, 2009). Recent discoveries in psychology have led to many new and renewed theories of learning. Science inquiry based curriculum and teaching techniques have emerged as a combination of several theories such as, 'constructivism', 'Blooms taxonomy of learning', 'multiple intelligences', 'whole-language' and 'accelerated learning' (Wilfred, 2003).

The importance of scientific enquiry is widely accepted and it is acknowledged that good quality scientific enquiry promotes the engagement and interest of students as well as developing a range of skills, science knowledge and conceptual understanding (SCORE, 2008). An understanding of the various aspects of 'scientific enquiry' has been a component of the National Curriculum for science since its launch in 1989 (SCORE, 2012). The content of this area of work and its place in the curriculum have, however, changed over the years.

The aim of this study is to analyse to one of the most dramatic changes to the science curriculum since the National Curriculum was introduced in England and Wales in 1989: that of scientific enquiry. It traces the historical moves behind the curriculum; reviews some of reasons for this change, and discuses it from various perspectives. In particular, this study will critically review the impact of good practice and effective pedagogy, and also the initial impact of this scientific enquiry on student achievement, attitudes towards scientific enquiry for their motivation and learning.

Chronological of Policy

The first National Curriculum was introduced in England in 1989 (DES/WO, 1989) and several revisions between 1989 and 2004 led to four main attainment targets that were essentially scientific enquiry, biological, chemical and physical processes (Rob, Charles and Anna, 2010). Science is to remain a core subject in the National Curriculum, and will remain part of the wider school curriculum (SCORE, 2012). Thus, school science curricula attempt to serve a dual purpose. first, science theories are presented for students to assimilate, and second a 'scientific attitude' is encouraged by teaching students how to think and act like professional scientists particularly in practical work (Michael, 2010).

Traditionally, a large part of the science curriculum has focused on the transmission of 'facts', which has typically occupied one-half to two-thirds of teaching time (Beatty and Woolnough, 1982). The remainder of curriculum time is spent doing 'experiments' (Michael, 2010). Rationales for the inclusion of practical lessons within the curriculum include the belief that the learning of science concepts is enhanced if students are given opportunity to do something hands-on (Millar, 1991). As a matter of fact, revisions to the National Curriculum have sought to broaden the range of scientific investigations carried out in science lessons (Justin, 2008).

However, views about the role processes in science education have been contested: some science educators have argued that practical work might help students to understand how scientists works, while others have argued that a process-based approach was likely to lead to better understanding of science concepts (Donnelly *et al.*, 1996). In addition, Critics of the impact of the National Curriculum in science pointed out that teachers were adopting a narrow range of teaching strategies when it came to doing investigations (Donnelly *et al.*, 1996).

In spite of this, *Beyond 2000* recommended that young people need an understanding of how scientific inquiry is conducted – to help then appreciate the reasoning which underpins scientific knowledge claims, so that they are better able to appreciate both the strength and the limitations of such claims, in a range of situations and contexts (Millar and Osborne, 1998). They also suggested an argument that an understanding of the methods of scientific inquiry is practically useful in everyday contexts has been over-emphasised. For most purposes a systematic, common sense approach will suffice.

Science enquiry finds specific support in the various national curricula in England. Scientific Enquiry was given an increased prominence in the 2000 revisions to the National Curriculum, which promoted a wider variety of enquiry and excellence and enjoyment' with its emphasis on enquiry, creativity, and group problem-solving at primary level (NESTA, 2005). Scientific enquiry considers two important, related questions i) How can our students carry out their own investigations in a scientific way? ii) How does the scientific community develop new ideas, supported by empirical evidence? (David and Valerie, 2002).

Up to the present time, curriculum changes that resulted in the 2004 National Curriculum originated at the instigation of science educators, with a series of open meetings in 1997 and 1998 that culminated in the document *Beyond 2000* (Millar and Osborne, 1998). This seminal document was the product of a desire to provide a vision science education that addressed the needs and interests of young people as a future citizen at the end of the twentieth century (Rob, Charles and Anna, 2010).

The next revision of the National Curriculum, introduced in 2005, established the term 'How Science Works' (HSW) to reflect that 'scientific enquiry' was not just a set of experimental skills but should also convey an understanding of how scientific knowledge has been and continues to be developed (SCORE, 2012). The original version 'How Science Works' was introduced with the revisions of the national curriculum that took place at key stage 4 in 2006 and key stage 3 in 2008 by the Qualifications and Curriculum Authority (QCA) (James, 2011).

'How Science Works' included the rather vague notion that it involves the 'scientific method'. Moreover, the Science National Curriculum features four 'How Science Works' elements in the Programme of Study, i) data, evidence, theories and explanations, ii) practical and enquiry skills, iii) communication skills, and iv) applications and implications of science (Vanessa and Per, 2008). Thus, with the revision of the curriculum at key stage 3 and key stage 4, How Science Works became a formal part of the science curriculum.

Despite changes that have now produced a curriculum for all pupils that are relevant, up to date and engaging, which is said to have contributed to How Science Works, there is still the nagging issue that this new curriculum remains dominated by assessment (Rob, 2010). Correspondingly, criticism is related to the wider area of science education policy and scientific literacy: What is science education for? The report Beyond 2000 (Millar and Osborne, 1998) states a growing inequality between the science education provided in schools and the needs and interest of pupils for the future.

At the present time, the new National Curriculum for England is to be taught in all maintained primary and secondary schools from September 2014 (DfE, 2013). The current national curriculum programmes of study for science at key stages 3 and 4 have been ceased with effect from 1 September 2013 and are no longer statutory. Currently, the statutory National Curriculum for Science will include a Programme of Study for Physics, Chemistry and Biology and will also encompass what is currently termed by the Department for Education (DfE) as 'working scientifically' (SCORE, 2012).

'Working scientifically' specifies the understanding of the nature, processes and methods of science for each year group and not be taught as a separate strand

(DfE, 2013). 'Working scientifically' is described separately at the beginning of the programme of study, but must always be taught through and clearly related to substantive science content in the programme of study. 'Working scientifically' will be developed further at key stages 3 and 4, once pupils have built up sufficient understanding of science to engage meaningfully in more sophisticated discussion of experimental design and control.

Furthermore, 'Working scientifically' might be embedded within the content of biology, chemistry and physics, focusing on the key features of scientific enquiry, so that pupils learn to use a variety of approaches to answer relevant scientific questions (DfE, 2013). These types of scientific enquiry should include: observing over time; pattern seeking; identifying, classifying and grouping; comparative and fair testing (controlled investigations); and researching using secondary sources. Pupils should seek answers to questions through collecting, analysing and presenting data.

Terminology

Since the National Curriculum was introduced, there is confusion in the broader science education community about the definition of 'practical work'. Additionally this confusion is underpinned by discussions about the value and difficulty of 'practical work' and many are frequently used with little clarification from a variety of terms exist to describe practical work (Justin, 2008). The National Curriculum uses several terms with little attempt to explain their meaning, for example: 'Practical and enquiry skills', 'practical and investigative activities', 'independent enquiry' and 'experimental work' (QCA, 2007).

Advocacy of 'scientific enquiry' is common in discussions of school science. However, according to Jim (2012), the meaning of this call is clouded by two issues.

Firstly there is often a failure to distinguish between scientific inquiry as a learning aim and as a set of teaching/learning approaches. And secondly, there is often insufficient detail about what teaching/learning approaches might count as scientific inquiry, and how these activities would fit within an extended teaching/learning sequence.

Although this may be true, in a statement that could correspondingly easily be made by UK science educators, Abrams *et al.* (2008) wrote:

> 'Surprisingly, the lack of a clear and commonly held definition of enquiry in the classroom, the ambiguity in terms of the kind of knowledge it is to engender, and even nagging questions regarding its effectiveness as a pedagogic tool have not stopped the push by those involved in science education reform to integrate enquiry into K-12 classrooms. This widespread acceptance by the research and teacher teaching education community in the face of such uncertainty leaves classroom teachers with the burden of crafting their own definitions of enquiry in the classroom, selecting their own approach to this method and determining its strengths and weaknesses for their particular students, context and content. Placing such a nebulous construct at the center of science education reform effort with such scant support for teacher thinking about these constructs calls into question the eventual success of these reforms'. (p. xii)

Comparatively, Lunetta *et al.* (2007) point to an ambiguity in the use of the term *'inquiry'*: Further complicating research into school laboratory practices have been ambiguous use of terms such as 'inquiry science teaching' which may refer to teaching science *as* inquiry (helping students understand how scientific knowledge is developed) or teaching science *through* inquiry (having students take part in inquiry investigations to help them acquire more meaningful conceptual science knowledge). (p. 396)

According to NESTA (2005), *'science enquiry'* learning is a type of science education that involves student raising questions and hypotheses, testing and revising these hypotheses based on experiments and observations, and presenting the conclusions to others. While *'scientific enquiry'* is essentially a thinking process; pupils need to develop thinking strategies to guide their practical activity and to make the most of the data they have collected (Anne *et al.*, 2000).

Even though there is a lack of consensus over the definition and usage of some words used in enquiry, David and Valerie (2002) suggested that it is advisable that all teachers within a school use the same terms, share the same meanings, use the terms consistently and avoid aggravating students' misconceptions which is this could be written into departmental policy and schemes of work, together with proposals for teaching ideas of evidence.

In the final analysis, what this part of the curriculum is called will be important. Ultimately, however, whatever title is given, it will be defined by what comes under it. The term How Science Works (HSW) was shrouded in confusion because of the lack of consensus among Awarding Organisations on what HSW is (SCORE, 2012). The problem with 'scientific enquiry' is that it is does not capture both the need to understand the ideas of science and how these ideas of science and how these ideas have developed, and scientific activity. Moreover, internationally 'scientific enquiry' is used to describe a pedagogy as well as curriculum content – e.g. – enquiry – based learning – so this term could lead to confusion.

What is the impact of good practise and effective pedagogy?

It is very clear that scientific enquiry in itself does not automatically improve learning in science rather it must be fully integrated as a major element of effective pedagogy in science (SCORE, 2008). The questions that are commonly asked about scientific enquiry are: *Does it work? Are the claims that it leads to understanding as well as the ability to use enquiry skills justified? Is there any evidence that enquiry-based activities are 'better' than traditional science activities?* (Wynne, 2007).

'Many scientists and science educators are convinced that scientific enquiry must play an important role in learning science, but the reasons for its prominence are less clear. This lack of clarity lies in the vagueness of the questions asked about the role of scientific enquiry. Asking about the effectiveness of scientific enquiry for learning is like asking whether children learn by reading. The answer lies in the nature and contents of the activities and the aims which they are trying to achieve'.

(Watson, 2000, p.57)

There is just a limited amount of evidence on these matters and most endeavours at contrasting the results of enquiry methodologies and different methodologies are uncertain. Comparison between the outcomes of enquiry and non-enquiry experiences would have to ensure that the enquiry experience is the only difference between groups whose learning is then compared (Wynne, 2007).

When science enquiry is newly introduced, prior questions are concerned whether students are actually experiencing enquiry. Ruiz-Primo *et al*, (2002) reported that classroom events showed few of the practices associated with enquiry learning, as intended. This is particularly likely to happen in experimental comparisons between enquiry and non-enquiry approaches. The results do not provide the basis for a valid judgment of the value of the principles of enquiry-based work. When there is evidence that the independent variable is in place, it needs to be in operation for at least a year before outcome measures are applied. Enquiry is aimed at changes in ways of learning that take time to establish (Wynne, 2007).

A good example of enquiry was the *spring bulbs'* study carried out by Welsh schools (Cowell and Watkins, 2007). It illustrates what 'enquiry' means in a real-life context, that is, asking questions about our surroundings and finding out answers. It is important that we let children lead the way because it really makes a difference when teachers let the children 'play' with the materials before they start discussing what they can investigate (Wynne, 2009). Once the children have explored parachutes (for example), they are able to pose questions and base predictions upon experience.

Equally important, it is often argued that scientific enquiry is central to teaching and learning in science and that good quality scientific enquiry helps develop pupils' understanding of scientific processes and concepts (Justin, 2008). By the same token, teachers also support the significance of science enquiry. A nationwide survey commissioned by NESTA (2005) shows that the overwhelming majority of science teachers 84% think that science enquiry is 'very important'. Further, teachers think that science enquiry can have a significant positive impact on the attainment of their students (83%), and on the development of problem-solving skills (85%).

Rob (2010) also agreed that scientific enquiry is a positive step that engages and challenges pupils, giving them a deeper understanding of, interest in and insight into the concepts and nature of science. In the research of how trainee teachers see the How Science Works strand in schools, Rob (2010) indicate that these pedagogies place greater emphasis on pupil participation and collaboration, on integrating practical enquiry into everyday teaching and learning, and on challenging pupils with higher order thinking skills while at the same time making the curriculum accessible for the less able in science.

The importance of scientific enquiry is supported by the DCSF (2002, p.11) on the grounds that it *'has a central place in science because it helps pupils to understand how scientific ideas are developed and because the skills and processes of scientific enquiry are useful in many everyday applications. Scientific enquiry provides opportunities for pupils to consider the benefits and drawbacks of applications of science in technological developments, and in the environment, health care and quality of life'*. Primary teachers in the 2008 NFER survey for NESTA provided wide support for this view.

However, in research done by Abrahams (2009) on a study of the affective value of practical work in secondary school science, the findings suggest that whilst practical work generates short-term engagement, it is relatively ineffective in generating motivation to study science post compulsion or longer-term personal interest in the subject, although it is often claimed to do so. This is supported by a study done by Pinar and Filiz (2010) in investigating the effects of Inquiry-Based Learning (IBL) environments, on students' conceptual understanding of matter, scientific process skills and attitudes towards science. This study indicated that IBL had a positive impact on students' conceptual understanding and scientific process skills, but did not make any difference on their attitudes towards science.

Other evidence of the impact of scientific enquiry comes from a study by Gibson and Chase (2002) who studied the impact of a Summer Science Exploration Program (SSEP), a two-week inquiry-based science camp in the US. The camp was designed to stimulate interest in science and scientific careers among middle-school students. From 79 SSEP students and 35 students who applied for the SSEP but were not accepted were taken the science opinion survey and the career decision-making revised surveys. The research report stated that *'the interviews and surveys suggested that SSEP students maintained a more positive attitude towards science and a higher interest in science careers than students who applied to the program but were not selected'* (p. 693).

Freedman (1997), investigating the use of a hands-on laboratory program as a means of improving student attitude towards science and increasing student achievement levels in science knowledge reported that:

> '... students who had regular laboratory instruction (a) scored significantly higher ($p < .01$) on the objective examination of achievement in science knowledge than those who had no laboratory experiences; (b) exhibited a moderate, positive correlation ($r = .406$) between their attitude toward science and their achievement; and (c) scored significantly higher ($p < .01$) on achievement in science knowledge after these scores were adjusted on the attitude toward science coverable'. (p. 343)

Furthermore, from the NESTA project conducted from 2001 until 2002, the on-going Planet Science website, which began as the portal for Science Year/Planet Science projects, impacted on students in three key ways: increased co-operation between students; higher levels of student motivation; and more engaged students (NESTA, 2005). This was proven by observation from many teachers who witnessed increased levels of co-operation when the students were involved in particular activities.

The impact of scientific enquiry also proven by Tony (2013), based on the feedback from schools who have followed this enquiry approach in the 'Get Science 11-14: Wikid Coursebook', where Tony reports it works fantastically well for many students. However, he continues... 'for some the challenge of learning skills and knowledge together in context can become too high, which results in less efficient learning'.

Millar (2004) identifies the value of scientific enquiry in school science, which is practical work is essential for giving students a 'feel' for the problematic nature of measurement and an appreciation of the ever-presence of uncertainty. It is also an important tool for teaching about experimental design. Notably research suggests that students should suggest better designs for investigations when they actually carry them out than and write these up rather than only being asked to write a plan; feedback from experience improves design.

Nevertheless, he adds a note of caution when he comments on the success of scaling up innovations across an education system; there are few examples of the successful implementation of extended practical projects or investigations as part of the science curriculum in the context of 'mass education', where large numbers of teachers and students are involved. This is because the teachers find it difficult to devise or to help students to generate enough project ideas, year on year and it is easy for the activity to become routinised, and become something very different from what was originally envisaged when it was included in the curriculum.

In either case the findings of their recent review of research into laboratory work, Lunetta *et al.* (2007) generally speaking; *'when well-planned and effectively implemented, science education laboratory and simulation experiences situate students' learning in varying levels of inquiry requiring students to be both mentally and physically engaged in ways that are not possible in other science education experiences'*. (p. 405)

They go onto explain that the laboratory can be *'an environment particularly well suited for providing a meaningful context for learning, determining and challenging students' deeply held ideas about natural phenomena, and constructing and reconstructing their ideas'* (Lunetta et al., 2007, p. 406). In terms of a pedagogical approach, they contend that: *'Social learning theory makes clear the importance of promoting group work in the laboratory so that meaningful conceptually focused dialogue takes place between students as well as between the teacher and students'* (p. 406).

Additionally, David *et al.* (2006) highlight four problems with implementing scientific inquiry in the classroom including the following; i) teachers may manipulate classroom science to obtain the expected results, ii) teachers' demonstrations merely simulate scientific inquiry, iii) the incomplete development of students' reasoning abilities may limit their ability to construct complex scientific arguments, and iv) scientific inquiry often requires detailed knowledge of a topic that students have yet to master.

Wynne (2007) also outlined the difficulties that are compounded when we come to think about what learning outcomes to assess, how to assess them and what timescales would give convincing evidence of real benefits to learning. As we know from the experience of the CASE Project (Adey and Shayer, 1990), some benefits of different learning experiences appear only after several years. There is a distinct danger of making judgments after too short time and failing to nurture approaches that need to be sustained for their benefits to show.

In another key point, Rob (2010) listed four challenges of scientific enquiry in How Science Works in schools falling into several categories; i) the practicalities of implementing a new curriculum, with reports of problems with pupils' responses to new approaches, ii) organisational problems, resulting from too many classes doing the same lessons at the same time and a lack of resources and guidance with schools being poorly equipped, and issues about having sufficient time to make new resources, iii) pupils' shortcomings with scientific vocabulary, including misinterpreting key words and definitions, and misunderstanding some terminology, such as accuracy and reliability, and iv) the content of the curriculum perceived as remaining too content-laden.

Conclusion

In conclusion, scientific enquiry is an important concept in science education, describing the way in which process skills (now more usually called enquiry skills) lead to understanding. The key feature of scientific enquiry, as opposed to more general enquiry, is the use of evidence from the natural and man-made world in testing ideas about how things work (Wynne, 2009). Often, but not always, this evidence is derived from first-hand manipulation of materials or direct observation of events.

In helping children to make sense of the world around them, other features of their learning experiences are important, in particular starting from their existing ideas and using information about their progress to adapt teaching and the pace of learning to ensure understanding (Wynne, 2009). So the term 'enquiry-based science education' is useful in signaling that there are other aspects of good science teaching in addition to enquiry.

There was agreement among the delegates of a seminar organised by SCORE that 'scientific enquiry' needs to be made explicit in the National Curriculum but how it is 'embedded' and contextualised will need further thought and guidance. Some teachers 'embed' this aspect of the curriculum into their teaching naturally but it cannot be assumed that all teachers, especially those without a science background, will do this (SCORE, 2012).

At the same time, Murat (2013) also suggested that science teachers need deeper understanding about enquiry and how to implement enquiry in the classroom environment. In order to foster a deeper understanding of enquiry instruction, pre-service and on-service science teachers will need well-developed opportunities to practice and reflect upon enquiry instruction.

This study has reviewed how scientific enquiry encompasses the statutory orders of the National Curriculum. It has traced the historical moves behind the curriculum and reviews some of the reasons for his change. In doing so, it has highlighted some of the main criticisms in the impact of good practice and effective pedagogy. This study successfully examined how changes to a radically altered curriculum – particularly how scientific enquiry – have been translated into practices in schools, as seen through the statutory order of the National Curriculum.

The potential of science enquiry to engage and motivate learners is clear from the broader research literature. Science enquiry can help learners to develop their understanding of the processes of science as well as the content of scientific knowledge (NESTA, 2005). As a result it can support gains in motivation and attainment, even by young people who have previously been unengaged by science education in schools in challenging circumstances.

References

Abrahams, I. (2009) 'Does Practical Work Really Motivate? A study of the affective value of practical work in secondary school science', *International Journal of Science Education*, 31(17), p. 2335-2353.

Abrams, E., Southerland, S. A. and Evans, C. (2008) Introduction: Inquiry in the classroom: identifying necessary components of a useful definition. In E. Abrams, S. A. Southerland and P. Silva (Eds) *Inquiry in the Classroom. Realities and Opportunities* (pp. xi–xlii). Charlotte, NC: Information Age Publishing.

Adey, P. and Shayer, M. (1990) 'Accelerating the development of formal thinking in middle and high school students', *Journal of Research in Science Teaching*, 27(3), p. 267-285.

Anne, G., Rod, W., Valerie, W. R. (2000) *Developing understanding in scientific enquiry: investigations*. London: King's College.

Beatty, J. W. and Woolnough, B. E. (1982) 'Practical work in 11-13 science', *British Educational Research Journal* 8, 23-30.

Cowell, D. and Watkins, R. (2007) 'Get out of the classroom to study climate change – the 'Spring bulbs for schools' project', *Primary Science Review*, 97, p. 25–28

David, I. H., Deborah, J-S., Marisa, L. P., Steven, G. C., Roger, W. H. and Graham, F. H. (2006) 'Teaching Scientific Inquiry', *Science Magazine*, 22 December 2006, p. 1880-1881.

David, S. and Valerie W. R. (2002) *Teaching Secondary Scientific Enquiry*. London: Association for Science Education.

DCSF (Department for Children, Schools and Families) (2002) *Framework for teaching science: years 7, 8 and 9*. Available at: http://http://webarchive.nationalarchives.gov.uk/ (Accessed: 21st December 2013).

Department for Education (2013) *'The national curriculum in England; Framework document'*. London: Department for Education (DfE)

DES/WO (Department of Education and Science and the Welsh Office) (1989) *Science in the National Curriculum*. London: HMSO.

Donnelly, J. (1995) 'Curriculum development in science: the lessons of Sc1', *School Science Review*, 76(227), pp.95-103.

Donnelly, J. F. and Jenkins, E. W. (1999) *Science teaching in Secondary School Under the National Curriculum*. Leeds: centre for Studies in Science and Mathematics Education, University of Leeds.

Freedman, M. P. (1997) 'Relation among Laboratory Instruction, Attitude toward Science, and Achievement in Science Knowledge', *Journal of Research in Science Teaching*. 34(4), p. 343-357.

Gibson, H. L. and Chase, C. (2002) 'Longitudinal impact of an inquiry-based science program on middle school students' attitudes toward science', *Science Education*, 86(5), 693-705.

James, D. W. (2011) *How Science Works; Teaching and Learning in the Science Classroom*. London: Continuum International Publishing Group.

Jim, R. (2012) *Perspectives: Scientific inquiry: learning about it and learning through it. London*: Wellcome Trust.

Justin, D. (2008) *A Review of The research on Practical Work in School Science*. London: King's College.

Lunetta, V. N., Hofstein, A. and Clough, M. P. (2007) Teaching and learning in the school science laboratory. An analysis of research, theory, and practice. In, S. K. Abell and N. G. Lederman (Eds), *Handbook of Research on Science Education* (pp. 393– 431). Mahwah, NJ: Lawrence Erlbaum Associates.

Michael, A. (2010) 'The place of scientific inquiry in the How Science Works curriculum', in Rob, T. (eds.) *How Science Works: Exploring effective pedagogy and practice*. Oxford: Routledge, pp. 44-55.

Millar, R. (1991) A means to an end: the role of processes in science education, in B. Woolnough (ed.) *Practical Science*, Milton Keynes: Open University Press.

Millar, R. (2004) *The Role of Practical Work in the Teaching and Learning of Science.* Paper prepared for the Committee: High School Science Laboratories: Role and Vision, National Academy of Sciences, Washington DC. York: University of York.

Millar, R. and J. Osborne (1998) *Beyond 2000*. London: King's College London School of Education.

Murat, O. (2013) 'Beginning secondary science teachers' conceptualization and enactment of inquiry-based instruction', *School Science and Mathematics*, 116(6), p. 308-316.

National Endowment for Science, Technology and the Arts (NESTA) (2005). 'Real science; Encouraging experimentation and investigation in school science learning', *NESTA Research Report*. London: NESTA.

Pinar, S. and Filiz, K. (2010) 'The effects of inquiry-based learning on elementary students' conceptual understanding of matter, scientific process skills and science attitudes', *Procedia Social and Behavioral Sciences 2*(2010), p.1190-1194.

Qualification and Curriculum Authority (QCA) (2007) *Science: Programme of study for key stage 3 and attainment targets*. London: QCA.

Rachel, S.-S. (2009) *Experiencing the Process of Knowledge Creation: The Nature and Use of Inquiry-Based Learning in Higher Education*. New Zealand: University of Otago.

Rob, T. (2010) 'How did we get here? Some background to How Science Works in the school curriculum', in Rob, T. (eds.) *How Science Works: Exploring effective pedagogy and practice*. Oxford: Routledge, pp. 1-13.

Rob, T., Charles, G. and Anna, C. (2010). 'Implementing a new science National Curriculum for England: how trainee teachers see the How Science Works strand in schools', *The Curriculum Journal*, 21(1), pp. 65-76.

Ruiz-Primo, M. A., Shavelson, R. J., Hamilton, L. and Klein, S. (2002) On the evaluation of Systemic Science Education Reform: searching for instructional sentivity, *Journal of Research in Science Teaching*, 39(5), p. 369-393.

SCORE – Science Community Representing Education (2008) *Practical Work I Science: A report and Proposal for a Strategic Framework*. London: Science Community Representing Education.

SCORE – Science Community Representing Education (2012) *Scientific Enquiry and its Place in the National Curriculum: Summary of a Seminar Organised by SCORE*. London: Science Community Representing Education.

Tony, S. (2013) 'Differentiated enquiry', *School Science Review*, 95(351), pp. 50-51.

Vanessa, K. and Per, M. K. (2008) *Teaching Secondary How Science Works*. London: Association for Science Education.

Wynne, H. (2007) 'Science education as enquiry: issues of evaluation', *Education in Science (EiS)*, April 2007, p. 22-23.

Wynne, H. (2009) 'Enquiry and good science teaching', *Primary Science*, Jan/Feb 2009.

13 ANNA WRIGHT

Anna Wright is a Manager, Lecturer in Business and Economics and Advanced Practitioner at Uxbridge College of Further Education. As an economist she was drawn to the idea of the marketisation of education as a result of the 1988 Education Reform Act. A former naval officer, she is passionate about and committed to the transformative effect that Further Education can have on young peoples' lives.

Literature Review

Chief Teacher or CEO? Seat of Learning or Business?
A Critical Evaluation of the Impact of the 1988 Education Reform Act on Leadership in Education

Abstract

This literature review critically evaluates the impact of the 1988 Education Reform Act on leadership in education exploring how the role evolved from lead teacher to 'manager' and how the introduction of market forces transformed schools into more business-like organisations. The conclusion is drawn that the policy has had a lasting impact on the headteachers' role and was a significant factor leading to the introduction of mandatory training for leaders in education by the subsequent Labour Government. The recommendation is made that future research could examine the presence of 'managers' rather than lead teachers in leadership roles in education today.

Introduction

That the Education Reform Act (ERA) 1988 had a huge impact on education in the UK seems largely undisputed (Creese, 1991; Dunning, 1993; Ferlie et al, 1996; Gerwitz, 2002; Jones and Hayes; 1991). However, it is arguable that a significant part of this impact was its influence on leadership practices. As Craig (1990), perhaps prophetically, wrote,

> 'In all the changes that will take place during the next decade, the key figure will be   the headteacher' (p.2).

The main themes of the ERA (Gorard et al, 2002) included the introduction of markets into education, more parental choice regarding school places, increased autonomy for individual schools and in particular the introduction of per capita funding, a scheme characterised by 'new public management' (Ferlie et al, 1996; Gerwitz, 2002). Where once teachers had been answerable to no-one the ERA 1988 imposed a prescriptive National Curriculum, a system of rigorous testing and an exacting inspection system, all of which undoubtedly had a significant effect on staff and school leadership (Creese, 1991; Dunning, 1993; Jones and Hayes; 1991).

This literature review will critically evaluate the context in which the policy was conceived and how this influenced the role of the headteacher. It will reflect on the diverse influences on the Conservative Government in the UK in the 1980s and other global stimuli that led to the implementation of the policy.

In the main body this review will critically evaluate the literature which considers the impact of the 1988 Education Reform Act (ERA) on leadership in education. It will consider the extent to which headteachers and teachers felt that the role of headteacher altered as a result of the ERA. It will assess the degree to which it was believed that headteachers required a new skillset and to what extent the size of the school had an impact. The effect of the introduction of Local Management of Schools (LMS) on headteachers' workload and focus will be examined. The review will then consider the extent to which staff and heads perceived that the ERA had impacted on student learning and review the evidence that the ERA had in fact had an impact on student success. The effect of the marketisation of education on the head teacher's workload will be examined, including the need to 'market' schools and enter into competition for 'consumers' (pupils). Other influences on heads' success in the wake of the ERA will also be considered. Finally the investigation will examine implications for the selection and training of headteachers and recommendations for further research will be made.

Commentary has been limited to that which is relevant to the effects of the ERA on headteachers in primary and secondary schools. That which relates to higher education will not be considered in this literature review.

Marketisation and Centralisation: context in which the policy was introduced

The 1988 ERA was conceived in a context in which Conservative mistrust of the 'liberal educational establishment' (Pierson, 1998, p.132) was rife. Secretary of State for Education, Kenneth Baker, described the education system as 'devoutly anti-excellence, anti-selection, and anti-market,' (Baker, 1993, p.168). Ball (2008) suggests Thatcher education policy was conceived within the context of attempts to dismantle the collectivism of the welfare state, 'reinvent a form of Victorian laissez-faire individualism' (ibid, p.84) and introduce market forces into the public sector. Maclure (1989) identified two factors which he considered to have had the most significant influence on the content of the ERA suggesting that in the 1980s educators had lost the confidence of 'consumers' and the Local Education Authorities had disappointed both consumers and the government. However, Jones and Hayes (1991) identified multifarious influences that they consider to have shaped the ERA:

> 'the strands of market forces, emphasis upon standards, criticisms of the LEA and perceived demands for local accountability and choice empowered the government to introduce to the education system an Act in which parental choice, competition, financial stringency, curriculum control and strong central direction would be strongly represented.' Jones and Hayes (1991, p.4)

Caldwell and Spinks (1988) maintain that the ERA should be viewed in the context of a global shift in education towards decentralisation and local 'consumer' control. However, this may be overstating the international aspect as their evidence cites change in Canada, North America, Australia and Britain only and is therefore restricted to the West (ibid).

Barker (2008) points to another international influence of the 1980s which was increasingly intense competition in global markets for high quality products and services, a view widely shared (Banker et al, 1998; Berry, 1982; Peapples, 1990). Wilkinson (2000) argues that every British government since has accepted without question the tenet that market competition and deregulation of labour markets are the route to economic success. Indeed, Shackleton (2007) commended the Blair governments' commitment to product market competition citing the greater anti-trust powers given to the Competition Commission in the 1998 Competition Act, increased outsourcing of government services and unwillingness to rescue failing businesses as evidence of this.

> 'Conservative policy was driven by a set of assumptions about choice, markets, standards, public management, accountability and the relationship between competitiveness, economic growth and the education system.'
>
> Pierson (1998, p.131)

Pierson (1998) suggests the Thatcher government was influenced by 'public choice' theory. According to Schug and Wentworth (1994) public choice theory proposes that it is beneficial to consider the role of producers and consumers in the public sector, as is done when studying the private sector. In economic terms it is argued that non-market forms of decision-making would always favour the interests of producers rather than consumers and that without competition the inevitable consequence would be 'monopolistic suppliers of education over-supplying a substandard good' (Pierson, 1998, p.132). Arguably this was a dramatic shift from the benevolent post-war aspiration for social justice and educational opportunity for all (Batteson, 1999).

Thus, Chitty and Dunford (1999) concluded that rather than improving what happened in the classroom the heads' task would be to influence efficiency and market their schools effectively. However, Jones and Hayes (1991: 2) suggest that it was believed that the ERA 1988 would in fact 'enhance the quality of the Education System'. According to Ranson (1990) the reason that Conservative government policy was based on public choice and accountability was that it was believed that quality of education would only improve if parents' trust was garnered. However, it would seem that it was not only the 'customers' (parents) who needed to be won over as Bell (1991) criticised educational management as lacking credibility with educators due to its continued reliance on ideas and models from the business-world. Arguably this concurs with Hood's (1995) identification of the changes in public sector accounting in a number of OECD countries during the 1980s that were key to the rise of the "New Public Management" (NPM) and its associated principles of public accountability and organisational best practice. It may be that this movement both influenced the design of the 1988 ERA and also the ensuing managerial style of leadership in education (ibid).

McLean (1989) suggests that the ERA overturned most of the education developments of the twentieth-century by 'cherry-picking' practices from the rest of the world, i.e. French national curriculum, West German assessment of students and American 'magnet' schools (ibid). However, the combination of policies incorporated into the ERA 1988 was hitherto unproven in any other country (ibid.).

A key aspect that will be considered in this literature review is how training impacted on how effectively heads could respond and adapt to the changes brought about by the ERA (ibid). Perhaps some confirmation that the ERA 1988 was the correct policy for the period is the Labour government's decision, rather than swinging back to more liberal policies as might have been expected (Brighouse, 1988), to push these developments further and introduce a mandatory leadership qualification (Bush, 2013).

Bridges and McLaughlin (1994) point to the inherent tension on which the ERA was designed between centralisation and devolution. They argue that although funding was now devolved to school heads the Secretary of State had removed control of the academic aspects of running a school by introducing a nationalised curriculum and testing arrangements (ibid). Indeed, this contradiction in political ideologies would appear to be a widely held view (Ranson, 1990; Salter and Tappe, 1985; Whitty, 1989). Even before the ERA 1988 Salter and Tapper (1985) commented that the influences on Conservative education policy appeared to confuse neo-liberal belief in the free market mechanism on the one hand with authority and traditional values on the other (ibid.) Further, Ranson (1990) submits that there was no unifying ideology that led to the ERA, suggesting it was a morass of contradiction.

This literature review will now consider how this seemly discordant policy impacted on the role of the headteacher.

From Chief teacher to CEO? A changed role and skillset for headteachers?

Arguably it is widely recognised that the main task of the headteacher changed dramatically as a direct result of the ERA to a more managerial role (Creese, 1991; Dunning, 1993; Jones and Hayes, 1991) and has been described as 'manager as opposed to master teacher' (McHugh and McMullan, 1995, p23). Craig (1989) asserted that the term 'headteacher' was misleading and that the work of a head was purely management. Jones and Hayes (1991) suggest that the ERA imposed tremendous change at breath-taking speed which transformed the way in which school organisations functioned and also the role of the headteacher. The government's consultants, Coopers and Lybrand (1989), coined the term 'Local School Management' to refer to the delegation of financial management to schools. This term is perhaps further evidence of the emphasis away from a lead teacher role to a managerial function.

However, McHugh and McMullan (1995) identified that educationalists considered the head's role to be inconsistent with that of a business manager and Lyons (1990) claimed that the culture within education was actually hostile towards business management ideas. Handy and Aitken (1986) add weight to these arguments with their suggestion that prior to the ERA promotion to headteacher was based on a perception that good teachers were likely to be the best managers. Conversely McHugh and McMullan (1995) questioned this assumption and suggested that as the role of the headteacher had altered so dramatically as a result of the ERA those recruited on the basis of outstanding ability as teachers would find themselves lacking the requisite skillset. This would seem to imply that some headteachers were ill-equipped to become effective 'managers' following the ERA and that their teaching background might be unhelpful in terms of the skillset they had developed (ibid). Further, Dunning (1993) identified that the need for more managerial ability, together with an increased portfolio of responsibilities, coincided with the demand that effectiveness be more transparent and measureable. It may be concluded that this confluence of new demands on ill-prepared heads would potentially lead to a poor outcome for students (ibid).

Kerry and Murdoch (1993) advocated that managerial 'competency' would henceforth be critical to the success of schools. Thomas (1988) had identified early on that at the same time as school leaders would be attempting to oversee implementation of a National Curriculum, new Assessment Programmes and Teacher Appraisal Systems they would be required to develop an entirely new skillset that would enable them to manage finance and competition. Arguably he was astute to foresee that some headteachers would respond to the challenge with great aplomb but that others might fail to conserve the existing quality of education. Perceptively he pointed out the irony that an act which had removed power from professionals and was dependent upon markets raising standards would in fact depend upon the strength and quality of professional commitment for its success (Thomas, 1988). Indeed, the Conservative Government's consultants, Coopers and Lybrand, had concluded that local management of schools would only succeed if there was 'a positive attitude to it from the head, the staff and the governing body' and that this approach would only come about if it was perceived that the benefits outweighed the additional workload and it was suitably shared (Coopers and Lybrand, 1989, p.13).

A common response to coping with the demands of the ERA was portrayed in Weindling's study (1992) by one headteacher:

> 'Being a head in the 1990s is like competing in a marathon held on a high sand dune and carrying a heavy load. As the race develops, the organisers reduce the number of feeding stations, increase the slope of the hill, and move the winning post. The racers have to be more efficient for they run on less calories.'
>
> Weindling, (1992, p13)

Weindling's study, which involved in-depth interviews with secondary headteachers, generated considerable evidence that heads believed their role to have altered significantly in terms of volume and focus, with more attention on external projects, paperwork and public image (ibid). McHugh and McMullan (1995) supported this view and cite evidence of headteachers complaining that the demand for them to be offsite and involved with external issues, together with being 'tied to the office much more' (ibid: 5) meant that 'they considered themselves to have lost touch with the real school world', (ibid, 5). Pierson supports this view, stating:

'Increasingly, headteachers were to be seen as 'chief executives' of their various educational enterprises with increased responsibility for budgets and the general economic management of their schools'. Pierson, (1998, p. 137)

However, Bush (2008) suggests that the sudden change in the role of the head and subsequent focus on financial and personnel management enforced by the ERA was not a permanent change. He suggests that after a decade school leaders began to reassert themselves as lead professionals once again. His proposition that this came about as a result of the Blair-led trend from 'management' to 'leadership' in education seems a logical conclusion to draw (Bush, 2008).

Although the pace of change as a result of the ERA was widely criticised as being too fast and Buchan (1990) warned that schools confronting change at a speed faster than their ability to respond would be destabilised, there is evidence that some saw an opportunity (Jones and Hayes, 1991). A number of headteachers identified that 'judicious use of the pace of change has produced opportunities, despite the problems' (ibid: 5). They cite the policy changes as a chance to restructure and introduce new co-ordinators' posts, decentralise budgets further and establish a senior management team (ibid). Kerry and Murdoch (1995) identified headteachers who felt that the speed of change actually offered the possibility to make improvements that they considered to be long overdue, including encouraging reactionary staff into early retirement.

McHugh and McMullan (1995) believed the impact of the ERA on headteachers was dependent upon the size of schools and resources available. They cite evidence that teaching heads in primary schools with 2/3 teaching staff felt the increased burden more keenly than those in large secondary schools who could delegate the new workload to a senior management team (ibid). Bush (2013) supports this pointing to the greatly expanded management role of senior colleagues in secondary schools as a result of the policy. Arguably this was a factor in deciding the effectiveness of individual headteachers following the implementation of the ERA (McHugh and McMullan, 1995).

This literature review will now consider the impact that the introduction of market forces, imposed by the 1988 ERA, had on head teachers.

Seat of learning or a business? The impact of market forces

Weindling's (1992) findings pointed to much greater concern on the part of head teachers for public relations and a focus on the marketing of schools. It would seem that the drive to be more market-orientated meant that many head teachers were taken up with the entrepreneurial business of attracting 'consumers' (ibid). Woods (1993) interviewed a secondary head who lamented the fact that there was now a focus on chasing the funding attached to each student as opposed to paying attention to their academic needs. Perhaps an even more concerning aspect was that the nature of the 'quasi-market' would vary according to geography and the social composition of the area (Woods, 1996). He suggested that this in turn would influence the extent to which the head's attention would be taken up with it (ibid). He cites evidence that schools were most likely intent on attracting parents from the higher social classes (ibid). Ball (1993) supports this view and goes further to imply that the middle classes used these quasi-markets to achieve social advantage. Herbert (2000) concluded that,

> 'local social geographies create an uneven playing field that significantly influences the relative success or failure of headteachers in this role' (ibid: 80).

From this evidence it may be inferred that the new focus on marketing effort in order to attract the 'right' sort of parents was diverting the attention and energy of heads (ibid). Assuming that the head's attention is a finite resource this presumes attention was being redirected to a greater or lesser extent from the academic needs of the students (ibid). This was possibly exacerbated by the other new demands on heads such as devolved financial control and implementation of a National Curriculum (Woods, 1996). Ultimately the extent of the diversion would seem to be dependent upon the challenge facing the head in terms of the social landscape of the school's locale (Herbert, 2000).

Jones and Hayes (1991) argue that the new emphasis on consumerism had the effect of reducing the head's ability to make decisions and the scope for risk-taking and introducing new ideas. They suggest that the possibility of losing a member of staff if insufficient numbers were on the roll paralysed the head and meant that most decisions were based on monetary considerations (ibid).

Brighouse (1988) described the Local Education Authorities (LEAs) as 'eunuchs' (ibid: 7) in terms of the financial power they could wield in the wake of the ERA. McHugh and McMullan (1995) suggest that prior to the ERA schools were virtually autonomous in academic matters but that organisational concerns such as cleaning and ground maintenance were the purview of the local education authority rather than individual schools. Maclure (1988) identifies the decision to devolve financial power to schools as being uncontentious and suggests that it was widely perceived as being supremely practical. He submits that it was widely thought that better value for money would be the result of releasing initiative that had hitherto been smothered by local bureaucracy (Maclure, 1988). However, research findings from a longitudinal national study to consider the impact of the 1988 ERA on secondary headteachers report mixed views regarding the changes to LMS (Weindling, 1992). Opinions of headteachers who were surveyed ranged from delight that there was potential for schools to be run more economically to horror at the increased administrative workload (ibid). Some headteachers felt that the demand for greater accountability as a result of the ERA created a burdensome level of recording and documentation in relation to the expectations of governors, parents and other bodies (ibid). Brighouse's (1988) early assessment of the changes was that there was potential for headteachers to learn from errors made by local authority Education Officers and he was optimistic that there was opportunity to make improvements to the way schools were run. However, perhaps also a realist, he hoped that the next government would recognise the short-sightedness of overwhelming headteachers with a potentially unmanageable workload (ibid). The Labour government did not in fact reverse the policy but did perhaps mitigate the challenge for heads to some extent by introducing leadership training in the form of the National Professional Qualification for Headship (NPQH) (Bush, 2013). Certainly the fact that compulsory training for headteachers was introduced suggests that it had been lacking (ibid). On the other hand it may be argued that it suited New Labour's emphasis on 'education, education, education' extremely well (ibid, 1) and in fact it reverted to optional status in 2012 (Bush, 2013).

Whitty and Power (1997) concluded that it was difficult to find decisive evidence of the effect of self-managing on learning and this would appear to the view of several commentators. The majority of head teachers surveyed believed that schools were able to make better use of resources thanks to local management but they considered that the additional administrative burden was distracting them from focussing on students' learning (ibid). However, there was no consensus as to whether children's learning was actually improving as a result of local management (ibid). Few teachers who were interviewed supported the view that self-management was improving overall standards and learning (Whitty and Power, 1997). Similarly, the research conducted by Jones and Hayes (1991) concluded that many heads were disturbed by some of the aims of the ERA. They were unconvinced that the drive to root out ineffectual teachers and reform inadequately performing schools was actually improving the education of children (ibid). Barker's (2008) review of the impact of the ERA some twenty years after its implementation concluded that there had been limited gains and Hoyle and Wallace (2007, p 11) argued that progress had been 'surprisingly limited'. On the other hand, Adonis (2005) believed the ERA had led to real improvements in examination results, better teaching and enhanced student commitment.

McHugh and McMullan (1995) identified a problem arising for secondary heads that did not appear to be so prevalent for heads of primary schools and that was the competition engendered between school departments for funding and pupil numbers as a result of the ERA. Heads were faced with the new challenge of managing this potential antagonism whilst remaining focussed on the whole school aims (ibid). A mixture of hierarchical and collegiate styles to manage this were observed and it was recommended that training was required to equip heads to be able to adopt an appropriate style to ensure effective outcomes (ibid).

Arguably the newly imposed imperative to compete for 'consumers' by means of marketing activity (Jones and Hayes, 1991, Weindling, 1992; Woods, 1993), the managing of a large budget to include upkeep of the fabric of the organisation (Brighouse, 1988; McHugh and McMullan, 1995) and the requirement for greater accountability (Hood, 1995; Jones and Hayes, 1991; Pierson, 1998; Ranson, 1990) would all seem to point to the transformation of the seat of learning to an organisation more akin to a business.

In light of the above findings this review will now consider the implications for the selection of headteachers for their new role as 'CEO' and the training required in the business skillset needed to manage a school.

Leadership in a market era: selection and training of headteachers

McHugh and McMullan (1995) suggest there was little evidence of planning on the part of the government architects of the ERA prior to its implementation in terms of retraining headteachers to be able to cope with a significantly altered role and the required skillset to be successful. They contend that the provision for training teachers up to that point did not include the management skills now required of headteachers and suggest that training was essential if heads were to meet the challenge effectively (ibid). They highlight the issue that those serving on interview panels to select new headteachers would need to be thoroughly acquainted with the new requirements for heads and were unlikely to be adequately prepared (ibid).

Kerry and Murdoch (1993: 10) advised that training for senior management and leadership required development in 'decision-making, problem-solving, creative thinking and communication', terms which arguably would all be recognised by trainee business managers. Jones and Hayes (1991) supported their view that in order to acquire these skills time had to be found to devote to training and for the training to be effective it had to be appropriate (Kerry and Murdoch, 1993). However, as was identified earlier (Weindling, 1992, McHugh and McMullan, 1995) lack of time due to the significant increase in the head's workload as a result of the ERA meant that training was extremely difficult to squeeze into the head's diary. Further, McHugh and McMullan (1995) identified that the provision of training was somewhat disjointed and inadequate. Many heads reported that their experience of training was disappointing and did not prepare them sufficiently for the task of leading in the wake of the ERA. These findings suggested that there was an urgent need for a 'more structured and more accessible training regime' (McHugh and McMullan, 1995). They prompted McHugh and McMullan (1995) to recommend that university business faculties be commissioned to assist with the training and development of the managerial skillset now required of headteachers. They advised that, as 'managers', heads could benefit enormously from the expertise of academics in areas such as marketing, accounting and organisational strategy (ibid: 12).

Bush (2010) argues that since the 1988 ERA there has been increased recognition that educational leadership is a specialist role which requires suitable preparation.

He suggests that expansion of the role arising from accountability requirements and devolved powers following the ERA 1988 together with greater complexity facing heads arising from globalization, technological and demographic changes has made it crucially important that they be adequately prepared for the role (ibid).

An opposing view is presented by Styan (1989) who purports that all teachers are managers as they must work with others to achieve defined aims with limited resources. Creese (1991) agrees with this opinion stating,

> 'the changes inherent in the Educational Reform Act do not change this basic fact. The very same skills and understanding which good teachers have always displayed are those most crucial now. The capacity to communicate, to delegate and to motivate remain paramount.' Creese, (1991, p 229)

Nevertheless Styan (1989) agrees that school improvement requires that those who manage them are trained, supported and developed.

Conclusion

It may be concluded that, to a large extent, commentators agreed that there were a number of converging influences, both global (Banker et al, 1998; Barker, 2008; Berry, 1982; Caldwell and Spinks, 1988; Peapples, 1990) and domestic (Ball, 2008; Baker, 1993; Jones and Hayes, 1991; Maclure, 1989; Pierson, 1998) which led to the ERA 1988. There would also appear to be much agreement that there were conflicting ideologies at work in the design of the policy (Bridges and McLaughlin, 1994; Ranson, 1990; Salter and Tappe, 1985; Whitty, 1989).
It is clear from the literature that much pain was endured by existing headteachers as a result of the immense changes imposed by the ERA (McHugh and McMullan, 1995; Weindling, 1992). There would appear to have been a significant shift in the

scope and focus of the head's role from that of lead teacher to 'manager' (Creese, 1991; Dunning, 1993; Jones and Hayes; 1991; Kerry and Murdoch 1993; McHugh and McMullan, 1995).

However, it would seem that many factors came into play in terms of mitigating the impact on individual heads (Brighouse, 1988; Herbert, 2000; Kerry and Murdoch, 1993; McHugh and McMullan, 1995; Thomas, 1988). Factors such as their capacity to embrace the change and see it as an opportunity rather than an inconvenience (Brighouse, 1988); their ability to adapt and learn a new skillset (Thomas, 1988); their skill in managing the response of their respective teaching staffs and the situation of the school in terms of its social geography (Woods, 1993).

The effect of the movement towards 'marketisation' of education undoubtedly affected the head's focus and the need to market individual schools in order to attract 'customers' could not be ignored (Ball, 1993; Ferlie et al, 1996; Gerwitz, 2002; Jones and Hayes, Pierson, 1998; 1991Weindling, 1992; Wood, 1993). However the extent to which this was a factor arguably depended upon the social landscape of the school's locale (Herbert, 2000). It may be concluded that this, together with the implementation of LMS (Brighouse, 1988; Maclure, 1988; Weindling, 1992), was one of the main factors which led to demands for formal training (McHugh and McMullan, 1995) for head teachers in areas such as marketing, accounting and organisational strategy, the skills required to operate a business. What appeared to be clear was the lack of planning on part the of the planners of the ERA with regards to how headteachers would implement the momentous changes of the ERA (McHugh and McMullan, 1995) and whether they were in fact equipped to do so (Jones and Hayes, 1991; Kerry and Murdoch, 1993; McHugh and McMullan, 1995).

Future research could examine the presence of 'managers' as opposed to lead teachers (Creese, 1991; Dunning, 1993; Jones and Hayes, 1991) in leadership roles in education. The incidence of 'managers' in the different stages of education, e.g. primary, secondary and further education, could be examined and if there is a proliferation in a particular stage the reasons for this could be analysed. The extent to which the lead teacher has evolved into a CEO and the transformation of the seat of learning into a business could be questioned.

References

Adonis, A. (2005) *Better schools, better results: Why our teenagers are making the grade*. Available at: http://www.theguardian.com/education/2005/aug/17/alevels.secondaryschools. Accessed: 24 December 2013

Baker, K. (1993) *The Turbulent Years*. London: Faber & Faber.

Ball, S. J. (2008) *The Education Debate*. Bristol: Policy Press.

Banker, R.D., Khosler, I. and Sinha, K. (1998) 'Quality and Competition', *Management Science,* 44(9), pp. 1179 – 1192.

Barker, B. (2008) 'School Reform policy in England since 1988: Relentless Pursuit of the Unattainable', *Journal of Education Policy*, 23(6), pp. 669 – 683.

Batteson, C. (1999) 'The 1944 Education Act Reconsidered', *Educational Review*, 51(1), pp. 5-15.

Bell, L. (1991) 'Educational Management: An Agenda for the 1990s', *Educational Management and Administration,* 19(3), pp. 136–40.

Berry, L.(1982) 'Retail positioning Strategies for the 1980s', *Business Horizons, 25(6), pp. 45 – 50.*

Bridges, D. and McLaughlin, T. (1994) *Education and the Market Place*. London: Falmer Press.

Brighouse, T. (1988) 'Politicising the Manager or Managing the Politicians? — Can the Headteacher succeed where the Education Officer failed?' *Educational Management Administration & Leadership*, 16(2), pp. 97-103.

Buchan, A. (1990) 'Follow Your Leader?' *Education,* 24 August 1990, p.153.

Bush, T. (2008) 'From Management to Leadership: Semantic or Meaningful Change? *Educational Management Administration & Leadership,* 36(2), pp. 271-288.

Bush, T. (2013) 'Preparing Headteachers in England: Professional Certification, not Academic Learning', *Educational Management Administration & Leadership,* 41(4), pp. 453 - 465.

Caldwell, B. J. and Spinks, J. M. (1988) *The Self-Managing School.* London: Falmer Press.

Chitty, C. and Dunford, J. (1999) *State Schools: New Labour and the Conservative Legacy.* London: Woburn Press.

Coopers and Lybrand (1989) 'Local Management of Schools', in Levacic, R. (Ed.) *Financial Management in Education.* Milton Keynes: Open University Press.

Craig, I. (1989) *Primary Headship in the 1990s.* Harrow: Longman.

Creese, M. J. (1991) 'Management Development: the way forward', *School Organisation,* 11(2), pp 223 – 229.

Dunning, G. (1993) 'Managing a small primary school: the problem of the headteacher', *Educational Management and Administration,* 21(2), pp. 79 – 89.

Evetts, J. (1994) 'The new headteacher: the changing work culture of secondary headship', *School Organization,* 14(1), pp. 37 - 47.

Ferlie, E., Ashburner, L., Fitzgerald, L. and Pettigrew, A. (1996) *The New Public Management in Action.* Oxford: Oxford University Press.

Gerwitz, S. (2002) *The Managerial School: Post Welfarism and Social Justice in Education.* London: Routledge.

Gorard, S., Taylor, C. and Fitz. J. (2002) 'Markets in Public policy: The case of the United Kingdom Education Reform Act 1988', *International Studies of Sociology in Education,* 12(1), pp. 23 – 41.

Handy, C. and Aitkin, R. (1986) *Understanding Schools as Organisations.* London: Penguin.

Herbert, D. (2000) 'School Choice in the Local Environment: Headteachers as gatekeepers on an uneven playing field', *School Leadership & Management*, 20(1), pp. 79-97.

Hood, C. (1995) 'The "new public management" in the 1980s: Variations on a theme', *Accounting, Organisations and Society*, 20(2-3), pp. 93 – 109.

Hoyle, E. and M. Wallace (2007) 'Educational reform: An ironic perspective', *Educational Management Administration & Leadership*, 35(1), pp. 9–25.

Jones, G. and Hayes, D. (1991) 'Primary headteachers and ERA two years on: The pace of change.' *School Organization*, 11(2), pp. 211 - 221.

Kerry, T. and Murdoch, A. (1992) 'The Art and Science of "Positive" Management: Some Implications for Training Education Managers', *School Organisation*, 12(3), pp. 247 – 253.

Lyons, J. (1990) The Decade Ahead: Learning to Manage, Managing to Learn, *Decision Maker*, 1, pp. 2 – 19.

Maclure, S. (1988) *Education Re-formed: a Guide to the Education Reform Act 1988.* Headway.

McHugh, M. and McMullan L. (1995) 'Headteacher or manager? Implications for training and development', *School Organisation*, 15(1), pp. 23 - 34.

McLean, M. (1988) "Populist" Centralism: The 1988 Education Reform Act in England and Wales', *Educational Policy*, 3(3), pp. 233 – 244.

Peapples, G. A. (1990) 'Competing in the Global Market', *Business Quarterly*, 55(2), pp. 80.

Pierson, C. (1991) *Beyond the Welfare State?* Cambridge: Polity Press.

Pierson, C. (1998) 'The New Governance of Education: the Conservatives and education 1988 – 1997', Oxford Review of Education, 24(1), pp. 131 - 142.

Salter, B. and Tapper, T. (1985) *Power and Policy in Education: The Case of Independent Schooling.* Lewes: Falmer Press.

Schug, M. and Wentworth, D. (1994) 'Public choice theory: A new perspective for social education research', *Social Studies*, 85(6), pp. 275 – 280.

Shackleton, J. R. (2007) 'Britain's Labour Market Under the Blair Governments', *Journal of Labour Research,* 28(3), pp. 454 – 476.

Sommefeldt, D. (2001) 'Nurturing environments? Reflections on leadership training: Development needs of new headteachers', *Management in Education,* 15(1), pp. 12-20.

Thomas, H. (1988) 'From Local Financial Management to Local Management of Schools', in Flude, M. and Hammer, M. (eds.) *The Education Reform Act, 1988: Its Origins and Implications.* Falmer Press.

Weindling, D. (1992) 'Marathon Running on a Sand Dune: The Changing Role of the Headteacher in England and Wales', *Journal of Educational Administration*, 30(3), pp. 63 – 76.

Whitty, G. (1989) 'The New Right and the National Curriculum: State Control or Market Forces? *Journal of Education Policy,* 4(4), pp. 329 - 341).

Whitty, G. and Power, S (1997) 'Quasi-markets and curriculum control: making sense of recent education reform in England and Wales', *Educational Administration Quarterly*, 33(2), pp. 219 – 40.

Wilkinson, R. (2000) 'New Labour and the Global Economy' in Coates, D. and Lawler, P. (eds.) *New Labour in Power.* Manchester: Manchester University Press, pp. 136 -148.

Woods, P. (1996) 'Choice, class and effectiveness', *School Effectiveness and School Improvement*, 7(4), pp. 324 - 341.

Printed in Great Britain
by Amazon